# BAKER BANDITS

# BAKER BANDITS

Korea's Band of Brothers

EMMETT SHELTON, JR.

Edited by Cynthia Shelton

CASEMATE
*Philadelphia & Oxford*

Published in the United States of America and Great Britain in 2020 by
CASEMATE PUBLISHERS
1950 Lawrence Road, Havertown, PA 19083, USA
and
The Old Music Hall, 106–108 Cowley Road, Oxford OX4 1JE, UK

Copyright 2020 © Emmett Shelton, Jr.

Hardback Edition: ISBN 978-1-61200-898-1
Digital Edition: ISBN 978-1-61200-899-8

A CIP record for this book is available from the British Library

Printed and bound in the United States of America by Sheridan

Typeset by Versatile PreMedia Services (P) Ltd

For a complete list of Casemate titles, please contact:

CASEMATE PUBLISHERS (US)
Telephone (610) 853-9131
Fax (610) 853-9146
Email: casemate@casematepublishers.com
www.casematepublishers.com

CASEMATE PUBLISHERS (UK)
Telephone (01865) 241249
Email: casemate-uk@casematepublishers.co.uk
www.casematepublishers.co.uk

We all need to be reminded, from time to time, what individual Marines have done for our country. Whether you were in Vietnam or Korea, whether it was for one day or two tours—you offered your life in defense of our country.

The real heroes never made it back alive, or they are still suffering from the wounds of war. I had the privilege of knowing and rubbing shoulders with some of these heroes, and I will never forget them.

You and I must live our lives so as to reflect good upon those whose lives were ended right there in combat. I have tried, and I hope I have succeeded. Each time I mention the name of one of these heroes, either in print or conversation, it shows that they live on, if only in our memories.

—Corporal Emmett Shelton, Jr.

# Contents

# Preface

I was raised by a hero. He never considered himself one, but I knew. When I was a kid, my father would tell us stories about being a Marine in Korea. But, today I realize his leadership and heroism was not limited to the battles of war, it was a lifelong journey.

When Emmett Shelton, Jr. returned home from the Korean War, he just wanted "to get back to a normal life". He raised a family and became a leader in our community. He was our volunteer police chief. He was the Commander of the Austin American Legion Post 76. He developed an Americanism speaker program in the schools. I was proud to be his daughter.

And then, 35 years after the Korean War, he undertook a new project reconnecting with his Baker Bandits, B-1-5 Marines from Korea. He tracked them down and gathered their stories. He published them in a newsletter, *The Guidon,* every month. He arranged annual reunions across the nation and honored the Baker Bandit heroes with awards.

The Bandits had an instant re-connection and bond with their brothers, from so many years before. They finished their buddy's stories and laughed at their shared memories. They cherished the old photos. They supported one another. When one Bandit developed cancer or lost his wife, the others rallied to support him and his family. When a Bandit died, Emmett "Posted Him to Heaven" in *The Guidon.* He truly lived the creed—Leave No Man Behind. The pride, love and caring was strong in every newsletter with every story and photo shared.

Emmett published *The Guidon* from 1986 through 2006. However, by 2008, many of the Baker Bandits had died, and most survivors were into their eighties. Cancer was endangering Emmett's health, so he had to discontinue publishing *The Guidon.* The A Company's newsletter, *The Able Cable,* continued for a few more years but discontinued publication in 2013.

Emmett's cancer grew worse at the end, but he refused hospice care—He Would Never Give Up. He died in spring 2015 at home, surrounded by his loving wife of 60 years and his children. As time grew short, Emmett changed to his Baker Bandit shirt so his Bandit Brothers could find him when he went to meet his maker.

***

On May 21, 2019, the Marine Corp Commandant, General Robert Neller, issued a letter saying the suicide rate for active duty Navy and Marines was at a 10-year high. In his four years as commandant, the corps had lost a company-sized group of Marines to their own hand. In 2019, 77 Marines died and another 354 attempted. He went on to say that, every day 20 veterans take their own lives. He resigned shortly after.

That same year, President Trump signed Executive Order (EO) 13861 mandating the development of the President's Roadmap to Empower Veterans and End the National Tragedy of Suicide.

I was heartbroken. Suicide was not an option taken by the Marines in Korea. I spent my entire career as a social worker working on public mental health issues. Suicide is one of the toughest and most tragic challenges. How had the men of Baker Company escaped this desperate choice? Could it have been the *Baker Bandits: Korea's Band of Brothers*—or the Marine pledge to never leave a man behind, not the dead, not the wounded, not the lonely, and not the troubled—Brothers for Life.

My father, Emmett, saved each edition of *The Guidon,* from 1986–2006. I have used his files to compile the treasured stories of each battle and the men's lives after war. I have indicated the men's ranks while they served in Korea, if known, even though several raised to the rank of general after the war.

In *The Guidon*, Emmett often included "A note from Ole Emmett" after many of the stories. I have included those here. Occasionally, I have seen the need to make a comment form 2020—those comments are from me.

The stories are compelling. It is my hope that readers also feel the Brotherhood, so many years later. Marines, families, military leaders, veteran supporters, mental health professionals and those who care, may be able to find that 'key' from the stories shared in these pages to find a way to build, or re-build, that Band of Brothers in each company.

***

As we worked to publish this book in 2020, the coronavirus hit the world. Suddenly, the limited lifelines for many vulnerable veterans are off-limits. No American Legion Hall, no VFW, no Reunions, no church and, for many, there are no family visits. Older veterans were at a high risk for suicide in 2019 and now they are also in the high-risk group for the complications of the virus. It is a good time for us all to reach out and Keep the Brotherhood Alive.

*Cynthia Shelton*

# Introduction

## Corporal Emmett Shelton, Jr.

I grew up in a Marine family. My Dad was a proud Marine, I went to military school at 14, and enlisted in the Marine Corp Reserves when I turned 17. In June 1950, I graduated high school with a new car and a sweetheart. But all my plans changed when the Korean War started. I was called to duty, trained and shipped to war.

By October, I was a Marine rifleman with B-1-5, the Baker Bandits. The deadly battles, endless casualties, and bitter cold were a living hell but we fought on, together. I was evacuated at Chosin due to frostbite in late December.

Emmett Shelton trained and ready for Korea, or so he thought (Shelton)

I came back home to Texas, married my high school sweetheart, started a business and raised four children. I tried to do good for my community and served as the Commander of Austin American Legion Post 76.

And then in 1984, I attended a Chosin Few Reunion and it changed my life. I saw the healing power of reuniting with "my" B-1-5 Marine brothers. I never realized my loneliness, before. They were not just any veterans – they were my Brothers from those battles in Korea. But that year, I also learned that, like many veterans, I was facing new battles: PTSD, frostbite disabilities and cancer. To find strength, I looked to "my" Marine brothers. I went through unit rosters and called my Baker Bandits. I sent them letters and ran ads in Marine magazines. In 1986, I had located 20 Bandits, and began publishing *The Guidon* as a monthly newsletter collecting and sharing stories of the Korean War and other news of their lives. Over the next twenty years, I built a contributing readership of over 340 Bandits.

I lived the creed—Leave no man behind—whether dead, disabled, or troubled, we Baker Bandits shared in each other's lives. We honored them when they died and kept touch with their widows. Our Brotherhood was a forever bond.

I believe every time we remember our heroes and share their experiences, they live on. Join us in keeping their memories alive.

Emmett was so proud of his work on *The Guidon*

# Baker Bandits: Korea's Band of Brothers

## Lieutenant General Charlie Cooper, USMC, Commanding Officer Baker Bandits, April–June 1951, Commanding General, Fleet Marine Force, Pacific 1983–85 (Retired)

Emmett,

I retired in August 1985 as the Commander General, Fleet Marine Force, Pacific. My leadership philosophy for over 35 years in the Marines was based on my experiences as a lieutenant in B Company 1/5 over seven intense weeks of combat. It was called the "Band of Brothers" concept. I would like to be able to address the Baker Bandits for a few minutes Saturday evening at the Reunion Banquet to tell them what this small unit's impact has been.

—*Gen Charlie*—

*A speech given at the first Baker Bandit reunion banquet on May 27, 1989*

My Brothers,

I can't tell you how moved I am to be a part of this gathering because all of my professional life, after my service in Korea, has been built on the theme of "The Band of Brothers" fostered by my association with you Baker Bandits, here today. I'd like to share with you what being a Platoon Commander of the 1st Division, 5th Regiment, meant to me and how I have tried to use that to guide my work as a Commander of the Marines.

I feel like I am a brother to all of those whose stories we share. I was the Commanding Officer of the Baker Bandits, 1st Division, 5th Regiment, B Company in April through June 1951 in the Korean War. We were bonded in combat over 40 years ago. Decades have gone by, our backs have gotten creaky, the memories fade, but we would still—if we had to today—die for each other.

How did we transform high school reservists and seasoned professionals into Brothers with such a lifetime bond?

Shakespeare spoke to the bond between men in combat when he wrote:

> We few, we happy few, we Band of Brothers, for he that sheds his blood with me shall always be my brother.

I came to Korea to join the 5th Regiment as a 23-year-old replacement officer back in April 1951, shortly after the 5th had faced the Chinese in the Chosin Reservoir. We were flown in because our regiment was surrounded by the enemy. We were then loaded on trucks and had to fight through the enemy lines all day just to get to the 5th Marines command post.

The Regimental Commander, Colonel Hayward, welcomed us to the 5th Regiment, "The family of the finest fighting regiment on the face of the Earth." He told us that "We" were going to make the 5th Regiment, better. He said, "However, for you to help us become a better regiment, there are a few rules that you've got to understand:"

> First, the 5th Regiment doesn't leave our dead, we don't leave our wounded. We take care of each other.

> Second, if we run short of ammunition—we redistribute, if we run short of rations—we share, if we run short of water—we share.

> Third, if the Regiment runs out of ammunition—we never surrender, we fix bayonets and attack. We will never give up, and we will never be beaten.

That's what I heard my first day in the 5th Regiment and I can never forget it. I've told it thousands of times to my combat Marines.

That simple, but unswerving, creed was burned into me and it only took me about two days after I joined B Company to find out what it was all about.

The "Band of Brothers" was a growing bond. I don't think it ever got slow for B Company in its history and it seemed to get faster each day. I know every piece of gear I owned got shot off of me, holes in my canteen, I got two helmets shot off of me, the heels of my boots had bullet holes. I began to think maybe I had a horseshoe that the Good Lord had given me, but then on May 28, I found out that wasn't right because I got blasted down a hill. I survived it, got patched up, and went back at it again that day.

Here tonight, with my B-1-5, Baker Bandits, former company commanders, former platoon commanders, former 1st sergeants, gunnys, platoon sergeants, squad leaders, mortarmen, rocketmen, just plain good Marines, I want to tell you that I got hit rather badly on the 17th of June 17, 1951 as we took a hill called Hill 907. It was almost an impossible mission, but we accomplished it, although we lost some good people that day. I was hit while briefing my men. I was so severely wounded that they told me I would never walk again. The doctors told

## Wallet Card

## Cut out, fold and keep in your wallet

## BAND OF BROTHERS

1. ALL MARINES ARE ENTITLED TO DIGNITY AND RESPECT AS INDIVIDUALS, BUT MUST ABIDE BY COMMON STANDARDS ESTABLISHED BY PROPER AUTHORITY.

2. A MARINE SHOULD NEVER LIE, CHEAT, OR STEAL FROM A FELLOW MARINE OR FAIL TO COME TO HIS AID IN TIME OF NEED.

3. ALL MARINES SHOULD CONTRIBUTE 100% OF THEIR ABILITIES TO THE UNIT'S MISSION. ANY LESS EFFORT BY AN INDIVIDUAL PASSES THE BUCK TO SOMEONE ELSE.

4. A UNIT, REGARDLESS OF SIZE, IS A DISCIPLINED FAMILY STRUCTURE, WITH SIMILAR RELATIONSHIPS BASED ON MUTUAL RESPECT AMONG MEMBERS.

5. IT IS ESSENTIAL THAT ISSUES AND PROBLEMS WHICH TEND TO LESSEN A UNIT'S EFFECTIVENESS BE ADDRESSED AND RESOLVED.

6. A BLENDING OF SEPARATE CULTURES, VARYING EDUCATIONAL LEVELS, AND DIFFERENT SOCIAL BACKGROUNDS IS POSSIBLE IN AN UNSELFISH ATMOSPHERE OF COMMON GOALS, ASPIRATIONS, AND MUTUAL UNDERSTANDING.

7. BEING THE BEST REQUIRES COMMON EFFORT, HARD WORK, AND TEAMWORK. NOTHING WORTHWHILE COMES EASY.

8. EVERY MARINE DESERVES JOB SATISFACTION, EQUAL CONSIDERATION AND RECOGNITION OF HIS ACCOMPLISHMENTS.

9. KNOWING YOUR FELLOW MARINE WELL ENABLES YOU TO LEARN TO LOOK AT THINGS "THROUGH HIS EYES", AS WELL AS YOUR OWN.

10. ISSUES DETRACTING FROM THE EFFICIENCY AND SENSE OF WELL-BEING OF AN INDIVIDUAL SHOULD BE SURFACED AND WEIGHED AGAINST THE IMPACT ON THE UNIT AS A WHOLE.

11. IT MUST BE RECOGNIZED THAT A BROTHERHOOD CONCEPT DEPENDS ON ALL MEMBERS "BELONGING" - - BEING FULLY ACCEPTED BY OTHERS WITHIN.

When I was promoted to Commander General of the 1st Division in 1977, we sent this wallet card to every Marine to carry as our "Band of Brothers" pledge (USMC) me that there wasn't any chance that I could ever get back to B Company, or the Marine Corps, for that matter.

I share this with all of you because all of you have suffered untold agonies and wounds and seen your friends die in combat. I was rather crude with those doctors when they told me I'd never walk again. I used some words I'd learned in B Company and told them to get the hell out of my room. I was in the room with a Marine Major aviator who had bailed out at about 300 feet and his parachute had not opened—he was broken from the chest down. My other roommate was a naval aviator whose napalm exploded on him and he was burned from the top to the bottom. I was in traction with a broken back and couldn't feel anything from my chest down. We didn't give each other much sympathy but we all knew—We Would Never Give Up.

The point I've realized is that I had seen what, at the age of 23, was the greatest miracle in my life. That was what that 18- to 21-year-old Marine could do in combat, the pain he could endure and the love and comradeship he showed for his fellow Marines. And yes, we even had Marines going "over the hill" from the hospital and the aid stations to get back to B Company when we were short handed in battle. I saw it again in Vietnam. But, that's the Marine way. In Korea, I heard the 1st sergeant tell the commanding officer that he had 13 extra men and he didn't know where they came from. They had "sneaked in" the night before with the supply train. They were all former members of B Company and some of them still had holes in them. I know one day, when we finally got a chance to get cleaned up in a river after about a month, and we all looked at our bodies, we found that about half of us still had holes in us. Some had wounds they hadn't reported. That was B Company.

Lying in that hospital and being told I would never walk again, I decided I had to put something on a piece of paper that would reflect my observations about what the corps was all about and at least I could leave something. I did a lot of praying too, and I told the Good Lord:

> Lord, if you'll help me heal, I'd like to spend the rest of my life leading Marines and giving them the kind of leadership they deserve. Up front leadership, because the 18- to 21-year-old Marine is the greatest weapon this country ever developed, when he is properly trained and supported, and led by the kind of leaders he deserves.

You know, the Good Lord heard me. My back started healing. I defied all the prognoses. I got stronger and returned to duty leading Marines. But this time, I had had time to reflect on my time with the Baker Bandits. I was convinced that those kids that had gone through Marine Boot Camp, if they were properly lead, trained and supported, could defeat any military force in this world. And that's still the philosophy that we believe in this corps. You've got to lead them right, you've got to train them right, and then give them the supporting arms they deserve and they can beat anybody, and you did. I finished up a wonderful career, made it to Lieutenant General, and commanded an awful lot of good Marines which is what I love the most.

Out of that great deal of trauma I put down some words about my experiences and later those words became a reality and a concept called the, "BAND OF BROTHERS" leadership principles that I've tried to preach my entire active service in the corps and I'm still preaching, teaching leadership at the Naval Academy and whenever the Marine Corps will invite me back. And it all comes from B Company. Tough, caring, just Marines with mud on their feet who loved each other, who would die for each other and would never let another Marine or navy corpsman down. And that's what it's all about. And I want to thank all of you for having given me that as heritage and I've done all I could to foster that.

I say to all of you, that my study of history, tactics, strategies and what's made this Marine Corps what it is and looking back at all the wars that we have fought in, such bitter battles where we suffered very heavy casualties, we never had a unit fail in combat. They never lost their identity, someone was always in charge, whether it be a corporal for a battalion or PFC for a rifle company.

It has always amazed me, with the stress of combat, the turmoil of bringing in replacements and people staying with the unit a short time and frequently not knowing the names of all the people in their unit, yet that closeness, that camaraderie, that total dedication to the unit and each other, the Band of Brothers, has always been there, if the leadership has let it happen. So I report to you, today this spirit is alive and well in the corps. You are the ones who have set the pace, you paid the price. God Bless You All!

*A note from Ole Emmett: Lieutenant General Charles Grafton Cooper, United States Marine Corps, was awarded the Navy Distinguished Service Medal for exceptionally meritorious and distinguished service in a position of great responsibility to the Government of the United States. His singularly distinctive accomplishments and his dedicated contributions in the service of his country reflect the highest credit upon himself and were in keeping with the highest traditions of the United States Marine Corps and the United States Naval Service. General Charlie died at the age of 81.*

General Charlie Cooper reflects on his time leading Baker Company (Cooper)

# All We Wanted Was to Be Marines

Our time in Korea was a defining time in our lives; a real test of our manhood and dedication. The dedication to country and corps were evidenced by the oath we swore when we enlisted. We gave life to that oath, and meaning to our manhood, under the most trying conditions of danger and stress.

In the end, it was as we acted and regarded one another, then and now, that makes the Marine Corps the unique fighting force it is.

You can enlist in the army, enlist in the air force, enlist in the navy; but you become a Marine. What a fine group of men the Baker Bandits are, I'm proud to have served with them.

—*Lt Bill Kerrigan*—

# All I Ever Wanted

## Private William G. Irwin

When I was 16, I took two big steps that shaped my life, without hesitation. I was baptized a Christian and a few months later, I persuaded my Mom and Dad to give their permission for me to join the Marine Corp Reserves.

It was no real surprise for them, because a Marine was all I had ever wanted to be. My friends all wanted to be firemen, policemen or doctors. Not me! I wanted to wear those Dress Blues, I loved that uniform. The day I was sworn in was one of the proudest days of my life.

In Boot Camp, they issued our Greens and Dungarees, but we didn't get our Blues. I was really disappointed and asked the Drill Instructor when we would get our Blues. His response was, "Boy, you're not fit to wear that uniform yet!" They had to do something about our talk, and our walk, and our attitude. They did something about it alright, and I'll never forget the day we received our Blues, boy was I proud! Finally, I was a Marine! Or, so I thought.

When the Korean War started, I shipped over. On one especially eventful day, in the life of this Marine, a hand grenade rolled against my side but failed to explode, a cigarette was shot out of my mouth, and my helmet had a hole shot through it. Each time, I thanked the Lord for His protection. I was impressed that God was watching out for me like that. That very night in a foxhole, I had an intimate moment with the Lord in which I felt that He was calling me for something special. I had no idea what that special thing was, but I was willing to do it, whatever it was. I didn't want to be like some I had heard about who promised God all this good stuff when they were scared, but when the emergency was over, they forget all about it.

I still haven't forgotten my promise!

—*Bill*—

# Found a Home in the Corps

## Private Madison Crosby

Up until I was 10 years old, I remember standing in the middle of the cotton fields in northeast Texas outside of Dallas. The sun always seemed to be at high noon. I would day dream of far away places like that Perry Como song I heard on the radio. I remember the passing trains with the dining cars and the white people laughing at us in the fields, especially the kids. Someday, I was going to those far away places. I spent a lifetime running away from the cotton fields. At the age of 10, I became a caddie at one of the local country clubs and never picked cotton again. Twelve days after my 17th birthday I became a Marine Reserve recruit.

I had one semester of college after graduating high school when I was 16 years old. Despite always enrolling five weeks late during the cotton season, and always having to catch up and keep up, I did graduate high school. During the school year, I only caddied on weekends. School was too much for my cousins and they worked as caddies full-time.

The Marine Corps took me away from this, the poverty, the cotton fields, the ghetto, the projects, the drugs, and violence. For the first time in my life, I felt like I belonged, the corps was a family who cared. In the Marine Corps I found a home. I ran into obstacles, prejudice, battles, bad equipment, and discrimination, but I just tried harder. In life you have to play the hand that's dealt you. Besides, where else could I be assured "three hots and a flop?" Semper Fi Brothers.

—*Madison*—

# A Young Reservist Gave His All

## Corporal Emmett Shelton, Jr.

Our hero is a 19-year-old Marine reservist, Private Roger Sturdevant. He graduated high school in May 1950. By November, he was a combat Marine in one of the fiercest and coldest battles of the Korean War, the Chosin Reservoir.

When Roger was 16, his buddies began to talk about joining the United States Marine Corp Reserve. They could make a little money each month and go on trips to California each summer for Marine training. On top of all that good stuff, it was right after World War II and everybody was patriotic. The Marine Corps had quite a reputation and was the place for Real Men to be—so he signed on.

At the first training camp, Roger believed the Marine Corps was everything he had hoped it would be—good men, good discipline and good training. Our young Marine was over six feet tall and strong as a young stallion, so the work and marching didn't even slow him down, he fit right in.

Emmett went to military school when his father went to fight in WWII (Shelton)

Right after his third summer camp at Camp Pendleton, his Reserve unit was put on alert for activation for Korea. He got his notice in July 1950. He took a bus in August, and then boarded a train and went back to Camp Pendleton. That month, trains from all over the country were snaking their way across the States carrying reservists, just like Sturtevant, to active duty.

Upon reaching Camp Pendleton, the units were split up. Most men were sent on to Boot Camp, but the need for Marines was so great at the front that those with two or three Summer Camps and good drill attendance, were sent to Tent Camp Two for combat training. Roger was one of these.

At Tent Camp Two, these young Marines were pushed to their limits, and then some. On one day, the Marines ran the Infiltration Course where they crawled 50 yards while machine guns shot over their heads and bombs exploded all around them. Next, they ran a very tough Obstacle Course. Then, the Close Combat Course where the Marines run obstacles while shooting dummies. Most of the instructors had seen combat and knew just what the Marines were in for so they did not spare danger or hardship. After this training, our young reservist was now a Real Marine.

Our young Marine was assigned to the 1st Replacement Draft in September and was trucked to San Diego where they boarded a ship. The USS *General Walker* crossed the ocean alone and, besides a rough crossing that had most Marines very sick at their stomach, it was an uneventful crossing.

The 1st Replacement Draft arrived in Japan and the Marines were taken by train to a small town called Otsu which is situated by a large lake with mountains all around. The 1st Draft would be in Japan for several weeks. Other units of the 1st Marine Division were on board a ship trying to make a landing at Wosan, North Korea, but the bay in Japan was heavily mined and the bigger ships could not approach. Finally, the 1st Draft left Japan aboard an old World War II *Liberty Ship* that floated higher and turned easily in its crossing of the Sea of Japan.

The night before they boarded the ship, no liberty was allowed. But being young Marines, some went "over the fence". The next night back on ship, one young Marine was stumbling and falling over the men while they were watching a movie on the deck. A corpsman finally took him below and it was determined that he had gone blind after he ingested some bad whiskey. Later that night, the word was passed that the Marine had died. Not much of a war for that young Marine.

The next evening, their ship pulled into Wosan harbor. The Replacement Draft debarked the *Liberty Ship* and was billeted in an old church school. The first night in Korea, Roger pulled guard duty. He was taken to a foxhole above the school where he could observe westward from his post, but it was a very dark night. Korea,

First time on a ship for most of us (Green)

being a backwards country, had no lights shining, like we had back home. When it got dark in North Korea, it got dark.

About midnight, our young Marine and his foxhole buddy, heard something crunching through the undergrowth down in the valley to their left. In a minute or two, they heard same crunching through the undergrowth to their right. These two crunchers got closer and closer to each other the "BUURP-BUURP—BANG-BANG" and everything was quite again. Nothing crunched away in either direction.

Way over on the horizon to the west front, they could see that some army unit was shooting it up with tracers sailing all over. Our young Marines wondered what the heck the army was shooting at?

The next day, the 1st Draft Marines found out what the shooting was about, the railroad that was to be used to transport them to the front had been blown up. It took a few days but, when the railroad was fixed, the Marines were loaded onto railroad coal cars. Away they went north with the wind in their faces and coal dust from the engine flying all over everything. A couple of ROK soldiers were stationed on the "cattle catcher" on the engine and shot everything that got in the way—dogs, people, anything they wanted to shoot at.

Our first look at battle (Schryver)

The Replacement Draft arrived at God-knows-where, North Korea, and the unit debarked from the train. Here again, our Marines were split up and sent to whichever units that needed them the most. Many went to the 7th Regiment, but a few went to the tried and true 5th Regiment. Our young Marine was assigned to B Company, 5th Regiment, of the 1st Division. He was assigned as a replacement on a Fire Team that had lost all but two men. Roger was introduced to the surviving leader of the fire team, Corporal Richard S. Cruz, who had also been a reservist. Next, he met the only other surviving member of Cruz's fire team, Private Ben Wray a reservist from Austin, Texas. I was the other replacement who arrived with him, Private Emmett Shelton, also from

Austin. As ranking officer, Cpl Cruz continued as Fire Team Leader. Wray would continue as Rifleman. Since Private Sturdevant was larger and stronger that any of the other members of the fire team, he would operate the Browning Automatic Rifle (BAR) and would be known as the BARman. I was made Assistant BARman.

The battalion was in a rear area and sent out patrols to keep watch on what was going on in the area. They had a few skirmishes. Then, they went up that 30-mile-long narrow dirt road to Hagaru-ri and turned right and went up the east side of Chosin Reservoir. It was getting dark, so we set up on a big potato field. It was cold and Roger's Fire Team lucked into a potato bunker. Winter was coming and the potato bunker was a warm and welcomed home.

In the daytime, they could see the Marine Air Wing across the reservoir diving and bombing and doing their best in support of the 7th Regiment. All was quiet on the east side, but local refugees kept pouring through their lines telling about large numbers of Chinese soldiers who were in their villages recruiting and scrounging what they could find. Their stories reminded the marines that the Chinese were very brutal.

Then one day, the 5th Regiment was ordered to saddle up and board the trucks to join the 7th Marines on the west side of Chosin Reservoir, which by then was ice-covered. Dark comes early that far north, and it was a cold and windy 30-mile trip over to Hagaru-ri then north over the icy road up and over Toktong Pass and into the Yudam-ni Valley. Baker Company debarked in an ice-covered rice paddy, no tents, no mess. Most of the men immediately crawled into their sleeping bags, clothes and all, eating whatever they had, in the warmth of their bags.

Along about midnight, all hell broke loose. The Chinese joined the war on the side of the North Koreans with orders to wipe out the 1st Marine Division. The Chinese felt that if they could wipe out this elite Marine Division, America would plead for peace, and knowing what we know now, they may have been right. They hadn't counted on the 5th and the 7th Regiments getting together, and they had not counted on the esprit de corps of the Marines. Not much sleeping went on that cold night in a furrowed field in the valley of Yudam-ni.

The next day, November 28, B-1-5 went up Hill 1240 to relieve what was left of D-2-7. Dog Company had been decimated. There were Chinese and Allied casualties all around. Dog Company had only a handful of men left alive out of over 200 men the day before. It was a difficult job evacuating all the dead and wounded. Some were just parts. It was hell on earth.

When we got back to company headquarters, there was fighting all around. It was out in "No-man's land" between the Chinese and Hill 1240. The Fire Team ate together that night and Cpl Cruz told the members of the team that he had had a premonition that he would be killed in his next battle. We listened—what could we say? Ben Wray and Shelton had dug a really nice foxhole that was so deep that we could stand up. As night fell, Cruz decided he wanted the bigger foxhole, so he switched for the night. Sure enough, the bigger foxhole was hit that night by a Chinese mortar round and Cpl Cruz was Killed in Action. He never knew what hit him. Cpl Richard S. Cruz was a reservist from Long Beach, California—he gave it all!

On December 1st, B-1-5 left their home up on Hill 1240 to fight their way to the sea and safety. There was one road in and one road out and the Chinese knew this quite well. The Chinese still had orders to wipe out the 1st Marine Division. B-1-5 along with the rest of the 5th Regiment fought its way to Hagaru-ri where the 1st Division headquarters were located.

A-1-5 had been hit real hard up on the line and partially overrun, so Baker Company was sent up to help them. Chinese dead and dying were all around. We had to assess, who was dead, who was alive, who still represented a threat and what to do about it. There were no questions—no doubts.

When B-1-5 returned to company headquarters on December 7, Roger and me, were assigned to share a foxhole. We chose one that had an earthen seat built in it and when we stood up, we could just see over the parapet. Unknown to

Casualties of battle (USMC)

us, we had a Chinese machine gunner as a neighbor. The machine gun was in a bunker with a top and was out of reach of Allied mortars, but not out of reach of the two young Marines.

The enemy machine gun opened up on the foxhole and then went silent. We knew the Chinese had spotted us. We sent a few 60mm mortar shells at the gun. I was standing up in the foxhole, looking over the parapet. We could hear the Chinese bugles and whistles out front, so we were on watch.

One of the mortar shells hit about a foot in front of the parapet. It shook me up. I sat down, shook my head and said "Boy, Roger that was close." There was no response from Sturtevant. I looked over and Roger had a startled look with blood coming out of his nose and then out of his mouth. I grabbed him, but our young Marine slumped forward. I called that now all too familiar call: "Corpsman." It was a long 30 minutes later that the young Marine, Roger Sturtevant, was carried away, silently. I waited for word and then, another Marine returned with Roger's ammo belt and the news that Sturtevant had died. I was now B-1-5 Fire Team BARman with no assistant.

Private Roger Van Duran Sturtevant would not suffer his wounds or the cold again, he was already home. Six months after graduation, his dreams were over. His friends, family and fiancé would miss him. In 1951, Sturtevant's family would look me up and visit me in Quantico as I recuperated from frostbite. But, their world would never be the same without Roger, their only son. Roger was buried in a mass grave in Hagaru-ri and has not been returned to the U.S.

When we fought our way to Koto-Ri, we were overloaded with wounded and dead Marines, so there was a mass burial at that location. Records show that Cruz was later recovered and buried at Fort Rosecrans National Cemetery. I believe Sturtevant's body is still buried at Hagaru-ri.

—*Emmett*—

GOD BLESS THOSE YOUNG MARINES
WHO GAVE THEIR ALL!

# Finally I Feel Like One of the Guys

## Sam "The Chopper" Corso

Art Markey was what we once called "Baby Marines," a 17-year-old reservist who had not been to Boot Camp or even Reserve summer camp. He came to B-1-5 and hardly knew how to load the M-1 machine gun. He came to my gun section and squad where Gunnery Sergeant Waldo Wolfe made him Number 4 Ammo Carrier. A fact I have teased him about, constantly. The truth is, he moved to assistant gunner and then gunner very quickly the way machine gunners move up—in other words, when the guy in front of you had a Wounded in Action or Killed in Action tag on him. One thing Waldo never told us was how short a machine gunner's life expectancy was.

Men of B-1-5 (Palatas)

Back to Art—and this addresses all those who bore the title Reservist—You, Art, You Emmett, You Corky, and all of the "Weekend Warriors" are Marines to the center of your being. Without you we, the so called "regulars" who chided you, would have been a sorry lot.

Corky Diels said to me "finally I feel like one of the guys." It is a sad commentary of ourselves that we allowed this Marine to feel "not quite a Marine" for all of these years. I can remember Corky who became our Section Leader, he made Corporal at 21 years old. He was often running back and forth between my gun and Harlan Pope's gun—re-setting our fields of fire—checking on sufficient ammo and yelling "MORE AMMO" to the carriers. I can remember Corky displaying a quiet leadership that gave comfort to us "regulars."

You Corky, and you Markey, and all of the Marine Corp reservists, we stand humbly before you and ask forgiveness for the years of anguish you suffered in thinking you were "not quite a Marine." You were, and are, Marines and we have always been proud to be your Brothers.

*—The Chopper—*

# Three Young Reservists from Austin

## Corporal Emmett Shelton, Jr.

In February of 1948, I reached the age of 17. I still needed to finish high school, but I wanted to be a Marine. So, in March, I joined the USMC Reserves here in Austin.

I enlisted for several reasons. First, my Dad had been a Marine in World War II. My whole family supported the Marines in the war and Dad had lots of stories. Second, I'd never been out of the State of Texas. The Recruiter said they'd give me a free trip to California each year and a small salary all year long. So, shortly after my 17th birthday, I signed up.

I'd been in the Reserves about a year and my buddies had heard all about Camp Pendleton. Two of my best buddies in high school, Oren Allen and Don Meyers, decided they would also like to get that free trip to California and that monthly salary. In those days, we were all patriotic as hell and a little money went a long way. I went with Owen and Don to the recruiter and they enlisted.

We attended our unit's summer camp at Camp Pendleton in early June 1950 (my third summer camp, their first). When we were at camp, Korea was under siege. We heard daily reports and each reservist began to realize what it meant to be a Marine.

Owen, Don and I had just returned home from camp in California when the North Koreans crossed the 38th Parallel and started the Korean War. After a little hemming and hawing, the Marines called the USMC Reserve to active duty.

Each of us Austin boys got our notice. We were mostly teens and our families knew the danger. They packed us a sack lunch, gave us

Shortly after my 17th birthday, I signed up for the Marines (Shelton)

words of encouragement and saw us off at the
bus depot. It was a hot Sunday night in August
in downtown Austin. My father drove us to the
station and we caught the bus together. It was
a long, quiet trip back to Camp Pendleton.

When we reached Camp Pendleton, our
Texas unit was broken up. I had three summer
camps, military school, and a good attendance
record at drills. I was a promising mechanic and
rifleman, so I was sent on to Advanced Combat
Training at Tent Camp Two. Don and Oren
did not have enough time in, so they went to
Boot Camp.

Dad saw me, Oren and Don off at the
bus station (Shelton)

After a few weeks of training, they shipped
my unit out as the 1st Replacement Draft and I wound up in Korea, just in time
for the winter of 1950.

Oren placed high in his Boot Camp Class and was sent on to Communications
School. Don was sent to Korea in 1951 and assigned to the 2nd Battalion, 1st
Marines, E Company, as a rifleman.

Six months after graduation, I was in Korea in time to serve as a BARman in
Chosin. It was brutally cold and the Chinese were fierce. My hands and feet were
frozen while we fought our way back. I was evacuated as soon as our Company
made it to "safety" at the Bean Patch. I thought I would lose my feet to frostbite
but I worked my way through the hospital system winding up in Jacksonville,
Florida. I took my convalescent leave and then went to Quantico, Virginia. I am
walking today but every step hurts.

I lost track of both Don and Oren until I received the letter below from Don.
It just shows how young Marines think:

S. Korea Sept. 6, 1951

Hello Emmett,

Gosh Bud, I was really glad to get your letter today. I have been trying to get your address
for quite some time, but all that I could find out was that you were at Quantico.

I am glad to hear that you are doing OK. I am sorry that you don't like it at Quantico,
but I am sure that you prefer that to Korea—Ha! If things should happen to work out
over here, without all out war, maybe you and I will be released from active duty before
too long, or has your enlistment been extended, too? I was extended a year, but it doesn't
bother me much.

Say Bud, I'm glad to hear that you finally found the right girl and that you are going
to be married soon. I would sure like to be there with you when you tie the knot, but that

seems impossible so I'll just wish you both the best of luck. The girl isn't that blonde we double-dated with Pop's car, is it?

You know from the looks of things that I'm going to be the last of the trio to tie the knot! First was Oren, now you. All that is stopping me is 6,000 miles of water!!

What have you heard about that girl in California?—straight scoop. I met her in Hollywood one weekend on liberty from Camp and I've been going with her ever since. Her name is Linda and we got along swell together. If, and when, I get back to the States, we are going to be married and take off for Texas on my 30-day leave.

I've been here in Korea nearly 7 months now and I'm still a long way down on the rotation list, so I look to spend at least three or four more months, here. I thought for a while that I might get out in November, but things don't look so promising, now.

At present, we are about 45 or 50 miles behind the lines, in Reserve. We have been here for quite some time.

From the scuttlebutt that I hear, we'll be making history before long, but you know how scuttlebutt gets started! I don't know what that "making history" means, but you can bet your boots it won't be fun!

Well Bud, I guess that's about all for now but I want to say again, it was really good to hear from you, Write every chance you get. Take things easy,

Your Buddy,
—*Donald*—

I replied to Don's letter, but before he could get it, Don was Killed in Action. My Dad got the notice and let me know that he had gone out to try to console Don's mother, but she was too distraught. She never did get over what happened to Don.

Corporal Don Meyer's remains were returned to Austin with full Marine Honors. He was buried in the Austin Memorial Park Cemetery. For years, my Dad and I would visit Don's grave on Veteran's Day and my Dad would play taps with his bugle and I'd place a new American flag on his grave. All of Don's hopes, and his plans that he shared with me, were buried with him.

Oren came back and followed his father's footsteps. He started selling wholesale auto parts all over west Texas, then moved to California and became a painting contractor. Both he and I married while still in the corps. I am so happy Oren stayed in touch with me!

—*Emmett*—

# Best Damn Machine Gunner in Korea

## Corporal E.C. "Corky" Diels

On January 17, 1951, I landed at Pusan, South Korea and was assigned to the B-1-5 Machine Gun Section. This is when I first met Charlie Webb, another reservist. Charlie had been with the 1st Brigade and fought his way out of the Chosin with B-1-5. He was quite a character. He took better care of his machine gun than he did of himself. He often stated that all he wanted to do was kill the enemy.

I can remember one time when Charlie dug steps up the hill to his gun position so the enemy would have an easier time getting to him, and oblivion! I can also remember how upset he got when told he was going to be rotated stateside. He said he had a lot of pay back to do and he couldn't fight the enemy in the States. He was rotated, against his will, April 8, 1951.

About three months later, we were heading north again, it was hotter than hell and we were taking five along the side of the road. I lit a smoke and glanced to

Bandits in the field ready to move when Charlie Webb walks up (Shelton)

the rear of the column and saw this guy walking hurriedly toward us. Jim Day was sitting there with me and I said, "Look at that guy coming up the road, he walks just like Charlie Webb." Jim agreed with me and said, "Yea, but that lucky guy is back stateside." We kept watching as this guy got closer and when he was about 20 feet away, he looked at me and yelled, "YOU BANDITS NEED A GOOD MACHINE GUNNER?" It was Charlie all right, after a couple of hugs and a few hand shakes I asked him what the hell he was doing back in Korea? He said, "Well I got a little problem, I'm AWOL." "From where?" I asked. "San Diego Recruit Depot," he replied. When I told the Captain about Charlie being back, he did not know what to do? He told Charlie to stand by until he talked to the major. They contacted San Diego, and it was verified that Charlie had been listed Absent With Out Leave (AWOL) for five weeks. Charlie was fined $50 and allowed to rejoin B Company.

Charlie Webb was still in Korea when I left on March 17, 1952. That's what I know about the best damn machine gunner in Korea—Charlie Webb.

—*"Corky"*—

*Charles E "Charlie" Webb first joined B-1-5 on September 4, 1950 and was first dropped April 8, 1951. Company Records show him returning to B-1-5 on November 23, 1951 and he was last dropped from company records February 9, 1953.*

—*Emmett*—

# Reservists Were Vitally Important

## "Mobilization of the Marine Corps Reserve in Korea 1950–51," USMC Historical Division

The role of the Marine Corps as a whole in Korea has been widely publicized. Not so well known, however, is the essential part played by the Marine Corps Reserve in such operations as the Inchon amphibious assault, the capture of Seoul, and the breakout from the Chosin Reservoir.

Many lessons have been learned from the Korean conflict, but there is no lesson more valuable to the Marine Corps than the one prescribing the vital importance of a large, readily available and high quality reserve. The significance of the reserve contribution to Marine achievements in Korea may be measured by just a few facts:

1. At the time of the Inchon–Seoul operations, 15 September to 7 October 1950, there were more Marines in Korea than there had been in the total Fleet Marine Force two and a half months earlier, and 20 percent of these were reservists only six to eight weeks removed from their civilian pursuits;
2. The first United Nations force, which early in November 1950 inflicted a first decisive defeat on a Chinese Communist division, was a Marine regiment including about 34 percent reservists;
3. By the end of March 1951, although the Marine Corps had almost tripled its active duty strength of 30 June 1950, reservists comprised 45 percent of the Marine Corps total active duty strength.
4. By the end of April 1951, the reserve had hit its peak strength during the Korean conflict—859,538 reserves on active duty.

# Pusan Perimeter August 1950

## A Message from the Commandant
## of the Marine Corps

In a democracy, the defense of its citizens and their way of life has always rested upon the shoulders of a small, dedicated, and disciplined force of brave men. These individuals have been willing to put their lives on the line and do what had to be done to protect their nation, their families, and their friends.

Such are the men of Baker Company, 1st Battalion, 5th Marines. In a strange, foreign land, among countless ridges and hilltops, you gave your all. You made the names of places like Pusan, and Chosin Reservoir a proud part of American history. You never failed your fellow Marines.

Yours is a legacy of unparalleled courage, valor and patriotism. I salute you. Semper Fidelis!

*—P. A. Kelley, General, U.S. Marine Corps, March 1987—*

# Bloody Battle of Pusan, August 12–13, 1950

## Corporal Emmett Shelton, Jr.

Private Herman C. Bohnke, Jr. was a short-timer when the Korean War started—he only had a few months left of his enlistment. When the 1st Provisional Marine Brigade was being formed, Marines from all over were being transferred into the companies making up the brigade to bring them up to strength as soon as possible. When the brigade was to be shipped over to Korea, they still couldn't make up a full regiment. They went into combat minus Companies C, F, and I because trained Marines were not available on such short notice.

On the other hand, the short-timers were being transferred, stateside. Only having a week or two left on his enlistment, Bohnke was being kidded a great deal with, "Hell, Bohnke, you've found a home in the corps, you'd better ship over with B Company."

Bohnke, along with the few other-short timers in our barracks, were ordered to get their gear together and fall out to the curb, a truck was to pick them up for their discharge. They fell out to the curb, but the truck didn't come. After waiting about two hours on that curb, Bohnke was heard coming back up the stairs with his gear and he said, "That truck is never going to come, so it will be better for me just to ship over to Korea with B Company," which he did.

Bohnke was assigned to the 3rd Section of Machine Guns in Baker Company and shipped out with the rest of us on July 13, 1950, on the USS *Henrico*. There were 202 Marines and 6 officers of B Company who embarked that day. The *Henrico* developed engine troubles out at about Santa Catalina Island and was detoured for repairs to San Francisco. After the repairs were

USS *Henrico* took B-1-5 to Korea (USMC)

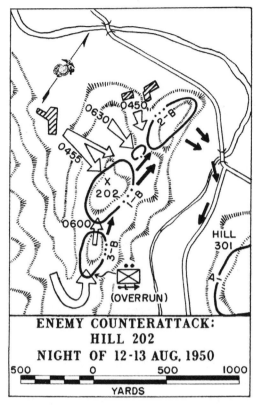

ENEMY COUNTERATTACK:
HILL 202
NIGHT OF 12-13 AUG. 1950

500      0      500      1000

YARDS

B Company set up defense in the high ground to the north (USMC Map)

completed, the already-loaded USS *Henrico* continued to chase the other brigade ships to Korea, in solo. They even had a submarine scare on the way.

The brigade landed at Pusan, Korea on August 2, 1950. Ten days later, on the morning of August 12, B Company and the rest of the brigade was fighting in the Sachon. We were moving up when Private Jerry Schultz was hit in the spine by a sniper and evacuated from the area, never again to rejoin our company in combat. Jerry was confined to a wheelchair for the rest of his life.

We lost Lieutenant Cowling, who was hit bad enough to require evacuation. Many other men were declared Killed in Action or Missing In Action in these two days. The wounded were placed on the back of the tanks and taken to the rear area medical facilities.

At about 1745 we received orders to set up our defenses for the night. The 2nd Platoon moved out under command of 1st Lieutenant Scotty Taylor who was ordered to take the right portion of the high ground which was B Company's objective. The 3rd Platoon was ordered to take the remaining portion.

The 1st Platoon would follow the 3rd Platoon as soon as it could reorganize. Our air support came in and worked over the ridgeline. The North Koreans pulled out and the gun that had been quite a problem previously was now silent. Only sniper fire was encountered as we moved up the hill. Unbeknownst to us, as we came up one side of the hill, the North Koreans were coming back up the other side. Fortunately, Lt Taylor's 2nd Platoon beat them to the top by about 10 minutes and set up an ambush. When the North Koreans reached the top, they left 38 of their men dead, and one wounded. The wounded man was the platoon leader and when headquarters heard that we had him we were ordered to bring him down the hill for interrogation.

We were new to Korea and did not know how the South Koreans treated North Korean prisoners. The prisoner was turned over to the squad of South Korean Police that was attached to B Company for the return to battalion command post. He never made it alive!

It was soon discovered that the 2nd and 3rd Rifle Platoons could not properly cover the entire ridge so the 1st Platoon was ordered on line too, but still quite a bit of the ridge had to be covered only by gun fire. Our Wireman, Bob Cook, didn't have enough wire for our phones and all but one of the radios were out, so our communications were poor, at best.

We had not yet learned of the order for a 50 percent watch which meant that at least 50 percent of the men must be awake at all times. We had been fighting hard these past 10 days and the men were extremely fatigued, so we only required a 25 percent watch.

The North Koreans had just been pushed off Hill 202 which we were now on, and they had prepared the fortifications, that we now manned. The enemy knew the terrain quite well.

At about 0450 August 13, we had a report from the 2nd Platoon that there was activity to their immediate front, feeling out a gap between 1st and 2nd Platoons. About that time, a flare went up to our immediate front and all hell broke loose on our left flank. The North Koreans evidently had moved up the hill under cover of darkness and right under the noses of our men who were supposed to be awake. That was the last mistake some of them would make.

Our entire left flank was overrun and the 3rd Section of machine guns, 10 men, were wiped out. The enemy turned those two machine guns on the rest of B Company.

Mortar Platoon, August 1951—always ready (USMC)

As soon as we were overrun on the left flank, a runner was sent to the 3rd Platoon ordering it to fall back into the company perimeter. The enemy had managed to cut our wire to the 3rd Platoon and runners were the only means of communication left.

The enemy had a small mortar and we were taking a lot of mortar rounds in B Company command post. We asked for 81mm, 4.2 mortar and artillery fire and told them not to hesitate in bringing it close to the company. They would have to bring it in right on top of us in order to hit the enemy.

After the 3rd Platoon had successfully pulled back within our perimeter, we spotted the machine guns the enemy had captured. We took one of our 3.5" rocket launchers, manned by Billie Rippy, and fired a round into one of their machine-gun emplacements, knocking it out and killing its crew. The use of this rocket proved so effective that we started employing all three of our 3.5" launchers on the enemy positions on our left flank. We succeeded in knocking out the other machine gun.

Daylight on August 14 was rapidly approaching and we could see the enemy had the upper hand from his positions on the high ground of the ridgeline. We decided to pull back to the Second Platoon's positions on the right portion of the ridge and reorganize to counterattack at daybreak.

We had called the artillery and mortars in to within 50 yards of our lines and they were doing a wonderful job. We took a round or two ourselves, but the fire had proved very effective.

At daybreak, we were reorganized and had enough artillery and mortars focused on the enemy positions, so we were ready to jump off in the counterattack, but when we requested permission to attack, we were ordered down off the hill!

We immediately notified battalion that we had some dead on the ridge, which was in enemy hands, and that we thought that we could go back up without too much difficulty and seize that ground and at least take our dead out. This request was not granted! The battalion commander stated that there was a great deal of urgency, which we must pull off, immediately. This was very demoralizing to us. We did not want to leave our dead—Our Brothers.

After we pulled down off the mountain, we loaded into the trucks back to Chindong-ni. We found that the enemy had penetrated the army lines on the Naktong River and we were to be rushed up to close the hole. We were being sent back to retake that portion of the Naktong River Perimeter, which we had taken the previous week and turned over to the army. The Marines we were forced to leave on the hill, were found later by another unit. Baker Company had 25 Marines Killed in Action, Missing in Action or Died of Wounds August 12–13, 1950. By these numbers, this appears to be the Baker Bandits' worst battle losses in the Korean War.

# Pusan Perimeter

## U.S. Marine Operations in Korea, Vol. 1

### Enemy Dawn Attack at Changchon

Baker Company had a return engagement before dawn on 13 August with the enemy in the Changchon area. Company commanders had received orders the night before to alert their units at 0400 for the withdrawal. General Craig's Operations Order 10-50 was a complete and well-planned field order, despite the need for haste; but the enemy interrupted with a surprise attack launched from concealed positions occupied under cover of darkness.

Baker Company's defense setup for the night on Hill 202 consisted of the 3rd, 1st, and 2nd Platoons tied in from left to right in that order. The action began on August 13, 1950 at 0450 with enemy automatic weapons fire. Marine 60mm mortar illuminating shells revealed a North Korean infiltration on the right in the area of the 2nd Platoon.

This effort soon proved to be a diversionary attack for the purpose of masking the main blow. At 0455 three enemy flares went up, two red and one green. They were the signal for an enemy assault on the left flank at the other end of the Baker Company position. The enemy, as a wounded Marine put it afterwards, was "right on top of the 3rd Platoon in a few seconds" with grenades and burp guns.

This was one of the occasions when the marines were painfully reminded that the North Korean 6th Division had been made up originally of veterans of the Chinese civil

Commanding Brigadier General Craig, 1st Provisional Brigade (USMC)

war and were conditioned by experience of the rigors of night fighting. Marine security had not been a fault, yet the enemy had managed to creep forward in uncanny silence to positions within grenade-throwing distance.

In an instant, the Marine position was overrun, with the machine-gun section being wiped out except for two men. Communication troubles added to the confusion. Platoon radios had been rendered inoperative by mud and water while crossing rice paddies, and telephone wires were believed to have been cut. Two runners were killed during Tobin's efforts to maintain contact with the hard-pressed troops on the left flank. A third runner got through with orders for the remnants of the platoon to fall back within the perimeter of the adjacent 1st Platoon.

The troubles of Baker Company were compounded at this stage when the enemy turned two of the Marines' own machine guns against them. During the next hour the fight became a slugging match. When the grey light of dawn permitted some visibility, Baker Company's 3.5" rocket launchers knocked out the two machine guns being fired by the enemy. The left flank was holding well when the 60mm mortars ran out of ammunition. To make matters worse, the artillery's radio took destructive hits from machine-gun fire just as the enemy changed the direction of his attack. At this point, the enemy's main effort was being channeled up the draw between the 1st and 2nd Platoons for the obvious purpose of splitting the company and beating it in detail. The attackers had been

B-1-5 machine gunners (USMC)

bled white by casualties, however, and Tobin's men had little difficulty in beating off the new assault.

## Breaking off Action

Battalion orders were received through A Company to disengage at 0630 and pull down from the high ground to the trucking point at Newton's Command Post. Captain Tobin, the B Company Commander, was now depending on A Company radios for 4.2" and 81mm mortar support which slowed up enemy efforts. As his first move toward breaking off action, Tobin ordered his 3rd and 1st Platoons to withdraw into the perimeter of the 2nd Platoon.

By this time, the enemy had fallen back toward the lower levels of Hill 202. Small-arms fire had slackened, but the Marines still received mortar bursts.

Tobin ordered his executive officer, Captain Francis "Ike" Fenton, to take the wounded across the rice paddies to the road with the 3rd Platoon and Headquarters troops. Tobin remained on the hill to cover this movement with the other two platoons. After Fenton got well underway, Tobin ordered the 2nd Platoon down to the road. Then, a squad at a time, the remaining Marines disengaged. The Baker Company commander came off Hill 202 with the last squad at 0815. The entire movement had been accomplished with precision, and a final airstrike kept the enemy quiet at the climax.

Considering the fury of the fighting on Hill 202, a Company casualty list of 25 Killed in Action in these two days might have been expected, but we initially only recovered three dead. The idea of men missing in action is always disturbing to Marine officers, but it was considered a moral certainty that the 21 MIAs were killed when the enemy overran the machine-gun section on the Baker Company left flank.

Before leaving Hill 202, Captain Tobin asked permission to lead an attack for the purpose of recovering the bodies. He believed that he could retake the lost ground in an hour, but his request could was not granted.

Just four days later, on August 17, 1950, Baker Company was redeployed.

# B-1-5 Casualties—August 12–13, 1950

## Killed in Action

*Confirmed through Korean War Project*

| | | |
|---|---|---|
| CPL Richard E. Hawley, from Portland, Oregon | MIA-KIA | 12AUG50 |
| PFC Edward A. Muntz, from Houston, Texas | MIA-KIA | 12AUG50 |
| SGT James R. Shepard, from Huntington, WV | MIA-KIA | 12AUG50 |
| SGT David M. Archer, from Dallas, Texas | DOW | 13AUG50 |
| PFC Patrick J. Berkey, from Twin Falls, Idaho | MIA-KIA | 13AUG50 |
| PFC Herman C. Bohnke Jr, from Carnegie, Penn | MIA-KIA | 13AUG50 |
| PFC Alfredo Carrizales, from San Benito, Texas | MIA-KIA | 13AUG50 |
| PFC Roger D. Fortenberry, from Houston, Texas | MIA-KIA | 13AUG50 |
| PFC Freddie Garcia, from Santa Paula, California | MIA-KIA | 13AUG50 |
| CPL Richard Garcia, from San Antonio, Texas | MIA-KIA | 13AUG50 |
| PFC Gilbert R. Gaudet, from New Orleans, Louisiana | MIA-KIA | 13AUG50 |
| PFC Gerald D. Hooper, from Athol, Kansas | MIA-KIA | 13AUG50 |
| SSGT Eugene L. Lawson, from Enid, Oklahoma | MIA-KIA | 13AUG50 |
| SGT Charles A. McCoy, from Hockerville, Oklahoma | MIA-KIA | 13AUG50 |
| PFC Spencer C. Meldrum, from Provo, Utah | MIA-KIA | 13AUG50 |
| PFC Joseph Ostergaard, from Richmond, California | MIA-KIA | 13AUG50 |
| PFC Arkie B. Parrish, from Norfolk, Virginia | MIA-KIA | 13AUG50 |
| PFC Bobby R. Poare, from Salinas, California | MIA-KIA | 13AUG50 |
| PFC Joseph W. Remine, from Leadville, Colorado | KIA | 13AUG50 |
| PFC Carlos L. Robles, from El Paso, Texas | MIA-KIA | 13AUG50 |
| PFC Jose R. Rodriguez, from Visalia, California | MIA-KIA | 13AUG50 |
| PFC Gerald A. Schick, from San Diego, California | MIA-KIA | 13AUG50 |
| PFC Bernard U. Stavely, from Hyattsville, Maryland | MIA-KIA | 13AUG50 |
| PFC Huey E. Upshaw, from Lillie, Louisiana | MIA-KIA | 13AUG50 |
| PFC Lawrence A. Wilcox, from Steinauer, Nebraska | MIA-KIA | 13AUG50 |

Many of these casualties were transferred from MIA to the KIA column in September 1950, after the enemy withdrew from the area and the Marines were allowed to recover their bodies. Others continued to be listed as MIA until November 1953, when they were assumed to be dead.

# A Day Rest and Move

## B Company Commanding Officer, Captain "Ike" Fenton

*This de-briefing is in the Question-and Answer-format. It was performed by The Historical Division, Headquarters USMC upon Captain Fenton's return from Korea and listed as Secret for years. It is no longer secret!*

Q. Let's move on to the next phase, including the period of 13–19 August. This phase was characterized by the first Naktong Bulge Battle, sometimes called Red Slash Hill Battle, or Obong-ni Ridge Battle. Tell us what happened to your unit after you were withdrawn and headed back toward Mirayang.

A. After we got back in the trucks at Changallon, we pulled back to Chindong-ni to an assembly area in a river bed. The 3rd Battalion had been committed to aid the army in this area and was already in the attack. We were more or less expecting to be committed in this area too. That night at 2400, August 13,

B-1-5 Platoon going back after a hard day's battle (Palatas)

1950, we received orders to move afoot to a point on the coast where we were to board a Landing Ship for Tanks (LST) and go to Masan. The reason we were to go by LST instead of trucks was that the North Koreans had infiltrated through the army's lines and had set up a road block on the Masan–Chindong-ni road restricting movement by that route. We started walking and boarded the Landing Ship (LST) about 0230 on the 14th. We arrived in Masan about 0930 or 1000. We immediately moved to the rail head where we had our first hot meal since our arrival in Korea. While in the middle of handing out dinner, the train came in, and we had to leave with only about half of the men having been fed.

We boarded the train and went to Miryang, arriving up there about 1930. We went immediately into a bivouac area "Bean Patch" which was located in a grove of trees by a fast-flowing river. This was our first opportunity to have a bath, wash clothes, and get cleaned up.

We were at Miryang all day the 15th. On August 16, 1950, we received orders to move out to the Yongsan area. The Brigade was going to be attached to the 24th Army Division for an attack. Formation: 2nd and 3rd Battalions in the assault and the 1st Battalion in Brigade Reserve. Due to shortage of trucks, it was an impossibility to take all battalions up at the same time, so the 2nd and 3rd Battalions moved up ahead of us.

Waiting for the next battle (Green)

# Obong-Ni Ridge: Captain Tobin Is Shot

## B Company Commanding Officer, Captain "Ike" Fenton

*This de-briefing is in the Question-and-Answer format. It was performed by The Historical Division Headquarters USMC upon Captain Fenton's return from Korea and listed as Secret for years. It is no longer secret!*

Q. Your B Company Commander was shot during this battle. Tell us about this incident.

A. On August 17, 1950, shortly after 1330, Captain Tobin deployed his 3rd Platoon and machine guns on the forward slopes of Observation Hill to support Company B's attack. The 1st and 2nd Platoons crossed the rice paddy and at 1500 passed through Company D on the slopes of the objective. Lieutenant Schryver led his 1st Platoon toward Hill 102, while Lt Taylor moved his 2nd Platoon up

B-1-5 Bazooka section rocket launcher (Sydman)

the gully leading to the saddle between Hill 102 and Hill109.

On Observation Hill, Captain Tobin noted how rapidly the enemy was advancing. This ridgeline was 400 yards to the southwest of Obong-ni Ridge, and where Captain Andy Zimmer, D Company's Commander, was located. While Tobin was obtaining information from the D Company Commander, Captain Zimmer and his radio operator were wounded and had to be evacuated. Captain Tobin immediately sent for me and the platoon leaders to come forward to where the road passed through the saddle of the ridgeline.

Captain Tobin met us there, and, while he was pointing out the area in which we were to attack, a North Korean machine gun opened up and severely wounded Captain Tobin in the chest and arms. Fenton directed the evacuation of the seriously wounded Tobin and then took command of B Company.

Captain Ike Fenton stepped in as commanding officer when Captain Tobin was hit (Duncan)

By this time, both assault platoons had been pinned down, the 1st Platoon was about two-thirds of the way up the slope, the 2nd Platoon only half that distance. The latter was taking heavy casualties from enemy guns on Hills 109, 117, and 143. Lieutenant Taylor himself sustaining a mortal wound on August 17.

Captain Fenton and his Gunnery Sergeant, Master Sergeant Edward A. Wright were stalled with the 2nd platoon. Since Lt Schryver's unit was also held up, the company commander radioed Observation Hill and committed his 3rd Platoon.

Lieutenant Schryver realized that the main obstacle to his advance was the fire hitting his flank from the village of Tugok, and he requested a fire mission from 1/5's Weapons Company. As 81mm mortar shells rained down on the village, the 1st Platoon worked westward to the spur above the Main Supply Route and outflanked the North Korean 18th Regiment. A quick assault carried Hill 102 at 1710.

With Lt Schryver's men driving down from the south and Company B's machine guns pouring fire on the peaks of Hill 117 and 143, the 2nd Platoon barreled its way up the draw and seized Hill 109 at 1725.

# First Naktong Bulge Battle:
# August 17–19, 1950

## B Company Commanding Officer, Captain "Ike" Fenton

*This de-briefing was performed by the Historical Division. Headquarters USMC upon Captain Fenton's return from Korea and listed as Secret for years. It is no longer secret!*

Q. The next phase is known as the first Naktong Bulge Battle. Tell us about this phase.

A. It wasn't until the morning of August 17, 1950 that we were able to load our battalion up and take off for Yongsan. This was about a 24-mile trip, and we made it in about two hours, arriving at Yongsan about 0730.

The 2nd Battalion was already in the attack, abreast of the 24th Division and the 9th Regimental Combat Team and headed toward Obong-ni Ridge which was the Objective-1 line. This attack was preceded by many heavy airstrikes and heavy artillery fire, but stubborn resistance continued. At 1100 we were in reserve about 1,000 yards to the rear of the 2nd Battalion when word was received that the 1st Battalion was to move forward and pass through the 2nd Battalion and continue to attack. The 2nd Battalion had run into a very heavy resistance and their casualties had been heavy. The enemy was well dug in on Obong-ni Ridge, and although the 2nd Battalion had managed to reach the ridgeline on two or three occasions they were not able to hold it due to their heavy casualties.

A Company, 1st Battalion, under the command of Captain John Stevens, was to be the battalion's left flank company and relieve E Company, 2nd Battalion. B Company, under the command of Captain John Tobin, was to pass through and relieve D Company, 2nd Battalion. Captain Tobin went forward to the ridgeline that ran parallel to Obong-ni Ridge. while he was pointing out the area in which we were to attack, a North Korean machine gun opened up and severely wounded Captain Tobin in the chest and arms. He had to be evacuated. I immediately notified the battalion commander and assumed command of B Company. We jumped off in attack with two platoons on line, one in support.

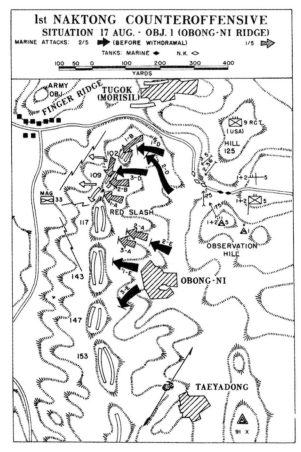

**1st NAKTONG COUNTEROFFENSIVE**
SITUATION 17 AUG. - OBJ. 1 (OBONG-NI RIDGE)

B Company seized Obong-ni Ridge at 1700 (USMC)

The 2nd Platoon was under heavy enemy fire as they moved up to what we called "Red Slash." This slash or wash was the boundary between A and B Companies. The 1st Platoon had moved to the base of the right side of Obong-ni but due to heavy fire from a village on their right flank, which was in the 9th Army RCT's sector, they were unable to advance without suffering heavy casualties. Because of the hilly terrain between the 1st Platoon and my position, I was unable to observe that village. Lieutenant Nick Schryver, who commanded the 1st Platoon, had to observe and adjust the mortar artillery fire by relaying over his SCR 536 radio. We fired continuously for about 20 minutes into this village before the 1st Platoon was able to move out and seize their portion of the ridge. Upon reaching the top, they were able to relieve the pressure on the 2nd Platoon's front, and the 2nd Platoon moved up and seized its portion of the ridge. B Company had seized Obong-ni Ridge on August 17, 1950 at approximately 1700.

In the meantime, A Company, on our left flank, was having a very tough time. B Company's seizure of the right portion of that ridge did relieve a little pressure on them, but their casualties were quite heavy and they were experiencing great difficulty securing the high points on the ridge.

About 1900, there was a great lull in the fighting and A and B Companies tied in and prepared for a night defense. I made my mind up that this was one night I would lay two lines of telephone wire to my platoons and to the battalion.

I had learned my lesson the hard way at Changallon. In the meantime, the 9th RCT had moved forward and occupied the ridgeline that was to my right front and which ran parallel to Obong-ni Ridge. Between their ridge and the one I was on, a road passed between us and curled back towards my rear. It was on this road that our platoon of M-26 tanks, which had supported our attack during the afternoon, were in position.

At approximately 2000, while we were digging in, one of my men called my attention to two enemy tanks about 5,000 yards to our immediate front. They were coming down the road toward our position. I immediately gave the "flash" and reported, "enemy tanks in the area." Just about this time, Air Force P-51s that had been in the area spotted the tanks and started to make runs on them. However, their runs were ineffective, and they did not score any hits or stop them. While informing the Battalion Commander of the presence of tanks, I spotted a third tank that was following the other two at a distance of approximately 1,000 yards. The Battalion Commander gave me orders to let the tanks pass through and that they would take care of them at the Command Post with the antitank weapons at his disposal. It was just like sitting on the 50-yard line of the Rose Bowl about 150 feet up. We had a good seat for the show that was about to take place. The three tanks came down the road as if they owned the world and with complete disregard for tactics. This was one time they could have maneuvered. There was firm ground to either side of the road. But they stuck to the road and continued towards the 1st Battalion Command Post (CP). The P-51s were still coming in, making their runs, since they were following the tanks they were shooting into our area. We finally managed to call them off the tanks and told them to leave the area. As the first tank rounded the corner down toward the 1st Battalion command post, it was met by 3.5" rocket fire from the antitank assault section, and fire from

our 75mm recoilless weapons in position on the high ground on either side of the road. The first tank was knocked out and the second tank immediately came up and tried to go around it. The second too was hit in the track and skidded off the road. Our M-26 tanks finished him off. The third tank made the same mistake that the second tank made; he too tried to go around the other two tanks. One of our M-26 tanks hit this third

One of our M-26 tanks hit this third tank with a direct hit (USMC)

tank with a direct hit. All three of these tanks were finished off by our M-26 tank platoon. I believe official credit was given to the antitank assault section for knocking out two tanks while the third tank was credited to 75mm recoilless and the M-26. No one escaped from any of these tanks.

We were quite worried that night about getting another night counterattack and cautioned all the men that this time we would have a 25 percent listening watch. We settled down to wait the night out. About 0230, August 18, 1950, my 2nd Platoon, which was on the left flank, reported enemy activity to the immediate front. A few minutes later, a flare went off and the enemy hit us with great force right where the two companies were tied in. Aided by the darkness, their ferocious attack managed to break through our lines. In the meantime, A Company was receiving counterattacks along their entire front. Their left flank was pushed back, and their right was turned by the enemy's penetration.

Upon receipt of the news that the enemy had broken through, I immediately ordered my 2nd Platoon to pull back towards the company and form company perimeter defense with my other platoons. The enemy took full advantage of their breakthrough, and a great number of them managed to overrun my 2nd Platoon. Some of them pushed into my B Company Command Post, where it was actually a case of hand-to-hand fighting. About then, the Battalion Commander notified me that it was of utmost importance that I "hold at all costs." A Company had three breakthroughs on their company front and, if B Company was pushed off the ridge, we'd have to do it all over again in the morning. The situation was confused. It was very dark, there was considerable firing going on, and it was impossible to see the enemy except at very close hand. Several of my non-commissioned officers displayed outstanding gallantry by personally reforming members of the company and leading them in a counterattack against the enemy. We finally pushed the enemy from our perimeter. Throughout the night, we received a great deal of small arms, and mortar fire. About an hour after our counterattack the Army 9th RCT received a counterattack which folded their left flank and drove them back about 200 or 300 yards. After reorganizing they launched an attack and retook their position.

When daylight arrived on August 19, 1950, I was the only officer left in the company and we had approximately 88 men left on line. When we went into combat the afternoon of August 18, 1950, we had a little better than 190 men and five officers. Captain Tobin had been wounded; Lieutenant Taylor had been killed; Lieutenant Schryver, my 1st Platoon Leader was wounded in the head by a hand grenade. Schryver was evacuated but returned shortly after daylight. The 2nd Platoon, which had borne the brunt of the attack, had but 11 men left. We were shot up but morale was good. The boys felt that they had done a pretty fine job in holding our line that night. With daylight's arrival, we were able to see groups of enemy on the high ground along the ridgeline on our left flank. A Company's right flank was down below the Red Slash.

During the night, a few stragglers from A Company had joined B Company. We reorganized 15 of them into a patrol and had them move down the ridgeline toward the enemy, while A Company moved up toward the ridgeline in a coordinated attack. Mortars and an airstrike supported their attack. However, there was one enemy machine gun that we couldn't knock out and it kept A Company's right flank pinned down.

Due to the situation, the Battalion Commander, on Captain Stevens's request, called in an airstrike, requesting a 500-pound bomb to hit this enemy position. The plane came in and actually pin-pointed the target with a direct hit. It landed at a distance no greater than 100 yards from the A Company lines. After this bomb hit, a few strafing runs and a napalm strike were called. A Company was able to move up and retake their sector of the ridge.

About 1000 we received orders to sweep down the ridge to the left and secure all high ground on the ridge. The 3rd Battalion was going to pass through us and take the Objective 2 (O-2) line, which was the high ground to our immediate front. The 3rd Battalion jumped off into the attack and seized O-2 without too much opposition. A lot of opposition had initially been expected at the O-2 line, but after Obong-ni fell, we knew we had cracked the enemy's main supply route. Immediately upon seizure of the O-2 line, the 3rd Battalion was ordered to continue the attack and seize the Objective 3 line which was the Brigade's final objective, the high ground that overlooked the Naktong River. The 2nd Battalion moved up into position and took over the Objective 2 line while the 3rd Battalion moved into position to attack the O-3 line.

By darkness the 3rd Battalion had managed to get two-thirds of the way up O-3 and dug in for the night. At daybreak on August 20, 1950, they continued the attack and secured the O-3 line.

To conclude the 1st Naktong Bulge battle, I would like to mention now that when Obong-ni was secured on the morning of August 18, 1950, B Company had only two officers and 88 men, left. I'd say, out of those 88 men, that approximately 20 men were wounded. A Company had but four officers and 100 men, effective. Full force would have been four officers and about 200 men.

In going over to the enemy positions on the ridge in a very brief inspection, we found about 25 heavy Browning machine guns, 15 light machine guns, numerous small arms and Browning automatic rifles, one 3.5" rocket launcher with nine rounds, four antitank rifles with large amounts of ammunition, and numerous hand grenades. The enemy also had one SCR 300 radio on our Battalion tactical net, and five or six SCR 536 radios laying around in the general area.

*—Ike—*

# Captain Tobin

## Lieutenant Nick Schryver

Captain Tobin was the first commanding officer of B Company in Korea, but his command did not last long. At the the first Naktong Bulge Battle he was severely wounded, never to return to battle.

The Brigade was given the mission of driving the North Koreans back across the Naktong River but to get there, they had to pass Obong-ni Ridge. The Second Battalion was ordered into the assault on the ridge. They suffered such heavy casualties that the 1st Battalion was ordered to pass through. Captain Tobin assigned my 1st Platoon on the right (as usual), 2nd Platoon on the left. We passed through Dog Company (2nd Battalion) and were successful in securing the objective. As we were "mopping up," a quick volley found Captain Tobin and he went down. Captain Fenton, until then our executive officer, radioed all units that Captain Tobin had been wounded and Fenton had assumed command. It was a real shocker. How could he have been wounded way back in the relative safe locality behind the front lines? It turned out a North Korean with a burp gun had hidden in the valley, apparently determined to gun down some high-ranking Marine Officers. Captain Tobin was conversing with General Craig and Colonel Murray. This was the target the Chinese had laid in wait for. He missed the general and colonel, but not Captain Tobin.

Somehow, I got possession of the map Captain Tobin had in the breast pocket of his dungarees. It was riddled with burp gun bullet holes and covered with his blood. I carried this map all through my tour in Korea and brought it back with me.

About 10 years later, when I was stationed at Marine Corp Headquarters, then Lieutenant Colonel Tobin came in for a few days of temporary duty. I was happy to return the map to him as memento of a more difficult time. And so another chapter comes to a close. Semper Fidelis,

—*Nick*—

# An Open Letter to Captain J. L. Tobin

## Fred R. Neuman

Dear Skipper

When you were wounded in action in August of 1950, the whole company felt a tremendous loss. You had the uncanny knack that few commanders possess. You made the troops feel comfortable in your presence and at the same time never let us forget you were the "boss." I was in your command in C-1-6 from May 1949 and when they formed B Company in September 49, I went with you to Pusan through September 50. As I recall, you never ordered anyone to do something but always "asked." It sure as hell got the same results and impressed the hell out of me and others in your command. It must be the mark of a true "mustang."

I have the greatest respect for you and the other company officers, who, under your direction, made B-1-5 the fine unit it became. I've talked to friends who had gone on to many different units after they left B-1-5 and they all agree that the old B-1-5 was the best unit they ever served in.

I just wanted to say "thank you" for being instrumental in putting together one of the finest units the corps has ever seen and I'm extremely proud to say that I was a part of that unit.

*—Fred—*

# B-1-5 Casualties and Medals— August 17–18, 1950

## Killed in Action

*Confirmed through Korean War Project*

| | | |
|---|---|---|
| PFC Herbert F. Huner from Blue Earth, Minnesota | KIA | 17AUG50 |
| PFC Lester H. Van Nort from Frankfort, New York | KIA | 17AUG50 |
| CPL Jewell C. Bruce from Mounds, Illinois | KIA | 18AUG50 |
| PFC Edward D. Darchuck from Scobey, Montana | KIA | 18AUG50 |
| PFC Donald E. Edwards from Richfield, Idaho | KIA | 18AUG50 |
| CPL Howard A. McDonough Jr. from Berkley, Mich. | KIA | 18AUG50 |
| PFC Kenneth J. Milligan Jr. from Galveston, Texas | KIA | 18AUG50 |
| PFC Joseph D. Moss from Pevely, Missouri | KIA | 18AUG50 |
| CPL Alejandro E. Salinas from Tucson, Arizona | KIA | 18AUG50 |
| PFC Robert B. Smith from San Pedro, California | KIA | 18AUG50 |
| 1LT David S. Taylor from Walla Walla, Wash. | KIA | 18AUG50 |
| | | Silver Star |

## Distinguished Service Cross

Corporal Jewell C. Bruce (Posthumously)

Corporal Jewell C. Bruce, United States Marine Corps, distinguished himself by extraordinary heroism against the enemy while serving with a Marine rifle company in Korea on August 18, 1950. Corporal BRUCE was a squad leader in a rifle platoon occupying a night defense position when the enemy suddenly launched a counterattack against his company's sector. With absolute disregard for his own safety, he dashed from foxhole to foxhole in an area swept by enemy machine-gun fire shouting encouragement as he rallied his disorganized squad. The determination of their leader to drive back the aggressors was instilled into his men as Corporal BRUCE led a charge against the point of enemy penetration. Assuming a forward position, he delivered accurate and destructive grenade volleys on the enemy as hand grenades were passed forward to him. His outstanding leadership and great courage contributed substantially to the successful counterassault that drove the enemy from the Obongi Ridge. In the course of this action, Corporal BRUCE gallantly gave his life for his country. His exemplary heroism and devotion to duty are in keeping with our most cherished ideals and reflect great credit on himself and the military service.

BY COMMAND OF GENERAL MacARTHUR the Distinguished Service Cross was awarded October 22, 1950 (Posthumously).

## Silver Star

First Lieutenant David Taylor (Posthumously)

First Lieutenant David Scott Taylor, United States Marine Corps, distinguished himself with gallantry in action against an armed enemy while serving with Company B, 1st Battalion, 5th Marines, 1st Provisional Marine Brigade, in action against enemy aggressor forces in Southern Korea on August 17, 1950. On this date, the B Company, 1st Battalion, 5th Marines (B-1-5), attacked elements of the 4th North Korean Army Division, located on Obangi Ridge, four and one-half miles west of Yongsan, Korea. At approximately 1630 hours, B-1-5 was halfway up the slope of the ridge. The 2nd Platoon, B Company, in the assault, was pinned down by heavy machine gun, automatic, and small-arms fire and was suffering heavy casualties. It was at this time that Lieutenant Taylor, Platoon Leader of the Second Platoon, personally led a portion of his platoon in a flanking maneuver to the top of the ridge to build up a base of fire on his platoon's right flank in order that the remainder of his platoon could advance. At this time, Lieutenant Taylor received a gunshot wound in his left thigh, but continued to supervise and direct the fire of his platoon until the majority of the remainder of his platoon had reached the crest of the ridge. Due to the pain and the great loss of blood, Lieutenant Taylor finally allowed himself to be evacuated. His actions materially contributed to his platoon's success and final attainment of the objective. The gallantry displayed by Lieutenant Taylor reflects great credit on himself and the United States Naval Service.

# This Is War!

## Corporal Emmett Shelton, Jr.

David Douglas Duncan was a Marine in World War II. He became a photographer after the war. In 1950, Duncan was working for *Life* magazine covering the Korean War since the outbreak. He sent his boss this message about the one story he wanted to do most:

GOING BACK THIS TIME TRYING GIVE YOU STORY WHICH IS TIMELESS, NAMELESS, DATELESS, AND WORDLESS STORY WHICH SAYS VERY SIMPLY AND QUIETLY "THIS IS WAR"

Duncan wrote:

I wanted to show what war did to a man. I wanted to show something of the comradeship that binds men together when they are fighting a common peril. I wanted to show the way men lived, and died when they know Death is among them, and yet they still find the strength to crawl forward armed with only bayonets to stop the advance of men they have never seen, with whom they have no immediate quarrel, men who will kill them on sight if given the first chance.

I wanted to show something of the agony, the suffering, the terrible confusion, the heroism which is every day currency among the men who actually pull the triggers of rifles aimed at other men known only as "the enemy."

I wanted to tell a story of war, as war has always been for men throughout the ages. Only the weapons, terrain, and the causes have changed.

Duncan joined the 1st Brigade's most forward unit B Company, 1st Division, 5th Regiment, on September 5, 1950. He ate,

Life photographer David Duncan came to B-1-5 to photograph war (Duncan)

C.O. Ike Fenton—"It's raining, no ammo, no radio, no air support, but don't let the men fall back" (Duncan)

lived, slept, and damn near died, with Baker Company during the intense battles in the Pusan Perimeter at the start of the war.

Duncan's book *This is War* was photographed during the Pusan Perimeter with B-1-5, Seoul with A-1-5, and a return visit to the 1st Division Marines during Chosin Reservoir.

The photo essay was first published September 15, 1950 in *Life* magazine. The book was first published in 1951. This book is one of the prized possessions of most veterans of that time.

In putting together the serialized version of "Ike" Fenton's de-briefing for *The Guidon*, I needed as many good pictures as possible. I called Mr. Duncan at his home in France to ask permission to use some of his excellent photos of the men of B-1-5. He said "Certainly." So you will see some of his photos intermixed with others I have from that period. My thanks go out to Mr. Duncan, his help will make our enjoyment and understanding of the Korean War much more fulfilling.

By the way, last year I covered the visit of Mr. Duncan to the University of Texas, where he opened an exhibit of his pictures. I met him then for the first time. Billy Rippy and "Ike" remembered him from Korea, and he even shared a foxhole with Duncan several times. Mr. Duncan was also given an award by USMC.

"Ike" Fenton and Mr. Duncan were best of friends. Duncan's lifetime retrospective, *My 20th Century* (2014) book cover features that famous picture of "Ike" on the 1st Naktong when, as the enemy attacked "Ike" had lost radio contact with battalion, it was raining, men were falling and battalion was out of ammo, just bayonets and grenades.

*—Emmett—*

# Second Naktong Bulge Battle, September 3–5, 1950

## B Company Commanding Officer, Captain "Ike" Fenton

*This de-briefing was performed by The Historical Division, Headquarters USMC upon Captain Fenton's return from Korea and listed as Secret for years. It is no longer secret!*

*Q. On September 1, 1950, B Company was in the Chang-won area, there was a general enemy attack at several points along the front. General Walker alerted the Marine Brigade at 1100 for a move to Miryang, again. The move was to begin at 1330. In view of the sudden change, is it fair to say you were quite surprised to again be called to the Naktong Bulge area?*

A. We had expected to remain in support of the 25th Division at Chindong-Ni. When we heard that we were going back to Miryang again, that the Koreans had recrossed the Naktong River, this time all the way to Yongsan, we were disgusted. It just seemed endless; down from the south up to the central front, from the central front back down south, from the south back up to the central front. We were beginning to feel like the queen on a chess board going around checkmating everything.

*Q. Describe the movement to the new assembly area and subsequent action.*

A. On September 1 we received the word to load out and board a train. We arrived about 1700 at Miryang. Owing to the shortage of trucks, we had to shuttle, and the entire battalion wasn't in the assembly area until 2400. Early September 2, 1950, we received a warning order to move to Yongsan. We pulled out at 0800 and moved to an assembly area near the 2nd Army Division Command Post. Men cleaned weapons and rested in preparation for a move later in the night to Yongsan with the 1st and 2nd Battalions. We moved out at 0030, September 3, into the approach march with the 2nd Battalion on the right and the 1st Battalion on the left. We were to follow the trace of the 2nd Battalion, which was to pass through the army and take their position. B Company was to move up abreast and jump off in the attack at 0800. The 2nd Battalion was held up at the outskirts of Yongsan by enemy mortar and small-arms fire. This caused a delay of about an hour in arriving at the line of departure. We were further delayed because the actual army defense lines, which the 1st and 2nd Battalions were to occupy prior to jumping off had moved back considerably. The Army 9th Regimental Combat Team (RCT), due to heavy pressure from the enemy during the night, had withdrawn to a new position.

About 0900, we were on line with the 2nd Battalion and ready to jump off. The 2nd had to cross a long rice paddy field which had little hills scattered throughout the center of it. We received

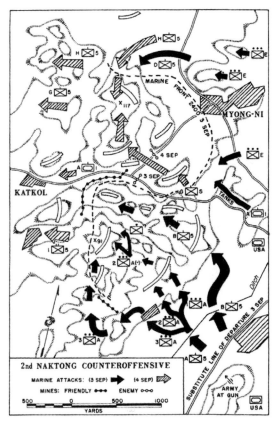

B Company's mission was to seize the high ground in front and the 2nd Battalion would take the ground in front (USMC)

intense small-arms, machine-gun, mortar and artillery fire and a very difficult time moving. The 1st Battalion, with A Company and B Company abreast, had to move across another rice paddy field, but it was only about half the length of that in front of the 2nd Battalion. B Company's mission was to seize the high ground to the immediate front, at which time the 2nd Battalion would move out and take the ground to our right front. It is interesting to note that this was the first time we actually employed two of our battalions abreast in an attack. Up to now, we had attacked with the battalions in column, one following another in trace.

The 2nd Battalion was pinned down and receiving heavy casualties but the 1st Battalion was able to move and seize the ridgeline without encountering heavy opposition. From our position, we were able to support the 2nd Battalion, but enemy defense was strong. By nightfall, orders were received for both battalions to hold what they had for the night. We had a few small counterattacks that

Gunnery Sgt Long (Palatas)

night but they were easily repulsed. We had a suspicion that the enemy was withdrawing. At 0800, on Sept 4, the battalion received an order to continue the attack. The 3rd Battalion moved up, passed through the 2nd Battalion and moved up on B Company's right flank. We moved out rapidly and in about 20 minutes overran the enemy's old command post. Tents were still up and equipment was all about. They pulled out in a hurry. We captured two T34 tanks unmanned in excellent condition. Nearly, was an ammunitions dump which we blew up. Our advance continued rapidly and we were meeting virtually no resistance. We had them on the run. We began taking prisoners and had 12 by noon.

By 1500 we had seized Objective 1. Next, we had to cross another big rice paddy, 1600 meters long, Tanks and vehicles could not cross the field and had to stay on the road. The plan was for the 1st Battalion to seize the left of the field by road and the 3rd Battalion would seize the left. B Company took over the lead. When we were about three-fourths of the way across the paddy, we received very heavy enfilade machine-gun, small-arms and mortar fire from our right flank. We were pinned down with little cover. I ordered a move forward under cover of close air support and sent our tanks between the small-arms fire and our troops. The amazing part is we had no casualties and I would say this was the most intense fire as any received in a daylight attack.

From our position, I could see Obong-Ni Ridge. It was the same ground that we had moved over in our first drive on the Naktong River in August. We felt we would get some enemy action that night, so I requested engineers and we mined the roads, and booby trapped every approach, and set up trip flares. We really tied ourselves in with demolitions.

During the night, the battalion command post received quite a bit of shelling. The black-out tent took a direct hit. Because it had been raining hard all afternoon and night, we were unable to get close air support. However, most was quiet that night.

The next morning, September 5, we received the order to continue the attack. This time my first phase was to be Obong-Ni ridge. We pulled up all of the demolitions we had set the previous night and then got word of a change in plans. B Company would right flank the 3rd Battalion. The Army 9th RCT was supposed to come abreast and jump off with us, however, at jump off time, the 9th hadn't arrived. We were ordered to jump off and continue the attack without them. It had been raining all night, and the battalion had managed to get some hot coffee up to us, but just as the coffee arrived, we got the word to move out. We were not able to distribute the coffee to the troops. This turn of events was not good for morale. The men were soaking wet. The men were getting anxious to get this thing over. We felt that we stood a good chance today, September 5, of running the enemy right back across the river. If we had any chance we were going to break their back. We moved out about 0800 against scattered resistance. It was enough to slow us down. The resistance fell back and we moved along rapidly. A and B Companies were working in close harmony, one taking the high ground, the other providing a base of fire.

B Company advanced about 3,000 yards to a ridgeline parallel to Obong-Ni Ridge. We had very little resistance and we thought we would be ordered to take Obong-Ni Ridge. New orders were to hold up until the adjacent units had come abreast. It is my belief, and the belief of the men, that the enemy had been withdrawn to the Obong-Ni Ridge to prepare a main line of resistance. I expected A and B Companies would come over the ridge and get down in the rice paddy and then the enemy would open up on them. I got word to stop and prepare a hasty defense. The men started digging in. And then, everything broke loose. We were pinned down and we could not move. The entire ridgeline was being swept by enemy fire.

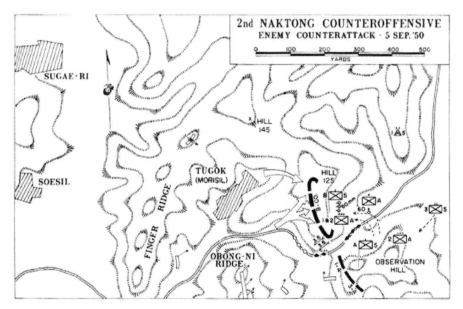

B Company's objective was Obong-Ni Ridge and would right flank the 3rd Battalion but the 9th Army had not arrived (USMC)

Unfortunately, it was raining very hard and we were unable to call in close air support. To make matters more difficult, the rain had knocked out all of my radios. The Battalion tactical radio also went out as did the artilleries. I was without communications to battalion. A runner reported to me that elements of the army were coming up on my right about 2,000 yards behind.

THEN, THE ENEMY LAUNCHED A STRONG COUNTERATTACK AGAINST B COMPANY. Three enemy tanks and about 350 enemy troops supported a well-planned counterattack, preceded by heavy mortar barrage and antitank high-velocity fire from the ridge. I sent a runner to the army unit for artillery support. I sent two runners back to Battalion Commander to notify him of what was taking place. I sent a third runner to notify our tanks and caution them about the enemy tanks up the road.

Our tanks were in the same position that they had been in on the first Obong-Ni Battle and at that time they destroyed three enemy tanks. While the positions were identical, this time the enemy caught out lead tank with its gun trained in the wrong direction. Just as out lead tank made the turn in the road, the enemy opened up and scored a direct hit on the turret, knocking out the tank. Our second tank made the same mistake and it too was knocked out.

Meanwhile a counterattack hit us. Heavy rain reduced visibility. We had a number of blind spots in our field of fire. I had every man in B Company on the line. Rocketmen, corpsmen, mortarmen, everyone. To make matters worse, we were running out of ammunition. I was almost out of grenades, and things did not look good for us.

Lieutenant Colonel George Newton guessed our situation and sent a much-welcomed platoon from A Company with five boxes of hand grenades. The enemy had closed so rapidly that we just took the grenades out of the case and threw them directly to the men in the line. They would pull the pins and throw them—the enemy was less than 100 yards.

I finally got a radio working and called in heavy 81mm fire. The counterattack began at 1420 and was over about 1500. It was hard to believe that, with the intense enemy fire, our number killed, in proportion to wounded, was very low. During that period, I had two men killed and 23 wounded, of which two later died of their wounds.

Men of the B-1-5 returning after a hard day of battle (Green)

# Just Another Fine Marine Private

## B Company Commanding Officer, Captain "Ike" Fenton

*This de-briefing was performed by The Historical Division, Headquarters USMC upon Captain Fenton's return from Korea and listed as Secret for years. It is no longer secret!*

During the Second Naktong, the rain knocked out our radios and we had to depend on runners to communicate. I sent one such runner to communicate with the army unit. This runner was Private William L. Wilson, 22, a graduate of Ohio State University. He made contact with the army company commander and asked for the artillery fire I had ordered. The commander did not have a fire officer and had to observe his own fire. Shortly after, Wilson saw the army officer crawling into a position from which to observe. He was hit and wounded severely and had to be evacuated.

Private Wilson calmly picked up the army radio and called in the fire mission for B Company. After the call, he spotted enemy on Obong-Ni Ridge dragging an antitank weapon into position. He called in another fire mission on them, after which he called in a third mission on a bunch of approaching enemy trucks. Private Wilson then gathered the army platoon leaders and brought them up to date on the situation, advised them as to the best location for their platoons, told them where to tie in, and where to place the army machine guns. Private Wilson then returned to B Company and reported to me of his army contact and the successful fires I had requested.

It was not until that afternoon that I found out what a wonderful job Wilson had done. The army officer told me "What a fine officer Wilson B Company had." I told him that man was not an officer he was just a Fine Marine Private.

*—Ike—*

# B-1-5 Casualties—September 3–5, 1950

## Killed in Action

*Confirmed through Korean War Project*

| | | |
|---|---|---|
| CPL James Aragon Jr, from Paguate, New Mexico | KIA | 5SEP50 |
| PFC Crocker, George A., from Eastboga, Ala. | KIA | 5SEP50 |
| CPL Fare, Kenneth W., from West Amana, Iowa | KIA | 3SEP50 |
| CPL Hoey, Weston W., from Baltimore, Md. | KIA | 5SEP50 |
| PFC Springstein, Myron H. Jr. from Montclaire, NJ | KIA | 4SEP50 |
| PFC Worley, Ronald, from Indianapolis, Ind. | KIA | 3SEP50 |

## Wounded in Action

*Confirmed through USMC Unit Diaries*

| | | |
|---|---|---|
| PFC Booth, Joe C. | WIA | 5SEP50 |
| PFC Brown, Coy G. | WIA | 3SEP50 |
| PFC Cerney, Melvin | WIA | 5SEP50 |
| PFC Dodge, Walter | WIA | 3SEP50 |
| SGT Fonsen, Keith L. | WIA | 5SEP50 |
| PFC Freiburger, Richard | WIA | 3SEP50 |
| CPL Gewitz, Charles E. | WIA | 5SEP50 |
| PFC Maltin, Murray | WIA | 3SEP50 |
| PFC Martinez, Arnulfo | WIA | 3SEP50 |
| PFC Mayes, Howard A. | WIA | 5SEP50 |
| CPL Mitchell, Donald R. | WIA | 5SEP50 |
| CPL Reynolds, Murell W. | WIA | 5SEP50 |
| PFC Shelton, Gillman L. | WIA | 5SEP50 |
| CPL Simpson, Richard J. | WIA | 3SEP50 |
| PFC Slavik, Ernest S. | WIA | 5SEP50 |
| PFC Snell, Chadwick L. | WIA | 5SEP50 |

| | | |
|---|---|---|
| PFC Tague, Robert R. | WIA | 3SEP50 |
| SGT Yates, Clifton B. | WIA | 3SEP50 |
| SGT Yesenko, Thomas | WIA | 3SEP50 |
| MSGT Young, Leonard R. | WIA | 5SEP50 |

# Inchon, Kimpo, Wosan
## September–October 1950

We have to give credit for the success of the attack on Red Slash Hill to the supporting arms, artillery, sir, mortar fire, and to the sheer determination and guts on the part of the men in getting up the hill. There was sweeping fire from machine guns the whole time we were trying to take that ridge. The courage displayed by the men was something to behold.

*—B-1-5 Commanding Officer, Captain "Ike" Fenton—*

# Inchon Landing

## B Company Commanding Officer, Captain "Ike" Fenton

*This de-briefing is in the Question-and-Answer format. It was performed by the Historical Division, Headquarters USMC, upon Captain Fenton's return from Korea and listed as Secret for years. It is no longer secret!*

*Q. What steps were taken to prepare your unit for the Inchon Landing?*

A. We arrived in Pusan on September 6, 1950. The battalion was immediately moved to one of the warehouses where the men were bedded down and given the opportunity to clean up. The following day, preparations commenced for re-equipping the men in clothing and small arms and getting them ready for the coming landing. At this time, we had no idea regarding our destination, whether it would be the east coast, the west coast, or Japan to join the 1st Marine Division. This information was still very highly classified.

We experienced great difficulties in equipping the men with 782 equipment, weapons, shoes and clothing. It was impossible to get Browning Automatic Rifle (BAR) magazines. The B Company rated 19 magazines per BAR, a total of 171 per company. But, we were only able to get enough to give each BAR man six magazines! We had lost a lot of these magazines when men were hit and evacuated—still in possession of their magazines. Many more were lost in rice paddy fields. There just weren't any replacements for BAR magazines in Pusan. Also, there were no replacements for BAR belts, so my BAR men had to carry the lower halves of packs hooked to their belts with telephone wire as their BAR magazine carriers.

There was also a shortage of Marine utility clothes so we had to outfit the men with army clothes. Shoes were a great problem. We still had difficulty getting odd sizes. We looked all over the town of Pusan at the army's various supply installations and the men picked up a pair here and a pair there, but we were unable to outfit all of our men in the correct sizes. We also tried to get new machine guns, but none were available. When we got our orders, we also got some replacement BARs and some new rifles.

The battalion was joined by C Company, which had just arrived from the States. B Company was joined by 17 men designated to form our third Machine Gun Section. In addition, we received replacement officers and men to bring B Company back to wartime strength. B Company strength after receiving these replacements was five officers and 215 men.

On September 11, B Company embarked aboard the USS *Henrico*. On September 12, we sailed for Inchon. It wasn't until that day that the maps and aerial photographs were distributed to the company commanders. At the same time, we received a detailed narrative of what was going to happen. This was our first knowledge of our landing beach and the plan.

I'd like to mention that, while we were in Pusan, the regiment had circulated a mimeographed sheet regarding a landing beach in Kasong. I believe this information was put out to mislead the enemy in the area. The papers were marked Confidential, but we had orders to read them to the troops in the warehouse, and I do believe that a copy or two managed to get lost.

Upon receipt of our operation order, and aerial photographs, I immediately started briefing my platoon leaders, squad leaders, and fire team leaders. The landing plan was so detailed that it was especially necessary for every man to know exactly where to go upon landing. The landing would be made directly against the downtown area of the city, at an hour which would allow just two hours of daylight and at a place where the tide rose and fell approximately 30 feet in a three-hour period.

Initially, B Company was to be in battalion reserve. A and C Companies would land in the assault on the left and right portions, respectively, of Red Beach 1. B Company was to land and follow in trace of A Company. Our reserve mission demanded that all platoon leaders, squad leaders, and fire team leaders, know the missions of both companies in case we had to take over their mission. This landing was so touchy, that even fire teams had objectives. In addition to brief

Marines waiting to land (USMC)

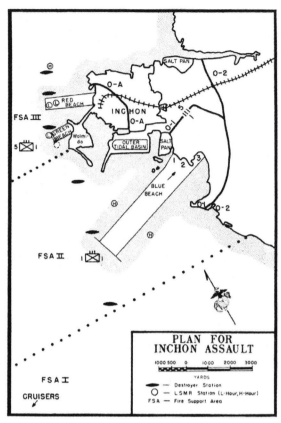

A and C companies would land in assault on the left and right portions of Red Beach 1 and B Company was to land next (USMC)

"dry net" drills and debarkation drills, we were given the opportunity to scale the ladders that we were going to use to get over the Inchon Seawall.

On the afternoon of 14 September, the USS *Henrico* and the ships carrying the 5th Regiment joined the rest of the Task Group and proceeded in column to the Inchon landing area. The 3rd Battalion, 5th Marines, was to make a landing in the early hours of the morning on Womi-do. Twelve hours later, the remainder of the Regiment would land on the sea wall at Inchon and continue the attack inland.

Everyone was very apprehensive about the landing at Inchon. It really looked dangerous, and the lack of security while down south had us worried. Everyone in Pusan knew the Marines were going on some kind of an amphibious landing, and we were afraid that the North Koreans had a pretty good idea that we were coming up their way. There was a finger pier and a causeway that extended out from Red Beach 1. If enemy machine guns were on the finger pier and causeway, we were going to have a tough time making that last 200 yards to the beach. We were also worried about what we were going to do if we were met by 200,000 hostile civilians when we landed.

Our landing had to be made against a sea wall which at that tide was 15 feet above the water level. That meant that we would have to use scaling ladders, however, a few boats in each wave would be able to locate holes in the sea wall and not bother with the ladders. The holes resulted from aerial bombing that had been conducted months earlier. Using scaling ladders meant that only two men could get out of the boats at a time and climb up on the sea wall. Heavy guns and communications equipment had to be lifted by lashing and lowering lines.

Captain Ike Fenton lead B Company in the landing (Duncan)

The ladders were of two types. One type was made of aluminum and had a big hook at the top which was a continuation of the ladder, itself. We had hoped to have enough of these ladders to place two in each boat. However, the factory that was making these ladders was damaged by a typhoon which hit Japan in the early week of September.

Inchon landing (USMC)

Only a few of the aluminum ladders were actually produced. The other type, a wooden ladder, was constructed aboard ship. It had a metal ring or hook nailed to it. We found that the hooks on the ladders were not wide enough to form a big enough arc and were of no use for hooking onto the sea wall.

A Company was to land first, followed by C Company, followed by B Company. This column formation was necessary because Red Beach was very narrow and two companies had to land abreast. Red Beach was not much longer than 600 yards. Captain Stevens, who commanded A Company, was quite worried about the trenches and bunkers that showed up on the aerial photographs about 15 yards inland from the sea wall. He knew that air, artillery and rockets were going to work that area over for two days, but he was wondering if we were going to be able to clear these bunkers out altogether.

*Q. Give a description of the terrain in the beach area.*

*A.* Upon getting on the beach, we faced a flat area of about 200 yards before we actually ran into the town itself. On the left side of the beach, our left flank, was a hill called Cemetery Hill. This feature, from the sea approach, was a sheer cliff. The only good approach to the hill was from the east side, 180 degrees from the coastline. Just off to the right (east) of Cemetery Hill there was a big beer factory, work shops and a cotton mill. To the right of that and about 600 yards inland from the beach was Observatory Hill.

Observatory Hill was the critical terrain feature in the area, overlooked the entire landing area, and was the Regimental Objective. On the right flank of Red Beach, in the 2nd Battalion's landing area, was a five-story office building. It was located right in the middle of their landing beach. The building was made of concrete and reinforced steel. Also on the right flank was a causeway that led out to Womi-do Island.

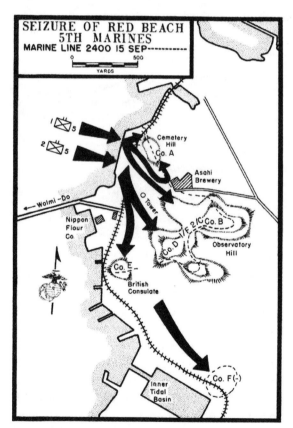

To the right of Observatory Hill, in the 2nd Battalion's area, was another piece of high ground. The whole landing beach was dotted with emplacements, bunkers, and connecting trenches that ran the entire length of the beach. About 200 yards inland from the beach was the town.

There was a great deal of confusion on landing sites and it was hazy—when A Company reached Cemetery Hill our gunners were firing on them (USMC Map)

*Q. Describe the September 15 landing and the subsequent activity of your unit.*

*A.* A Company hit Red Beach 1 at approximately 1730 and disembarked with the use of the scaling ladders. Some of the landing craft utilized holes blasted in the sea wall to unload their troops. A Company made up the first three waves. The left flank of Red Beach 1 was strongly defended in contrast to the fairly weak defense on the right flank. A Company started to assault O-1 which was Cemetery Hill.

Landing ships unloading at Red Beach (USMC)

In the fourth and 5th waves, C Company landed about 20 minutes late. Because of a motor failure in a boat, Lt Peterson, the company commander, was left at the rendezvous area, and his entire wave was delayed until Lt. Peterson's boat was ready to move. The organization of C Company on the beach was again delayed inasmuch as the units from the 2nd Battalion were overlapping into the 1st Battalion's zone of action.

There was a great deal of confusion on Red Beach due to the failure of the coxswains to land in their assigned areas. Units were intermingled and unit commanders had difficulty organizing their commands. I believe this failure to land at the proper beach on the part of the coxswains was due to the fact that enemy fire coming from Observatory Hill, and the beach itself, pushed them a little off course. I also feel that the coxswains of the boats were not well briefed on the beach itself. They knew where Red Beach 1 was, but they had no idea as to where Red Beach 1 and 2 met. I think that about all they were concerned with was getting everyone on Red Beach, wherever they could find an opening. Added confusion was caused when a beached Landing Ship Tank (LST) arrived shortly after the 9th wave and started firing over the heads of the troops into Cemetery Hill. It was approaching dusk at this time and the haze made it difficult to identify the people on Cemetery Hill. I imagine that the gunners on the LST knew that Cemetery Hill would probably be occupied, and they started shooting. However, by then A Company had reached the top of Cemetery Hill, and the LST gunners were shooting into them.

Owing to the difficulty that C Company was experiencing in reorganizing, the battalion commander deemed it necessary to commit his reserve. I received orders for B Company to pass through C Company, and continue the attack to seize Observatory Hill. C Company was to reorganize and assume the mission of battalion reserve. I found in passing through C Company that darkness was more of an aid to me than to the enemy, and the cover and concealment that the town afforded, aided me greatly in obtaining my objective. The men had been very well briefed; they knew all the streets, knew where each house was, and consequently, even in darkness, were able to make their way with good speed and seize the objective. We managed to get to the top of the Observatory Hill around 2000, but it was not until approximately 2330 that we were tied in with the 2nd Battalion on our right and A Company on the left. Resistance had been very light. The total B-1-5 company casualties for this landing were six wounded in action.

During the landing itself the volume of fire was very heavy; everything—anti-tank weapons, machine guns, mortars and artillery—was fired at us. As soon as darkness arrived, the fire subsided. After seizing Observatory Hill, we found that it had been the location of the enemy battalion command post. There were a number of gun emplacements up there, and a number of enemy dead. We had very little activity during the night and patrolled forward about 500 or 600 yards. The patrols encountered no opposition. The town people stayed in their houses, off the streets, which was a great help to us. When daylight arrived, there was no sign of the enemy in the area.

First Lieutenant John R. Hancock joined B Company on September 4, 1950 as Executive Officer.

# B-1-5 Casualties—September 9–15, 1950

## Killed in Action

*Confirmed through Korean War Project*

| | | |
|---|---|---|
| PFC Arulfo Martinez, from Brownsville, Texas | DOW | 9SEP50 |
| CPL Alvis Clowers, Pittsburg, Oklahoma | KIA | 15SEP50 |

## Wounded in Action

*Confirmed through USMC Unit Diaries*

| | | |
|---|---|---|
| Walter D. Hicks | WIA | 15SEP50 |
| Joseph A. Horvath | WIA | 15SEP50 |
| Thomas A. Roberts Jr. | WIA | 15SEP50 |
| Thomas S. Watkins | WIA | 15SEP50 |

# On to Kimpo Airfield

## B Company Commanding Officer, Captain "Ike" Fenton

*This de-briefing was performed by The Historical Div. Headquarters USMC upon Captain Fenton's return from Korea and listed as Secret for years. It is no longer secret!*

*Q. The attack continued the next day. Describe the progress of the attack from Inchon to Kimpo Airfield.*

*A.* The initial plan from Inchon to the Kimpo Airfield called for the battalion to sweep right through the heart of Inchon. It was evident that resistance had fallen off, and it was decided that the 3rd Battalion would move across the causeway from Womi-do Island, pass through the 2nd Battalion, and move up and tie in with the 1st Marine Regiment, which had landed on the outskirts of the city. The 1st Marine Regiment was moving quite rapidly, so the 2nd Battalion moved out following the 3rd Battalion with the 1st Battalion bringing up the rear. We moved rapidly through the city and cleared it at approximately 1300 or 1400. We continued to move along the Inchon–Seoul highway, the 1st Marines on the right, the 5th Marines on the left. By nightfall the regiment had traveled a good seven miles east of Inchon, where we tied in with the 1st Marines on the high ground just west of Ascom City. The 2nd and 3rd Battalions were on line, the 1st Battalion was in reserve. The ROK Marines were to swing out to the left, check the high ground, and cover our advance the following day. During the early hours of the morning, enemy tank activity was reported to our front. Three North Korean sailors were captured. They had driven from Seoul to Inchon to pick up medical supplies and had no idea that a landing had been made at Inchon two days previously. No one had told them anything about it and they were amazed to find us there.

The tank activity increased, and, when daylight rolled around, the 2nd Battalion took the tanks and the infantry following them under fire. There were approximately 200–300 infantry following the tanks. A combination of the 2nd Battalion's fire, and the Marine air that was on station, destroyed all tanks. I believe that a total of five tanks were destroyed.

Our attack continued that morning, and we moved very rapidly against scattered resistance. The enemy was very definitely withdrawing toward Kimpo Airfield. We were really amazed to find the Inchon area so lightly defended.

After passing Ascom city the 1st Marines encountered some heavy resistance to the right of the Seoul highway. The resistance in the 5th Marines' zone, on the left of the highway, was practically negligible. Several snipers had to be wiped out, and a few houses had to be flushed, but there was no real resistance. The 2nd Battalion had orders to attack the Kimpo field, while the 1st Battalion would continue towards Yong-Dungpo and secure the high ground east of Kimpo.

About dusk, the 2nd Battalion reached Kimpo Airfield. There the enemy resistance stiffened, and the 2nd Battalion was engaged in a number of firefights. Our battalion continued to move. We took the high ground just east and southeast of Kimpo. There, A and B Companies went on line with C Company in reserve. In the meantime, the 1st Marines were still engaged in a heavy firefight and were a good 2,000 yards to our immediate right rear.

At dawn on 18 September, I noticed many enemy troops on my left flank advancing in the direction of Kimpo Airfield to attack the 2nd Battalion. I immediately notified my battalion commander, who in turn notified the 2nd Battalion. Evidently the enemy did not know that B Company was on the high ground and, therefore, were completely unaware of our presence. After they had moved past me and the 2nd Battalion opened fire, we also opened up and were able to deliver enfilade fire into the enemy flanks. Between the 2nd Battalion's

A tank and soldier on way to Seoul (Sydman)

and our fire, we practically wiped out the enemy force to a man. I'd say that this enemy group was about 200 strong. While all this was going on, the battalion commander moved C Company off around my left flank, completely cutting off any enemy that might still be in the Kimpo Airfield area. C Company had moved into position on the high ground about 700 yards to my immediate left and about 300 yards to my left front.

We remained in position all day the 18th (while Kimpo Airfield was secured), and on the morning of the 19th, we continued the attack toward Yongdunpo. We had all three companies on line, and the order called for A Company to hold its present position and protect our right flank. The 1st Marines were moving slowly and were still encountering stubborn resistance.

B and C Companies were to continue the attack to Hill 118, the high ground which overlooked the city of YONGDUNPO. At jump-off time, C Company was unable to move out because, during the night, a number of Koreans had come across the Han River and had built up a sizeable force on the battalion's left flank directly in front of C Company. Instead, B Company was ordered to jump off and attack anyway and outflank the enemy. We moved out, utilizing all the concealment available, and reached Hill 118, a distance of about 2,300 yards in a little over an hour. We didn't have a single casualty and completely outflanked the enemy which had prevented C Company from moving. Once again, the enemy had failed to watch his flank and was caught with his pants down.

C Company was continually calling for air support and artillery, and they started to move under its cover. The enemy started withdrawing and ran into us. We were able to wipe out most of them and take many prisoners. In the afternoon, C Company passed through A Company and seized two points of high ground on my left flank, Hills 80 and 85, which overlooked Yongdunpo.

On two occasions that afternoon, I called for close air support. Since the battalion Operational Command Post had not yet moved forward and was instead approximately 1,000 yards to my rear, I controlled these airstrikes through the battalion tactical net. This method proved very successful, and I continued to work this way for the remainder of the Inchon–Seoul operation. That evening the 1st Marines sent A Company, 1st Battalion, under the command of Captain Bob Barrow, to relieve B Company. C Company was also relieved, and we had orders to pull back to Kimpo Airfield, where we were to go into an assembly area and prepare to make a river crossing in the morning. We made this move under the cover of darkness, arriving at Kimpo Airfield around 0300.

We were to be ready to move around 1100. The 3rd Battalion was to cross the Han River in covered LVTs at dawn, followed by the 2d Battalion, then the 1st Battalion. The 3rd Battalion made the crossing and took the regimental intermediate objectives. The 2nd Battalion crossed the river, passed through the

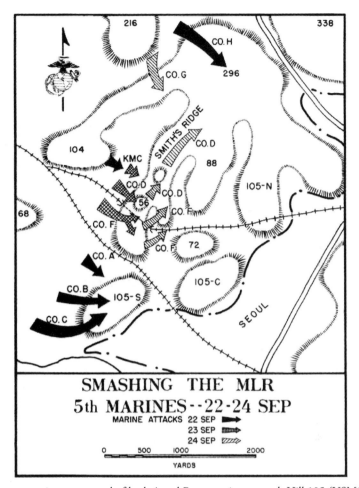

Ike Fenton was given command of both A and B companies to attack Hill 105 (USMC Map)

3rd Battalion, and seized two other pieces of high ground. The 1st Battalion crossed the river and remained in regimental reserve.

From this time until September 22, we continued to advance with the 2nd and 3rd Battalions toward Seoul. In the meantime, the 1st Battalion had been committed on the regimental right flank. Opposition was scattered, although there was some sniper fire and a great deal of mortar fire, which was very accurate. They could really drop it in your lap.

The morning of September 22 found the 2nd Battalion on the regimental right flank with a ROK Marine regiment on the high ground on the 1st Battalion's left flank, and the 3rd Battalion, 5th Marines, on the high ground, Hill 296, overlooking the city of Seoul. The plan of attack was as follows: the 1st Battalion and the ROK

Marines would jump off while the 3rd Battalion remained on Hill 296; the attack would swing to the left on a pivot so that we would swing into the city of Seoul itself. However, during the night of September 21 and in the early morning hours of September 22, the ROKs were engaged in a heavy firefight and receiving a great deal of pressure. Consequently, the attack did not jump off at 0730 as scheduled.

The ROKs claimed they could not move and called for all types of air support and artillery. The target for all this support was a very insignificant-appearing ridge that extended from Hill 296 to Hill 105. At approximately 0815 it was decided that the 1st Battalion would make an enveloping maneuver far to the right, cut through a rice paddy field, and seize Hill 105 from the western slope. This maneuver would bypass the ridge that was holding up the ROKs. Initially, B Company, which was on the battalion's left, was to move out and take this ridge, but because of the heavy volume of fire that we were receiving from this ridgeline in front of the ROKs, the battalion commander decided to pass A Company through C Company, and swing it far to the right where it could move in on the western slope of Hill 105.

A Company was able to get to within 500 yards of Hill 105, at which point it was pinned down. There was a lot of enemy activity on Hill 105. An antitank gun and several machine guns were really raising Cain and A Company was unable to advance. C Company, which had followed A Company in trace, moved up on A's right flank and attempted to move up the slope of the hill. However, they too were pinned down, and their casualties were very heavy. At 1645, it was decided that B Company would pass through A Company and, in a coordinated attack with C Company, seize Hill 105. This was done after 30 minutes of artillery fire and a heavy airstrike. The hill was declared secured at approximately 1900. Upon securing the hill, we could find no dead or wounded, and not a trace of the enemy having been up there. By that I mean, we found no empty cartridges and things of that nature. However, during the afternoon, we had seen groups of 10–20 at four or five different times and had called artillery and air down on them. The North Koreans had evidently dragged their wounded and their dead off the hill and down the eastern slope. We didn't know it at the time, but on the eastern slope of the hill there was a big cave which probably afforded them a handy burial site.

A Company was ordered to fall back across the rice paddy field to protect the battalion Command

That tattered flag in Seoul (USMC)

Post, and I, Ike Fenton, was given command of both A and B Companies for the defense of Hill 105C.

Casualties had been fairly heavy in taking the Hill 105: B Company had one killed and six wounded; C Company had nine killed and 17 wounded; and A Company had two killed and eight wounded.

Hill 105C was very barren, had a very flat top, and looked like an egg that was flattened on the top. We were subjected to a great deal of fire from the ridgeline that the enemy still held, and also from the high ground in Seoul, which was to our immediate front. The enemy was firing a great deal of antitank and high-velocity fire at us, and the ridge was continually swept with machine-gun fire. It was unsafe for the men to venture out of their holes during daylight hours.

During the night the North Koreans counterattacked up the eastern slope of the hill and overran a platoon of C Company, killed a machine-gun crew, and took their gun before being driven off. The enemy started moving down to the base of the hill and around the hill, firing the captured gun into our lines to draw fire. When no fire was returned, the enemy got a little bolder and started up the hill. When the enemy got close, every Marine on the line cut loose with a hand grenade. That discouraged the enemy and he withdrew. We estimated that the counterattack consisted of approximately 50 men.

Throughout the following day, we were ordered to remain in position. We were subjected to enemy small-arms fire and sporadic enemy mortar and high-velocity fire. Movement was impossible during the daylight hours. Water, rations, and ammunition had to be supplied to us after darkness, when the enemy small-arms fire subsided.

During the early hours of the 24th, we had another counterattack in the same spot as the previous one. This counterattack force was practically wiped out to a man, and we counted a little more than 50 dead when daylight arrived.

About 0700 we received word that the 1st Marines were going to make a river crossing, swing up and pass through my position, and continue the attack into Seoul. We were to be relieved. In the meantime, on the afternoon of the 23rd and the morning of the 24th, the 2nd Battalion had passed through the ROKs in an attempt

Raising the flag over Seoul's Embassy (USMC)

to seize the ridgeline that extended from Hill 105 to Hill 296. The 2nd Battalion had suffered a great many casualties and, in the early hours of the morning, we could see the Koreans on the slope on one side of the ridge and the Marines on the other side. The ridge was very heavily defended. It was probably one of the strongest points we had encountered during our entire operations in Korea.

Casualties had been extremely heavy for the 2nd Battalion. I understand that in one day's fighting they lost 69 killed and 268 wounded. Two of their companies were down to less than 50 men apiece. Despite their heavy casualties, the battalion managed to break through and seize the ridgeline on the afternoon of the 24th. By actual count, they found a little more than 1,200 enemy dead on the ridge. This ridge had been subjected to intense artillery fire and a great number of airstrikes, both napalm and rockets. The air-artillery effort proved very effective.

During the two days Companies B and C had remained on Hill 105, total casualties for the two companies were seven killed and 17 wounded. All of these Marines were <u>hit in their foxholes</u>. The men were not exposing themselves, but there was no way to keep the enemy from plunging fire right in the top of us. At 1630, September 24, Company A, 1st Battalion, passed through us and we were relieved. We moved back to an assembly area near the 1st Battalion's Command Post.

From this time until the fall of Seoul on September 27, the 1st Battalion saw very little action. The 3rd Battalion continued the attack until it was pinched out by the 1st and 7th Regiments. We followed in trace of the 3rd Battalion and moved into the city of Seoul, where the battalion had one last firefight near the Government Palace. We suffered only minor difficulties before defeating the enemy.

While in Seoul, we bivouacked in a school and conducted daily patrols. Our patrols found a number of warehouses filled with American arms, winter clothing, communications gear, medical supplies, motor transport equipment, and things of that nature. These supplies had evidently fallen into the hands of North Koreans when the South Koreans had retreated from Seoul earlier in the war. All the equipment was in good shape and had not been used.

On October 5, we received word to entruck and head back to Inchon and prepare to load out for another amphibious operation on the east coast.

*On October 13, 1950, Captain Francis I. "Ike" Fenton, Jr. was relieved as company commander by 1st Lieutenant John Hancock. Capt. Fenton was a sole surviving son and his mother had exercised her prerogative to have him moved out of combat. Several times, Ike told me that B Company had been so well trained by Capt. John Tobin, that even his privates could run a fire team, his corporals, a squad and his sergeants, a platoon. Ike had great praise for the men of B Company.*

*—Emmett—*

# B-1-5 Casualties and Medals—
# Kimpo–Seoul, September 16–26, 1950

## Killed in Action

*Confirmed through Korean War Project*

| | | |
|---|---|---|
| PFC Richard Q. Braman, from Danbury, Conn. | KIA | 22SEP50 |
| CPL Leonard E. Hayworth, from Crown Point, Ind. | KIA | 24SEP50 |

## Wounded in Action

*Confirmed through USMC Unit Diaries*

| | | |
|---|---|---|
| 1LT John H. Hancock | WIA | 26SEP50 |
| PFC Alva L. Christeson | WIA | 22SEP50 |
| PFC Jerry M. Ferrell | WIA | 24SEP50 |
| PFC Floyd F. Frey | WIA | 22SEP50 |
| SGT Eugene L. Funk | WIA | 24SEP50 |
| PFC Abraham Gomez | WIA | 24SEP50 |
| PFC Robert L. Hale | WIA | 22SEP50 |
| CPL Francis P. Hogan | WIA | 23SEP50 |
| TSGT Eugene Horn | WIA | 22SEP50 |
| PFC Victor J. Horvath | WIA | 26SEP50 |
| SSGT Lawrence Lemon | WIA | 22SEP50 |
| PFC Edward L. Linder Jr. | WIA | 23SEP50 |
| PFC Francis H Morzinski | WIA | 19SEP50 |
| PFC Lonnie E. Prince Jr. | WIA | 22SEP50 |
| PFC Harlan L. Smith Jr. | WIA | 26SEP50 |
| PFC John J. Thomas | WIA | 22SEP50 |
| CPL William Timbrook | WIA | 26SEP50 |
| PFC John L. Williams | WIA | 23SEP50 |

# Silver Star

Sergeant Lucius E. Hanes

Lucius Hanes, left (Schryver)

The President of the United States of America, authorized by Act of Congress July 9, 1918, takes pleasure in presenting the Silver Star (Army Award) to Sergeant Lucius E. Hanes, United States Marine Corps, for gallantry in action against an armed enemy while serving as Squad Leader, First Squad, Second Platoon, Company B, 1st Battalion, 5th Marines, 1st Marine Division (Reinforced), in action against enemy aggressor forces in Korea on September 22, 1950 during the assault on Hill 105 in the outskirts of Seoul. Sergeant Hanes was assigned the mission of the initial assault of Hill 105, a vital terrain feature in the 1st Battalion and Regimental Zone of action, defended by heavily entrenched enemy forces and covered by enemy machine-gun, mortar and artillery fire. With a high degree of courage, skill, and outstanding leadership, he led his squad up the side of the hill against fierce enemy fire. Upon capturing the hill, Sergeant Hanes was ordered back off the hill because of intense enemy artillery and mortar fire. A concentration of our own artillery fire was placed on the hill and again Sergeant Hanes led his squad up the hill under intense enemy machine-gun and small-arms fire from his left flank, destroyed the enemy thereon, and reoccupied Hill 105. Upon successful completion of his assignment he reorganized his squad and continued the attack. Sergeant Hanes's heroic actions were instrumental in enabling the 1st Battalion to capture the objective and was in keeping with the highest traditions of the United States Naval Service.

# On to Wosan—Operation *Yo-Yo*

## B Company Commanding Officer, Captain "Ike" Fenton

On October 9, 1950, B-1-5 boarded the USS *Bayfield* in Inchon Harbor for a landing somewhere on the northeast coast of Korea. It was part of a 250-ship armada taking the 1st Marine Division and other units of the X Corps to the east coast of Korea. The bay at their planned landing location, Wosan, had been mined with Soviet-manufactured mines. On October 10, minesweeping operations of Wosan harbor were commenced. Unfortunately, the three large minesweepers: *Pledge, Pirate,* and *Incredible,* were not well adapted for sweeping the shallow waters around Wosan, so more dependence was placed on seven wooden-hulled minesweepers: *Mocking Bird, Osprey, Chatterer, Merganser, Kite* and *Partridge* which were rugged, even though low-powered.

On October 12, both the *Pledge* and *Pirate* were blown up by mines with a total of 13 Killed in Action and 87 Wounded in Action. Flying boats were brought in to fly low. They could see the mines and guide the sweepers.

We had a lot of sick Marines on the ship (Green)

We boarded the USS *Bayfield* (Schryver)

On October 13, Captain Francis I. "Ike" Fenton, Jr. was relieved as commander by First Lieutenant John Hancock. Capt. Fenton was a sole surviving son and his mother exercised her prerogative to have him moved out of combat. Lt Hancock had been wounded September 26, but returned to command B Company.

On October 18, one of the Japanese sweepers hit a mine and went down. On October 19, the Republic of Korea (ROK) forces disintegrated after a terrific explosion in a cleared area.

After 10 days at sea, most of us did not know what the delay was, but our ships just went back and forth out in the deep water, waiting for the "Mines All Clear" to be sounded, hence, we called it "Operation *Yo-Yo*".

The situation aboard the ships had become serious. The Landing Ship Tanks (LSTs) and transports were not prepared for a voyage around the Korean Peninsula taking nearly as long as a Pacific crossing. Food supplies ran low and gastro-enteritis and dysentery swept through the crowded transports in spite of strict medical precautions. The transport USS *Phoenix* alone had a sick list of 750 during this epidemic. A case of smallpox was discovered on our ship, the USS *Bayfield*, and all crewmen and passengers were vaccinated the same day. "Heck, this was our ship! Which one of B Company had smallpox?"

Meanwhile, the Marine Air Wing beat us to Wosan by 12 days and the ROK forces had taken the harbor with little resistance. They could fly over those mines, but the navy couldn't take us through them.

Lieutenant John Hancock took over as the B Company Commander October 13 onboard the USS *Bayfield*. B Company's 194 enlisted men and six officers disembarked the USS *Bayfield* at Wosan October 29, 1950.

—*Ike*—

# A Female in Korea

## Lieutenant Mike Palatas

On September 7, 1950 the dock area of Pusan was a beehive of activity. It was congested with military traffic and piles of combat stores of all descriptions.

The USS *Henrico* was one of the Task Force ships tied up or anchored in the harbor. She was moored to the pier on her port (left) side by 2-inch hawsers. She was our ship and the "Bandits" of B-1-5 were already embarked. Our destination, although we did not know it at the time, was Inchon. We were heading halfway up the west side of the Korean peninsula for an amphibious assault there and eventual re-capture of the capital city of Seoul.

The "Bandits" weren't the only troops on board. The entire battalion landing team (BLT) 1/5 and supporting units were billeted in the five hold compartments.

The battalion had just returned to Pusan docks from the Miriyang area where it was engaged in the battle of the "Second Naktong River."

Lieutenant Colonel George Newton was the battalion commander and now aboard ship, he would also wear the hat of "Commanding Officer of Troops Onboard." When we would put to sea, our "Brigade" designation would cease and we would become part of the newly designated 1st Marine Division, joining with "Chesty" Puller's 1st Marines and Colonel Litzenburger's 7th Marines. These latter regiments recently arriving in the West Pac area under Major General O.P. Smith, USMC.

It was about 3pm now and the ship's quartermaster on the bridge was observing the deck below on the starboard (right) side taking on the last of the LCVPs and "M" boats using booms fore and aft. He walked back into the wheelhouse and observed the duty bosin's mate piping "chow" bumps into the ship's intercom PA system. As he glanced about the bridge, his eyes fell on the clinometer and he was puzzled. Just 15 minutes earlier, the ship was on an even keel, but now it registered a 10-degree list to the port side!

At the same time, he was aware of a heightening roar of howling, squeals and whistles. Then he noted Marines topside on all decks at the life lines were responsible for the racket. Their noise drowned out the noise of the sailors working the booms on the starboard side.

From the port wing of the bridge he looked down to the pier for the cause of the commotion?

There it was, A FEMALE, and a round-eye at that! She wore a one-piece light tan coverall and was standing alongside one of "Rocky" Williams's Jeeps. Lt Col's Murray and Stewart were with her chatting. Corporal Pendergast, the driver, was seen to pick up her canvas expeditionary bag and disappear up the USS *Henrico*'s gangway. A <u>woman</u> aboard our troopship? It sure was to be! Lt Col. Newton and Major Olsen were on the quarter deck, as was "Ike" Fenton and Major Russell to greet the comer and it was the only time in Korea that I saw a grin on the face of our battalion commander.

Caption Maggie Higgins, a dedicated reporter (Palatas)

The personality, carefully holding on to the rails of the gangway as she enjoyed her "reception," was a female war correspondent. Her name was "Maggie" Higgins and she would accompany us landing at Inchon and fighting toward Seoul. It was on the run to Inchon that the ship's company on the bridge could tell which side of the ship Maggie was on by the standard 10-degree list it would take because of our Marines jockeying for position to get a close-up look of a different format.

"Maggie" Higgins was rather comely. The gentlemen I was, I presented her with a suit of our two-piece dungarees. She expressed that desire to me one evening after mess. I saw her at a distance on two occasions after landing and enroute to Seoul.

In 1951, The Pulitzer Prize jury report cited Higgins's "fine front line reporting showing enterprise and courage," adding: "She is entitled to special consideration by reason of being a woman, since she had to work under unusual dangers."

As the *Herald Tribune*'s Tokyo correspondent in 1950, Higgins was one of the first reporters to reach Korea when hostilities broke out. The *Herald Tribune* published Higgins's report on landing with the Marines at Inchon on September 18, 1950, three days after it happened.

She later reported from Vietnam, where she contracted a tropical disease that proved to be mortal. She died on January 3, 1966, at the age of 45.

Like many good correspondents, at another time and place and another combat situation, she would die covering actions of Marines!

—*M.V.P.*—

# Second War—Second Purple Heart

## Lieutenant Mike Palatas

I had come to Korea at the end of August 1950 with Lieutenant John Hancock, two other lieutenants and 36 enlisted men. We arrived from Marine Barracks, Guam, as replacements to the 1st Marine Brigade. I had served in World War II and now in Korea began my second war.

We joined the 5th Marines right after the First Battle of the Naktong. Lieutenant Colonel Murray was the Regimental Commander.

Our battalion command post was located in a town name was Miriyang. In getting there, we passed several hulks of still-burning enemy tanks and when artillery rounds passed overhead to the south and splashed in the rice paddies, it signaled for me that I was in combat again.

Lt Mike Palatas (Palatas)

I met our wild-looking battalion commander and his freckled Executive Officer, Major Olsen. They assigned me to the battalion staff and I would plan the logistics for the upcoming assault on Inchon.

Shortly, we made our battalion retrograde movement back to the Pusan docks, where we would embark on the USS *Henrico*. It was here that I met "Rocky" Williams, the Battalion Motor Transport Chief. Rocky was a most affable individual and capable leader. He was also an artist at "cumshaw." We had a common bond and the battalion was lucky to have him. In the battalion S-2, was a scout, "Red Dog" Keller, a young non-com who would eventually be commissioned and go on to be legendary in the corps.

We landed at the Inchon sea wall to a hot small-arms fire beach. We pressed the attack, assembled near Kimpo airfield, then pushed on across the Han River in Amtracs.

On September 21, I took two jeeploads of ammo to Hill 105, north of Seoul, where B Company had its command post. As I set out, the driver of the first Jeep hit a land mine in the road. *Life* magazine photographer Dave Duncan, "Ike" Fenton, our "Top" Phil Dierickx and the rest of the command post group, witnessed the detonation that spiraled the windshield high in the air and lifted and spun the Jeep over in a smoldering hulk. I was unhurt, but minutes later, shrapnel from a mortar barrage sent me to the U.S. Naval Hospital in Japan. It gave me my Second Purple Heart in my Second War.

Ole Top and Doc examine casualties (Duncan)

*"As entered in the Congressional Record: Lieutenant Palatas received several awards from his service in the Marine Corp, including: a Silver Star, a Legion of Merit, a Bronze Star, two Purple Hearts, six Presidential Unit Citations, a Combat Action Ribbon, a Good Conduct Medal, two Navy Unit Commendations and a Meritorious Unit Commendation. His pride for his nation was demonstrated by the thirty-four years he spent in active duty for our nation's military."*

CONGRESSIONAL RECORD,
Hon. Scott McGinnis of Colorado,
July 15, 2004

# Chosin Reservoir Campaign
# November–December 1950

Together the B-1-5 Marines of 1950–51 confronted danger and endured terrible hardships. Together, you rose to the challenge; you never faltered. Many of your Brothers gave their full measure of devotion so that others might live in freedom. Your accomplishments in the defense of liberty will never be forgotten, and America's debt to you will remain far more than we can ever repay.

Some people spend an entire lifetime wondering if they made a difference. The MARINES don't have that problem.

*—President Ronald Reagan, 1987—*

# On the Way to Chosin

What manner of men are these young, gaunt, and weary looking Marines with their huge packs, rifles, ammunition belts, and canteens? While many in the States chose not to sign up, these men did. And, here in the middle of hell on earth, almost daily several of these youngsters are sneaking a ride aboard Marine helicopters to return to their units, hoping the sergeant major or I won't recognize them. They're deserting, but in a different direction, as they escape from medical treatment and return to their combat unit. They try to lose themselves in the groups of replacements flying out to the companies. There's the drive, the calling, the need to return, return to your buddies because they need you and you need them. The Band of Brothers, that's what it is all about.

—*Lieutenant Charles Cooper*—

# B-1-5 Missing in Action

## USMC Historical Diary for the Period November 12–14, 1950 ~~SECRET~~ Declassified

**Nov. 12** Upon arrival at MAJON-DONG the battalion reverted to control of the 5th Marines. During the day, four local and two motorized patrols were conducted with no enemy contact. Five outposts were established around the battalion perimeter.

**Nov. 13** At 0745, local patrols were dispatched from the battalion area in accordance with Regimental order. All patrols, with the exception of one motorized from B Company, patrolled their assigned areas and returned with negative contact. The motorized patrol from B Company, consisted of six Jeeps and 20 men, departed the battalion area with orders to make a reconnaissance patrol west to the village of SIMPUNG-NI. The patrol proceeded to the village of UNBONG-NI, establishing a radio relay station on Hill 688. One prisoner was taken at this village who stated there were enemy in the vicinity. The patrol, less two Jeeps which remained at the radio relay station, proceeded on to the village of SIMPUNG-NI. As they approached the village, the men in the lead Jeeps disembarked and proceeded on foot. The patrol leader, with an interpreter, moved up a hill on the right to make a reconnaissance.

At this time the enemy, estimated to be between 50 and 150, opened fire on the patrol from three sides. The patrol leader, evidently realizing that the enemy had the advantage of surprise and superiority of numbers and fire power, tried to disengage the patrol from the enemy. This enemy contact was first reported to the battalion by an observer aircraft which was on station in that area. Later a few men who had succeeded in returning to the radio relay station reported the action to battalion headquarters.

At 1200 a reinforced platoon from B Company was dispatched to the relief of the patrol. Upon reaching the area they discovered the enemy had withdrawn.

They recovered all casualties, three Jeeps and one SCR-300 and some of the weapons.

At 1810 the relief platoon returned to the battalion area. <u>Patrol casualties were seven (7) KIA, five (5) WIA, and one (1) MIA.</u>

**Nov. 14** Local and motorized patrols were conducted with negative enemy contact. <u>A patrol to SIMPUNG-NI recovered the man who was missing from the patrol the day before. He was suffering from exposure, but otherwise in good condition.</u>

# Hey! Bandit Over Here!

### Private John Rukstelis

On a cold Sunday morning, November 13, 1950, approximately 24 to 30 of us were sent out on a mounted reconnaissance patrol to rendezvous with a 7th Marine patrol in the vicinity of Majon-Dong.

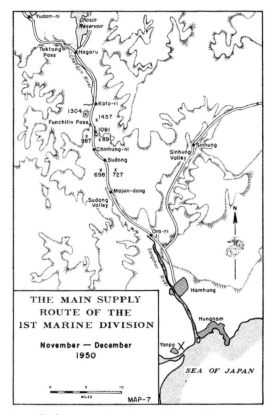

THE MAIN SUPPLY
ROUTE OF THE
1ST MARINE DIVISION

November — December
1950

MAP-7

Guerrilla forces were heavily armed as we left on patrol from Majon-Dong (USMC Map)

About an hour after we left the camp area, we picked up a Korean who began telling our interpreter about an enemy force ahead. Staff Sergeant Gordon Gardner, our patrol leader, checked his map and then gave the order to move out. We proceeded approximately two more miles and halted at a point where the road curved to the left. To the right of the roadway was high ground where, unbeknown to us, a hidden guerrilla band was laying in wait for a signal to attack.

To the left of the roadway was a river partly iced over with high ground beyond. Down the road, there was a valley and past the valley more high ground. There was a transmission tower on top of this high ground at the end of the valley. Unbeknown to us, another enemy force was hidden near this tower.

The smoking lamp was lit and we were all watching the hills unaware the enemy was right there. SSgt Gardner came up and told me to relieve Corporal Don Durst on the point. He then said to continue on further around the bend in the road. I went out about 100 yards and stopped where the ridge with the tower was. A few minutes later, Private Joe Smulley came out and joined me and, as usual, a couple of men began griping because we were walking instead of riding on the Jeeps and trailers.

All of the sudden all hell broke loose. There was machine-gun fire from above my position. Then at least 60 guerrillas above the main body opened up with small-arms and automatic weapons fire. They tossed grenades into the Jeeps. The gasoline tanks exploded and our men had no cover. Smulley and I started running back to the main body when bullets started kicking up the dirt road behind us. Instinctively, we jumped into the half-frozen river where we would have some cover. I started up river thinking Private Smulley was right behind me, but he headed down river. I got behind some large rocks and took about five shots at the top of the ridge from which the machine gun was firing. I don't know if I hit anyone, but the shooting stopped suddenly and the screaming enemy came down the hills above the main body to take what they wanted and kill any wounded that moved.

Three Chinese appeared on top of the ridge that I had fired at. One was pointing right where I was so I crawled to a better place for cover and concealment and waited with my rifle ready. Half of my parka and my shoes and socks were all soaked from the river water. I guess I wasn't worth the trouble, because they never came looking for me.

I watched four enemy about 2,000 to 3,000 yards away burying weapons in the valley. One of our observation planes circled the area and the enemy took cover and waited until the plane disappeared. They then took to the hills. Minutes later, I watched one of the prettiest artillery barrages comb the ridges and valley.

I finally realized I was beginning to freeze. I removed my shoes and socks. I had a field jacket under my parka so I took it off and wrapped my feet in it and kept the shoes and socks inside the parka hoping they would dry out with my body heat.

My plan was to wait for darkness and start back to the camp area. It was bitter cold and dark now! My socks were almost dry and the shoes were warm. I put them on and tried to stand. I could not, my legs were too stiff and my feet were numb so I just sat back and waited and prayed.

Sometime the next day I heard troops on the road. This scared the pure hell out of me. Then I heard "Hold it up." I rose up and it was Lieutenant Hancock leading a B Company patrol. I yelled, "HEY! I'M OVER HERE!" and started waving my hands. Two Marines came charging across the river. I learned at the Austin B-1-5 reunion in 1987 that Ed Kennison was one of the two Marines that carried me out.

I was taken to the regimental hospital where I learned my toes and heels were severely frostbitten. My hopes of rejoining the company and 3rd platoon faded. I met Joe Smulley at the hospital and he had wounds in both legs, but not serious enough to keep him out of the war. He informed me that my good buddy Private Gene Bowden was Killed in Action as was Corporal Durst, Corporal McDowell and others. These and many other heroes will never come back.

One last thing, I'm damn glad I was a Marine!

*—John—*

# It Took a Team

## Lieutenant Mike Palatas

Our rifle company could not have operated alone for any length of time. That is to say, we have to have a supply and support group—an umbilical cord to the battalion command post.

Not all members of B Company (about 235 men) are infantry men. About 95 percent are infantry but the non-infantry men are no less important. They are essential to support the riflemen, BAR men, mortar men and machine gunners. They let us infantrymen get on with the nitty gritty of battle and are held in the highest esteem.

Top on our list is the corpsman, a navy man who wears our uniform with pride. Another would be a radio operator. He is always with the Skipper, gets little rest, and carries the heavy back load of the SCR-300 radio, which is temperamental. He keeps in touch with the battalion commander and his staff.

We may have two wiremen and they will try to give us a landline to battalion. They will also assist in wiring-in of the company's platoons at night in a combat situation. The devices had no ringer in combat. It was a net of sound-powered handsets—you whisper into them to gain the other's attention. Charlie Lyles, though an infantryman, knew these communications devices well.

Another essential member of the team would be the Supply Sergeant. And we needed a Jeep driver and usually he will stay with the Battalion Motor Transport Platoon. The company clerk or mail orderly is essential for communications and would stay close to the 1st Sergeant… the same for the field musician or Bugler, an essential messenger in combat.

We would have other team members with us, as the situation dictates. These may be the 81mm Mortar Forward Observers, Artillery Liaisons, Naval Gunfire Liaison, and a tanker team, maybe even some engineering personnel and the S-2 scouts and interpreters.

So thus we are a team, capable of almost anything under the most challenging circumstances—in the war field!

# Speculations of a Rifleman:
# On the Way to Chosin

## Corporal H. J. "Syd" Sydnam

I got orders to ship out to Korea. I had a short somber pause before the next challenge in life. Here I am, half drunk in Hawaii headed for war with the people my previous Marine Corps duty had taught me to love.

Now, we must forget the Chinese sense of humor that survives the terror of war. We must forget that they are fighting, either for a cause that promises better conditions, or because they may have unwillingly been pressed into service.

Choe was one of the finest, most intelligent young Chinese men I met in China. To think that I may, one day, face Choe She Ming and that one of us must kill the other. Or perhaps, it might be that young boy with the "American eyes" that I met in Peking, who in return for help with the English Speller, taught me the abacus. He, too, would be of age to fight for the Chinese Red Army.

How can God expect that a man will see, and do, good when he also expects us to move as political pawns in warfare, first killing Cain then Abel? One day we must fight beside, the next, against. No fear that I will not kill with vigor—I must, or be killed. Besides, it seems that there is <u>right</u> on our side—it must always be so. One must help the politicians, diplomats, and militarists to ensure that HE is in the right before He sends us to battle. For in the end, it remains for us to kill or be killed.

Personal desires and beliefs must be disregarded until our present enemy is again on OUR side, the right side, in conflict or in commerce.

Now, the fighting is very far away, thus it gives a moment to pause for meditation and moralizing. Short pause. Next month I may be dead, in a hospital, or still in combat. I am doubtful that I will survive a month of combat without loss of limb or life.

In this war, many of the casualties are caused by cold weather and inadequate clothes. We are well trained to fight, but few know how to stay warm and dry. Fewer still are able to fight and keep from freezing at the same time.

I don't know if I will stay whole and can fight in the battle for the whole winter? Already I am weary to death of it all. Where others lead—ye shall go.

—*"Syd"*—

# B-1-5 Casualties—November 13, 1950

## Killed in Action

*Confirmed through Korean War Project*

| | | |
|---|---|---|
| PFC Eugene Bowden, from Jacksonville, Florida | KIA | 13NOV50 |
| CPL Donald J. Durst, from Bethlehem, Pennsylvania | KIA | 13NOV50 |
| SSGT Gorden Garner, from Portsmouth, Virginia | KIA | 13NOV50 |
| CPL Maynard L. Highly, from Houston, Texas | KIA | 13NOV50 |
| CPL George M. Hudson, from Fort Valley, Georgia | KIA | 13NOV50 |
| CPL John F. Mc Dowell, from Farwell, Minnesota | KIA | 13NOV50 |
| PFC Secundino V. Olivares, from San Antonio, Texas | KIA | 13NOV50 |

## Wounded in Action

*Confirmed through USMC Unit Diaries*

| | | |
|---|---|---|
| PFC John W. Gordon | WIA | 13NOV50 |
| PFC Joseph Smulley | WIA | 13NOV50 |
| PFC Robert C. Stewart | WIA | 13NOV50 |

## Missing in Action—Returned

PFC John A Rukstelis

# Chosin

The performance of the officers and men in this operation was magnificent. Rarely have all hands in a division participated so intimately in the combat phase of operation. Every Marine can be justly proud of his participation. In Korea, Tokyo, and Washington, there is full appreciation of the remarkable feat of the division. With the knowledge of the determination, professional competence, heroism, devotion to duty, and the self-sacrifice displayed by the officers and men of this division, my feeling is one of humble pride. No division commander has ever been privileged to command a finer body of men.

*—Major General Oliver P. Smith, Commanding General 1st Marine Division, December 19, 1950, Division Memo. 238-50—Distributed to each member of 1st Division*

# Chosin

## USMC Historical Diary for the Period
## November 26–December 15, 1950 ~~SECRET~~ Declassified

**Nov. 26** 5th and 7th Marine Regiments assembled forces in YUDAM-RI.

At 2000, the Battalion Commander issued his verbal attack order for November 27. The general plan of attack was to move out in a column of companies (Fox Company, Dog Company 75mm Recoilless Platoon, Forward Company Post Group, Weapons Company, and Easy Company) along the Main Supply Route (MSR). At this point, Fox Company was to move to the high ground and proceed along north side of the MSR to the Battalion objective with Dog Company. The remainder of the battalion was to proceed along the MSR, unless Dog Company should be fired upon from the high ground south of the MSR, at which point Dog Company should move to the high ground on the south side of the MSR and proceed to the next battalion objective.

Weather was cloudy and cold. Low temperature was 20 degrees. Light snow flurries all night. Terrain was very mountainous.

**Nov. 27** At 0700, the battalion moved out as planned. Nine roadblocks were encountered on the MSR. Fox Company bypassed the roadblocks and the engineers cleared them with cover from Dog Company.

At 0930, Fox Company began receiving small-weapons enemy fire and automatic-weapons fire from the ridge. 81mm and 4.2 mortars were ordered into position and began firing on the enemy. B Battery, 11th Marines began firing missions at 1023. 75mm recoilless was called in to reduce pillboxes. Under cover of artillery and mortar barrages, Fox Company moved to high ground and C, D, E and Dog Companies moved to the valley.

At 1115, an airstrike was called on the ridge. Results of the airstrike were undetermined and the command post was displaced. Fox Company moved to the valley and up the next hill where they began receiving a small amount of 60mm mortar fire.

By 1430, Fox Company cleared the ridge of enemy troops. Dog Company moved to high ground. The battalion began consolidating positions and established a command post. Supporting units were in position by 1600. 31 wounded and evacuated. Five sick evacuated.

At 2125, enemy soldiers estimated to be about two battalions attacked attempting to penetrate between Easy and Fox Companies. The enemy was creeping close to our lines, throwing hand grenades, and then rushing our lines firing small arms. It was noted the enemy was firing with Sub-Thompson Machine Guns. The first attack lasted until 2400 and was repulsed by machine-gun, small-arm, mortar and artillery fire.

**Nov. 28** At 0315 the second attack hit on a wider front. This attack lasted until 0600 at which time the enemy withdrew.

At 0730 a third enemy attack was attempted in the center of Fox Company line and lasted until 0815. The battalion withdrew from position on order of Regimental Commander. Weather was partly cloudy and sunny and freezing with light snow.

Seven killed in action. 25 wounded and evacuated. 60 sick and evacuated (most due to frostbite). Three Chinese prisoners of war taken. 500 Chinese killed.

**Nov. 29** At 1035, Dog Company spotted enemy troops and called for artillery fire on them. At 1055, Battalion Commanders went to inspect the defense.

At 1255, Fox Company received mortar fire. Three provisional platoons from the 1st Battalion, 11th Marines, were attached to reinforce the defense of the Battalion.

Weather was cold with a little wind and light snow. Two men returned to duty. Joined by one replacement. One Chinese prisoner of war taken.

**Nov. 30** At 0110, received orders to prepare to move to a new position, all companies were alerted.

At 0300 received oral orders for the battalion to relieve the 7th Marines on the left and establish a new defense line.

At 0430, all Company Commanders were notified of the move. Easy Company was directed to assume responsibility for the right half of the new defense line. Dog Company was directed to cover the 7th Marines' withdrawal. The remainder of the company moved back to cover the left half of the new defense line. All companies were instructed to make these moves in such a manner that it would not appear to the enemy as a general withdrawal. The move was immediate and completed by 1000. A new command post was established. One wounded and evacuated. Six returned to duty. Seven sick and evacuated.

# Baker Bandits at Chosin

## B Company Commanding Officer, Lieutenant John Hancock [in his own hand writing from the battlefield]

This is the story of Baker Company, 5th Regiment. I write this as the Commanding Officer of B-1-5 during the Chosin campaign. It attempts to tell how the company carried itself in one operation of its long, operation-filled history. How its members died, how and why they suffered, and in what manner the survivors survived.

I tell this story because I believe in Baker Company with a belief that transcends all other faith; because the men of Baker Company deserve to learn of the deeds they did, unknowingly and unquestioningly.

On December 27, 1950, we moved from our battalion perimeter on the east side of the Chosin Reservoir and moved through HAGARU-RI northwestwards to YUDAM-NI, from where, it was understood, we would attack westward some 20 miles with the 7th Marines. We were not aware of the Chinese Communist

Hancock presents B Company to General Craig (Palatas)

buildup to the west, nor of their proximity to the 7th Marines perimeter, inside which we were to reach that night.

Riding that 34 miles in covered trucks that freezing night, we little knew how welcome the sight of the icy, windswept pass was to be, a seeming eternity later. At that time, having read the week-old news, we were letting our minds dwell on a comparatively cozy winter defensive line on the YALU. "Who knew—maybe Xmas in Japan? or at home?"—if the army became overly magnanimous and relinquished our services to the navy.

Riding that truck to YUDAM-NI was to be, for many men, their last ride. We were ready for a fight, feeling that an all-out push was the only means to the end in sight—reaching the YALU. Up until now, except for heavy patrolling and some occasional scrapes during the same, the 5th had literally—and actually—been left out in the cold. Reading about the 7th Marines' battles was only a bit better than reading about the Republic of Korea's forces (ROK) and the army. At night, we had watched the tracers arching across the black sky above the 7th Marines zone on the west side of the Reservoir; seen the Corsairs hovering and swooping low over hidden targets lurking behind the menacing grey mountains to the west; and these goings-on were subjects of many remarks about the rugged 7th calling airstrikes against enemy fire teams. Now, at long last it appeared that the 5th was going to be in on the last drive in a big way—meaning Baker would have its chance.

We had grown accustomed to arriving at a new position at night, shivering all night in hastily made "oochies," and waking at dawn to learn just where we were. So we expected nothing more, nor less when we arrived at YUDAM-NI at about 2100, to find our advance party had barely managed to get one tent per platoon erected in our assigned bivouac area. This area was immediately adjacent to the 7th Marines command post and inside a perimeter manned by the 7th on the high ground around our position on the valley floor.

Frostbite had already made its deadly presence known, many men having had their toes and heels nipped on the icy ride over the pass. It was at least 15 degrees colder than it had been on the east side, and tonight it was to reach 10 degrees below before dawn.

In this weather, if conditions permit, a man is in his sack 10 minutes after it drops from his back. 25 percent watch was established and soon the remainder were warming up their bags by the simplest method—crawling inside.

No sooner had we swallowed our frozen cans of meat and beans and begun to doze off, than the foreboding cracks of enemy rifle fire erupted. The muffled crunch of grenades coming from the top of the surrounding high ground informed us that the Chinese were in contact with our outer perimeter—very close. It is typical of the trained Marine that ricochets and the crack of spent rounds flying hundreds of feet overhead, make him nervous when he is in a bivouac or semi tactical position—much more so than do near misses when he's on line. He'd much rather his own unit be in position to bear the brunt of an enemy assault. To be in reserve, is to rely on another to make your way in the terrifying dark in an attempt to curtail a breakthrough. So, Baker Company waited out the night—a night that, in that frozen hell, was all out of proportion to time.

I, the Baker Company commander, was summoned to the battalion command post where Colonel Stevens informs me that, he will take command of B Company, and keep them in reserve. I stayed with the colonel. While he relayed the word to the executive officer, Cronin relays the dope to platoon command post by runner:

0030: Easy Co, 7th is being overrun on Hill 1282, behind us. Able Company sends two platoons up the mountain, which in the night doubles in size and rises straight up from our position. Dog Co, 7th is being pushed off Hill 1240, to the north. Charlie Company dispatches one platoon to reinforce.

0200: D-7 and A-5 are in big trouble on the high ground behind us. Post 100 percent watch. All troops out of their bags. Standby to move—anywhere—at any time!

The rest of Charlie and Able Companies double-time up the hill with all the ammo they can carry. Colonel Stevens now has B Company left under his control. He won't let it be committed—if he does, the men know it's the Big Show and the Last Card. Mortars keep dropping into the valley, sporadically

0500: Everyone holding. The enemy does not retreat from his positions on the reverse slope of the hill crests. He has good cover and is within grenade range of the perimeter.

Daylight: Mortars still drop in. Casualties continue to stream down the gash in the mountainside that is the perimeter Main Supply Route. Marines have head wounds, bullet wounds, gashes, and the deep, bloodless incisions of the chest and torso that come from stopping grenades.

Regiment says it cannot evacuate any but the most serious casualties. The full import of that message doesn't seem to strike anyone—but me. Clerks, drivers, and the other men of headquarters and company commanders take on a new grim look—enemy mortars are searching them out, hoping to knock out, and cut off, the life blood of the infantryman.

Baker Company comes alive. We crawl nimbly out of our positions on the valley perimeter. Groups congregate around the aggressive ones who have scrounged a few boards for a fire. The next couple of hours is consumed in eating ravenously half-thawed cans of chow, drying socks and squaring away gear for the inevitable move—"Battalion won't let us stay here; they were getting fired on last night."

Around 1300, the executive officer passes the word to deck all tents and prepare for a move. In short order, I return from a fast, cursory reconnaissance and pick up the Gunny and his runners, and take off in a cloud of snow with orders for B Company to follow, on foot. From the casualties we've seen and the grenade bursts we can hear on the crests of the hills surrounding us, we assume that wherever we're going is going to be closer to the Chinese.

The word that we're only moving a mile—to relieve Dog Company, 7th. "Jeez, we've never relieved anyone in broad daylight, how do you do it?"

Mortars landing! Sounds like they are near the Second Platoon sector. "Corpsman!" Into the night goes "Doc" Christman.—Fisher, Robert J. & Dobbs, Robert. Four others were bringing in the wounded and stumbled across the frozen, wash-board rice paddy to the aid station in the rear of us...

*This is where Lt Hancock's manuscript ended. He gave it to Lt. Palatas to review. Lt. Hancock was Killed in Action in a raid on February 7, 1951, before he could get back to it. When Lt. Palatas found out about Lt. Hancock's fate, he put the manuscript in his pack until he got back to the States.*

# To Chosin

## Lieutenant Mike Palatas

In mid-November, I was back in Korea at Wonsan and enroute again to join the 5th Marines. Our weather was turning cold. At some supply point, I was issued my ration of cold weather gear. The twill dungarees, leggings and the tankers jacket that I had, would no longer be needed. I was given long johns, woolen socks, shoepacs, green trousers, wind-proof trousers, field jacket, parka and a down-filled sleeping bag.

I stayed in the regimental command post for one night. I was introduced to the bitter cold of Korea on my first head call and peeling off layers of clothing. The next day, I made it to the 1st Battalion Command Post and saw many new faces.

On joining B Company, "Ike" Fenton was gone and Lieutenant Hancock was now the Commanding Officer of B Company. Jim Cronin was Executive Officer, but he would come and go, being assigned to liaison duties periodically with the Republic of Korea (ROK) Marines.

Men of B-1-5 with orders to move out (Palatas)

The 5th Marines were preparing for a move northward to the Changjin Plateau and I was asked by Lt Hancock to represent B Company with the battalion's advance party. We would precede the battalion's move by perhaps two days and select a command post site and assembly area on the east side of the Changjin (Chosin) Reservoir, some 50 miles north of the present positions.

The 7th Marines were already up there and attacking along the west side of the reservoir. We, the 5th Marines, would "leap frog" battalions up the east side of the Chosin probably headed for the Yalu River and the China border.

Our Top, First Sergeant Phil Dierickx, was part of this advance group. He, himself, could take on an enemy platoon. We departed in several Jeeps from "Rocky's" motor transport unit and headed up a steep-walled canyon on a tortuous twisting dirt road. We passed the huge pipe lines which carried water down to the hydroelectric plant and we crested out on Fuchlin Pass, some miles south of Koto-ri. Somewhere between Koto-ri and Hagaru-ri, at the southern tip of the reservoir, we made our small encampment.

I was a bit apprehensive that night on the barren landscape. We didn't know but we were sitting ducks to the Chinese who were already hidden in the area. In retrospect, considering the situation, it's a wonder our small group was not ambushed, taken prisoner and destroyed.

In a few days, a unit designated as Task Force Drysdale would be ambushed in this very area with a great loss of men and equipment and with prisoners taken by the Chinese. I'm certain we were under constant observation but for whatever reason, we were left unmolested.

We took turns at night security, rose early the next day and departed. We passed through Hagaru-ri (which would become the 1st Division's Advance Command Post) and went northward to a point halfway to the reservoir's east side. Here in the patchy snow, we would await the arrival of the battalion which would come up in a convoy of 6×6 trucks.

For me, now, this was the beginning of my seventh major campaign—CHOSIN.

Marines wait for the road north to be cleared (Palatas)

# Chosin

## Lieutenant "Bud" Kohler

Just prior to Thanksgiving, this battalion took up position in a perimeter defense north of Sinhung-ni on the east shore of the Chosin Reservoir. My platoon (B Company, 2nd rifle Platoon) was assigned as a combat outpost and located on the high ground above the river bed two miles north of the battalion defense perimeter. We had a machine-gun section and a 610 radio attached in addition to our own units. Weapons Co., which was set up on the road (the Main Supply Route to the north, east of the Chosin Reservoir) was prepared to deliver 81mm mortar fire or illumination shells to our front if we needed them.

About 1300 on November 27, an army battalion relieved us in the area of my platoon's combat outpost. We had held the outpost three nights, but had made little contact. The only contact was with an enemy patrol of six men one time. This patrol fired on us as they fled, we returned fire—resulting in no casualties for either side. The army battalion set up a perimeter and B Company joined the rest of our battalion and moved by truck to Yudam-ni on the west side of the reservoir. We arrived in our assembly area in darkness with the intention of getting a night's sleep, then begin our "Big Push" to the north. The 7th Marines were in a perimeter defense at Yudam-ni when we arrived. We were to move through them at dawn. However, several companies of the 7th were engaged in a firefight on the high ground surrounding our assembly area. The intensity of the fire increased greatly about midnight. I moved my platoon out into the flat valley floor and spread them out in an effort to prevent more than one man being hit at a time by the mortar shells which were beginning to land all around us.

The ground was frozen so solid that when enemy bullets struck the earth, sparks flew and the bullet did not penetrate. It was impossible to dig in for our own protection. We had no cover except prayer, and prayers were used very effectively!

Just at dawn on November 28, an American-made 81mm mortar shell landed in the center of my platoon line killing two men and wounding two others. There was still no place to take cover. We removed the men, and I managed to say a brief prayer for the two that were obviously dying. I had to yell constantly to prevent the men from bunching up. It is amazing how human beings feel safe when they bunch up in small groups.

The count had been 41, but now, Baker Company's, 2nd Rifle Platoon had 37. We stayed on the low ground until late in the afternoon. We managed to scrounge a box of C-rations, but we could find nothing to burn, consequently we ate frozen beans, crackers, and a cookie. For dessert we had frozen fruit cocktail, delicious! It actually was—we were very, very hungry. Cold weather makes a man feel the need of food—exaggerates hunger.

At 1500 Jim Cronin, Executive Officer of B Company, took me on a reconnaissance of the area my platoon was to occupy. We were to relieve D Company, 7th Marines on a hill they had fought all night to hold. They had only 55 men left, after having climbed the hill with over 200. They were receiving very heavy small-arms fire from the high ground ahead of the ridge, and an occasional round of high velocity, probably a 76mm weapon. After completing our reconnaissance, I called for my platoon leader Sergeant Frank Lischeski, "Ski," to bring up the platoon. One by one they crossed the crest of the hill, climbing over the bodies of some twenty Marines and about sixty Chinese. In the fifteen minutes it took me to place my men, we suffered 10 more casualties. Sergeant Ed Morris moved his 3rd platoon through our lines and tied in with our left flank. Austin "Swede" Jenson kept his 1st platoon on the road below the hill because of very intense fire which was being delivered on them from the high ground they were supposed to occupy.

By dark, "Ski" had found a convenient hole which the Chinese dug that made a fine platoon command post. It was L-shaped, covered except for an entrance at each end, and about 4' deep. We got our phone communication in with the B Company Command Post and I squeezed the whole platoon into the trench. The enemy ceased firing at dark, after we called an airstrike on the hill Swede was trying to take, and all was quiet. Sergeant Stanley, my platoon guide, "Ski," "Doc" Yolinsky, "Pat" Patton (my runner) and I squeezed into the hole along with Sergeant Wolfe who was section leader of the 2nd Section Machine Guns, attached to my platoon. It was crowded, but warm and we managed to catch a few minutes sleep, even with the firefights and the constant artillery barrage being delivered by our own people and the enemy.

Executive Officer Jim Cronin (Palatas)

Sergeant Frank Lischeski (Wray)

At dawn the fire of the enemy increased greatly and "Baker 2" returned the fire. We called another airstrike on the hill Swede was still trying to take. We plastered it with bombs, napalm, .50 caliber machine-gun fire, rockets and 75mm recoilless fire. It seemed impossible that anyone could live through such a barrage! Swede led his platoon up the hill while his machine guns and 4.2" mortars gave him support. Swede charged the hill like a madman, firing from the hip and throwing grenades. He got to the top and over the crest with eight of his men, then some enemy popped up out of spider holes and knocked him down with grenades. Other enemy troops pulled a single envelopment, moving around the lower slope of the hill. Two other men of his platoon died there and we had to leave the bodies. Four of the remainder that returned were wounded. We never did take that hill.

My platoon was still receiving small-arms fire and occasionally a mortar or rifle grenade landed in our area. I stayed near the platoon command post, which was also the O.P. for the artillery forward observers as it was the highest point that we held. Occasionally I trooped the line to see how the boys were doing. Corporal West had located three enemy pill boxes so I called for a rocket team to try to knock them out. I stopped to talk to Corporal Cruz and kid him about digging such a deep hole. He said, "Lieutenant, if they hit me they'll have to drop one right in my hole." I laughed and crawled back to the high ground when a shell landed between two of my boys. They were both hit hard, but I'm afraid Corporal Timbrook was hit, really bad. While "Doc" was treating the wounded, a shell landed in the hole with Corporal Cruz. Poor guy never knew what hit him.

Later in the day, Lieutenant John Hancock, the Company Commander, came up to my combination outpost–command post and informed me of the latest S-2 reports. We were fighting 4 Chinese divisions and perhaps more! We were also cut off to the rear by at least two divisions of Chinese. About that time, some "flying box cars" came in and parachuted supplies to us.

The fighting continued through the day and although our troops inflicted terrific casualties, and our aircraft and artillery accounted for many more, we could not advance one step. At night the enemy stopped firing at us. We could hear

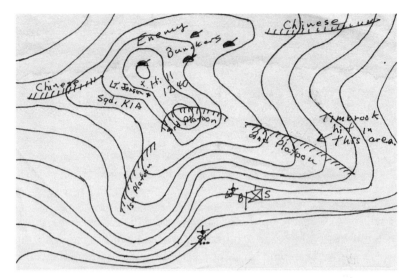

Map of the day Timbrook was hit (Yolinksy)

them digging in new emplacements, whistle at each other and yell commands. Finally somebody blew a bugle and they launched another attack. We repulsed that one easily, and the Chinese army returned to their digging. We fired an occasional shot in their direction just to let them know we were still there, and they acknowledged by firing a few rounds back at us. About 4am they blew what sounded like a Chinese version of taps and all was quite until dawn.

When the firing started I decided to leave the sitting position I tried to sleep in for a couple of hours and troop the line again. I couldn't get out of my usual entrance to the command post as the bullets kept breaking off the scrub brush and throwing snow down the hole. So I sneaked out of the other hole, and a mortar shell landed on the roof of the command post. It didn't penetrate the roof and didn't hit me, I cannot imagine why?

At the outpost (10 yards from the command post) Sergeant Underhill was acting as artillery observer. We were looking for an enemy mortar position when a bullet sounded especially loud. After we took cover we found a hole in Sgt Underhill's parka—it came between us and we were only two feet apart at the most. There were a lot of close ones. A cartridge belt I was carrying was shot out of my hand. Cpl. West had his leg scratched as one tore through his pants. One of my machine gunners got what looked like a floor burn on his arm from a bullet.

—*"Bud"*—

# And the Chinese Came!!

## Lieutenant Mike Palatas

The battalion's 6×6's came up the primitive road which fringed the east side of the Changjin Reservoir, found a suitable spot, wide and flat enough to make a large circular turn, then come back out on the dirt road to where they now faced south—the direction from which they had come. The exhaust from their engines was vaporized and visible as it hung in the cold still air. I saw a few "Bandits" use the opportunity to warm their hands at the end of the tailpipe. The truck motors, left to idle, drowned the sounds of the continuing fighting west across the reservoir and landscape. That was our destination.

The platoon leaders would oversee the loading of their platoons, about 13 men to a truck and our Skipper, Lieutenant John Hancock, directed Gunny Wright to oversee the loading of the entire company—then report to him. He did not want

We were ready to MOVE OUT! (Palatas)

the troops sitting idle in the bitter cold for fear of frostbite! Our "Top," 1st Sgt Dierickx, the walking personnel and unit diary file, reported to the Skipper that our strength was at 213 with six men on "light duty" because of injury or wounds. Those would remain with the B Company command post. The Top was then

Waiting to leave for Chosin (Sydman)

directed to find a seat in the rear of the Jeep at the end of the convoy with our company executive officer, Lieutenant Jim Cronin. The Skipper and Gunny would ride in the lead Jeep which carried a front bumper sign reading "Roadmaster." In a short time, Gunny Wright reported the company had loaded onto trucks and the Skipper gave word to Rocky Williams (head of the motor transport contingent) to get his show on the road—MOVE OUT!

It was not far down the winding narrow road to Hagaru-ri at the reservoir's southernmost end. Here, about 11 days from now, B Company would be in hand-to-hand combat at dawn on a ridge north of the village against the Chinese threatening to break through our lines.

The convoy swung west and north and in about 10km we were over Toktong Pass where tonight F-2-7 would be encircled and battered for the next week. In about a week's time, we would be passing back through here, cross country and on foot breaking a trail through knee deep snow on our way "out."

We continued on the ridge for another dozen "clicks" then stopped just north of a spot on the map named Yudam-ni. It was at the western tip of another finger of the Changjin Reservoir. It was about dark now, but for us, huddled against each other in the canvas covered 6×6s, it was dark for the entire trip, we saw no scenery.

On de-trucking, we were stiff and began the "Chosin stomp" to get the circulation going and to ward off the shivers. The side of the road along the parked convoy became one long instant "benjo" (ditch-urinal). The company was led into the cultivated but now barren and snow-covered field a matter of yards off the road. This was temporary staging area for our next move.

Three pyramidal tents were set up by someone earlier and these would serve as warming huts with their small diesel-fueled pot-bellied stoves centered in them. The troops would rotate in and out, five or 10 minutes, depending on the temperament of the overseeing non-com. We would catnap through much of the night in this open field and would watch in wonder the ridgeline a few hundred yards to our NE where continuous lines of tracer bullets flew across the sky above. The Chinese were attacking the Marines who were holding the high ground from the air and in hand-to-hand combat. An occasional 60mm Chinese mortar would over shoot the ridge and land in our vicinity with a whistle and splatter on the frozen ground. These caused more tension than casualties.

As I stood along side a 6×6, there was a tug at my arm and a gentle shove—the voice said, "Get your ass moving, Marine," I turned to see the apologetic face of Sergeant Waldo Wolfe. He took the cigarette out of his mouth and said, "I'm sorry sir, I didn't know it was you!" Charlie Lyles, the Skipper's radioman had an embarrassing moment, too. He followed a form he thought to be Lieutenant Hancock and near the end of the parked trucks, the form turned around and it was the stubbled face of Sergeant Shimmel, the Battalion Police Sergeant, who was looking for Sergeant Shoemaker. Charles scampered back and found Lt Hancock

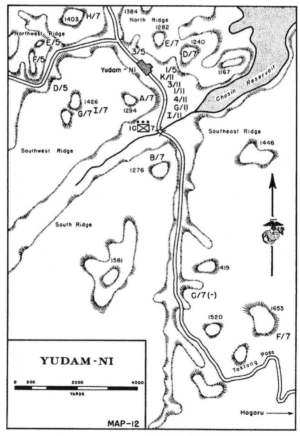

Lt Jenson lead the 1st Platoon in assault of the knoll to his front on which he was killed (USMC Map)

in time to accompany him to the battalion command post for a briefing on the situation above us on the ridgeline.

At 0100, D-2-7 was being overrun by the Chinese on the ridge's southeast flank. Only a handful of the company hung on. Our Skipper had Charlie Lyles radio our executive officer to prepare to move out on his return.

Not many B Company men could describe Yudam-ni. To us, it was a frozen field that was under cultivation in the summer. There were a few scattered single-storied square structures, presumably dwellings, but now vacated and in different states of shambles, yet good enough to serve as mini-command post for the Marine units in the area. Yudam-ni was the main hub for the 5th and 7th Regiments.

Lieutenant Hancock informed the platoon leaders, the Gunny and the "Top" that we would be moving out. He would take the 2nd and 3rd Platoons and the mortars around the base of the mountain (about ½ mile) and establish our command post there. Our machine-gun sections were now attached to their respective rifle platoons. He would then have Lieutenant Morris and the 3rd Platoon followed by Lieutenant Kohler's 2nd Platoon move up the hill onto the ridgeline still held by fragments of D-2-7.

Lieutenant Austin "Swede" Jenson and his 1st Platoon would enter the draw to our immediate front and climb the trail to the top, when there, went single-file a hundred or more yards to link up with the 3rd Platoon. Once atop the ridge, our line would follow the slight curvature of the ridge. Our right flank would be open, but visibility was excellent to the finger of the frozen reservoir which was a short distance away over the flat ground. Lt Jenson was to "tie in" with E-2-5 on B Company's left, but the distance was too great and we left a gap—leaving it to visual tie-in rather than thin out our line.

All went well. I accompanied the 1st Platoon with Lt Jenson and Sergeant Schmidt in the lead. We got to about 150 yards off the ridge top and I observed two forms moving, taking cover and looking down on us. We continued advancing, slowly. One of our men yelled out, "Jesus Christ, they're behind us now!" The two got up and fired random rifle shots at us then moved out of our sight. In no time flat, Waldo had one of his machine guns

Mortar men of B-1-5

in action and the gunner let go half a 250-round belt before I got back to him yelling "Cease Fire, our Marines are up there, too!" Fortunately, no one was hurt in the brief encounter, but the adrenaline began to flow. We moved on up without further incident.

Atop the ridge, I recall seeing the aftermath of the D-2-7 fracas the night before. Bodies of Marines and Chinese still lay where they fell. I noticed the parkas missing from the Marines' bodies. The acrid smell of the battle still permeated the air as we began to organize our position. We couldn't dig in—the ground was frozen hard. I told a wild-eyed D Company Marine to gather his remaining men (16) and go to the bottom of the hill where he would get a ride to our command post. The next day, he went back out to the road to Yudam-ni to search for other 7th Marine units.

Until our last day on this ridge, we were unaware of the plight of the 1st Marine Division and the folding of the entire front in Korea.

Members of the 1st and 3rd Platoons of B Company will vividly recall Lieutenant Jenson's assault of the knoll to his front on which he was killed. We never took that knoll, we saw it re-fortified the next morning, and we could all feel the heat of the napalm dropped by airstrike.

We wondered about the D Company tent, Jeep, and supplies which were now 200 yards in front of the 2nd Platoon. From the 1st Platoon's line, we could watch E-2-5 in hand-to-hand combat on the hillside 500 yards to our northwest. It was quite a grenade-throwing contest, with the Chinese fighting uphill. From our high position, we could look back south and down in the flats and see the Artillery Support unit. However, the direct support artillery was mostly ineffective for us because of the lay of the land. Mortars were our best fire support in this location.

There was a dearth of information trickling down to us from battalion. I wondered aloud to the Skipper, Lt Hancock, as to why we weren't getting orders to move out in the attack. A rifle unit gets uneasy when it stays in one position for more than a day. When word came, it said to lighten our basic load. We, the division, were in bad shape and encircled. Shed <u>and destroy</u> any unnecessary gear, keep one sleeping bag for every two men—pile and burn the rest. Re-supply now would come via code name "Baldwin" for air drop. Tootsie rolls in the air drops would be the main entree for the next dozen or so days.

Still ahead of us were night marches, isolated attacks, frost-bitten extremities, cat naps on our feet when stopped in sometimes knee-deep snow, hand-to-hand combat at Hagaru-ri and that was only the halfway mark! By the time we re-group at Hagaru-ri, Sergeant Zollinger reported our machine-gun platoon strength at 24, we were at less than 50 percent strength for the six guns and still had a long way to go!

# God, Don't Let this Bandit Die!

## Corpsman Phil "Doc" Yolinsky

I was a retread from the South Pacific in World War II who made the mistake of volunteering, again. I'm really not sorry. I wouldn't have missed it for a million dollars. I am real proud to have served with the best. I joined the division at Wonsan assigned to the 2nd Platoon, B-1-5 somewhere north of Wonsan, North Korea. We made a little train ride north. You remember the train that rambled and shook so much, we thought it would fall off the tracks, no fear of that. My battle station was behind a pile of 105mm ammo. We were riding shotgun. We stopped approximately every hundred yards or so and rifle squads went out and cleared the enemy out who were trying to keep us from reaching our destination. We made it to the rear echelon of the 5th Marines.

They loaded me on a Jeep and went for another joy ride north to find Lieutenant L.B. "Bud" Kohler's 2nd Platoon command post which had the point at the base of a small mountain. We stopped and I checked my gear, carefully. My sea bag was left at the rear echelon so it didn't take long. Sleeping bag, carbine and medical supplies. Before climbing up to the company, I was handed a five-gallon can of

We took a little train ride north to battle (Schryver)

Corpsman Phil "Doc" Yolinsky, 2nd platoon (Yolinksy)

Corporal Bill Timbrook right before he shipped over (Timbrook)

water to take along. It seemed there was no water up there and the people were dry. I made the top, a little pooped. I met Lt Kohler and he turned me over to one of the platoon sergeants who introduced me to the platoon.

This is where I started my new job. I picked myself a spot to dig in and settled down to rest behind one of those funny-looking mounds. How was I to know it was a graveyard, so I was told, and they buried their dead sitting up, those ant hills made good cover.

It was at this point that my friend Corporal Bill Timbrook, who was to become my life-long friend, showed me the ropes. He was one hell of a nice skinny kid. He was always there when I needed him. We were dug in overlooking a bridge and a lake. That night I was baptized with my first firefight and that became a nightly routine. One of my first casualties happened one morning after firing at some stumps. There was a strip-and-clean weapons order and one of the 10 percent asked another guy to check his rifle and "bam" it went off. The owner had a beaut. The bullet hit his forearm, went through his elbow and then out his lower arm. We loaded him on a Jeep and drove him to the rear area where I picked up my first 12 1oz. bottles of brandy.

When I returned to the platoon, this was my first giveaway of cough medicine. I was not a drinker of the finer spirits. Now, I was getting to know the men a mite better and Timbrook and I became close buddies.

The 2nd Platoon remained on the point until Thanksgiving. We were relieved and sent to the rear for our turkey dinner and rest, we thought. I picked up another 12 bottles of "cough medicine" and boy was I getting popular.

"Saddle up, we're going back on point," was ordered, and that we did. A few days later we were relieved again and sent back to rejoin the battalion.

Timbrook, his squad and I, set tent halves next to our holes and made a G.I. stove out of an empty drum. We just laid around and relaxed, went on patrols and naturally we had our nightly firefights. Each morning I remember the enemy soldiers we killed were the same ones that were helping us during the day, NICE PEOPLE!

Timbrook and the men of B-1-5 staying warm (Sydman)

Those were the days, relaxing by the stove, C-rations and drinking bouillon soup. I used to make bouillon soup and pass it out during the day and I'd crawl around at night from foxhole to foxhole passing out a tin cup of broth. The habit I picked up when we were on point. I had picked up a can of bouillon cubes and a can of cheese somewhere along the line from an army unit that had passed by us one time.

The only thing that really bugged me to hell, was Timbrook. Every damn time a sergeant needed a recon patrol my buddy Timbrook would volunteer, and naturally no patrol goes out without a corpsman. "Come on Phil, Let's go," I can still hear him. I kept telling him, "Don't keep volunteering us, you're pressing our luck."

Boy, was I glad when the word came down, "Saddle up, we're moving up to a place called the Chosin Reservoir." Man, how lucky can you get? No more volunteering for patrols that kept getting ambushed. Poor Timbrook, what would he do now? After a nice long truck ride up a winding mountain road, yea wide, we arrived at the valley. Remember those beautiful frozen rice paddies? It was almost dusk when we got there. We tried to dig in, but the ground was frozen solid making it impossible to dig. Then all hell broke loose, it was one hell of a night. Machine-gun fire, tracers and mortar fire under the bright flares coming in the whole night. I sure was busy that night, that yell or call, what ever it was, "CORPSMAN! CORPSMAN!" I would say I earned my pay that night. I also learned a good lesson. Never get up or move when you look up. Those tracers all look like they are coming straight at you. I yelled to all around me, "Don't run, lay down in the furrows and stay put!"

The next morning we got the word again, "Saddle up, we're going up and take the hills." We started up and along the way we found our perimeter defense. We all know what happened to those poor guys. I believe they were 7th Marines.

Second Platoon, led by Lt "Bud" Kohler, started up the mountain, I believe it was Hill 1240, and I was behind my buddy Timbrook. We almost made the top when we had a clear gap. Old Timbrook was taking pop shots at some Chinese soldiers along the ridge and everything was moving fast. Then we were pinned down by mortar fire, you know, wait two minutes then send two or three men through the gap, then wait again and send the next group.

My friend Timbrook was doing a fine job and enjoying his work. He didn't make the count, he, with me behind him, jumped off too soon. I write this with tears in my eyes. Timbrook caught a mortar hit close by and he was one hell of a mess. I crawled over and pulled him to safety, ha. I didn't know where to start, he was hit from head to toe. His head looked worst as it was open so I started there and worked down. We still kid each other to this day because I threw his finger away. He was bleeding from a dozen wounds. I put a battle dressing on his head and tied it under his chin. By this time he was starting to come to. I took one of the morphine syrettes out of my mouth, pulled the top off and gave him a shot of 1941 vintage (because of the extreme cold the corpsmen often had to carry morphine syrettes in their mouths to thaw them out enough for use). I put his head on my lap and finished patching him up. Now conscious, he asked me what happened, how bad was he hit and why was it dark out? He couldn't see, even at best without those thick glasses he wore. He was blind without them. "Sorry Tim, I'm not funning you," I told him the sun had gone down and it was getting dark. Timbrook said, "Who the hell are you kidding, it was light a little bit ago?" We were both crying and he asked me how bad he was hit? I told him he had been hit by shrapnel a little and you're OK. To this he said, "Doc, what the hell are you crying for?" I answered, "Well, you're my buddy and I feel bad about you getting hit." He started complaining of the pain and I had a little more checking to do. I told him to bite on his dog tag while I finished up. (About six years after the police action, I went down to visit Timbrook and his family. He gave me the dog tag with his teeth marks on it.)

Helicopters saved lives by quick evacuation (USMC)

Well anyway, I grabbed a couple of jarheads and told them to take Timbrook down the hill. He had a chance of making it if I could get him to the aid station. Out of nowhere some officer said, "Leave him be, you guys get back to your positions." I told him Timbrook had a chance and we had to get him off the hill, but he wouldn't listen. So I put him on a tent half and started down the hill dragging Tim after me. The officer yelled for me to stop and said I was the only corpsman left on the hill. We need you to take care of the wounded up here. We're short of people. Take care of the ones that can still handle a weapon. Take care of the critical ones later. I didn't stop, so he pulled his weapon on me and said, "Stop or I'll fire." I kept going, and I got Timbrook down the hill and turned him over to the collecting station or what ever they called it. He was handled with tender loving care and strapped to a helicopter and away he went.

I went back up the hill, took care of the wounded and in between was directing the ammo carriers to the various gun positions along the whole ridge. I knew where they were from answering the calls of, "CORPSMAN, CORPSMAN!" Two forward observer officers called me over to their hole and asked my name. "What for?" I asked? "You're doing one hell of a job up here and we are going to recommend you for a field promotion and a star," they said. I told them my name, said BS and went back to work. ["Doc" got a Silver Star many years later.]

Some time in the next few days, a mortar dropped in near me and I picked up shrapnel, concussion and on the way out, frostbite. Lieutenant Kohler called for a replacement and when I reached the bottom of the hill I reported to sick bay. The Doctor told me that Lt Kohler had called him and said that I had done a damn good job, thanks "Bud." The next day or so the order came down to saddle up to form a convoy to break out of the trap at the reservoir. The rest is history, Cpl. Bill Timbrook and I have kept in touch and been close friends these many, many years. There were some more incidents, but Tim took the cake.

—*"Doc" Phil*—

*A note from Ole Emmett: Although disabled from his war injuries, Timbrook came home and raised a family. Tim is one of the true heroes who truly suffered the wounds of war.*

# The Premonition

## Corporal Emmett Shelton, Jr.

When I got to Korea in the 1st Replacement Draft, I was assigned to the fire team led by Corporal Richard Cruz. He was from California, where his new wife lived. The other members of the fire team were Private Roger Sturtevant from Nashville, Tennessee (later Killed in Action at Hagaru-Ri), Private Ben Wray, and me. Ben and I were both from Austin, although we had never met prior to Korea.

In mid-November 1950 while Baker Company was still on the east side of the reservoir, Cpl Cruz told us that he felt his number was up, he would not make it back from Korea.

Corporal Cruz was very concerned about his premonition, it was real to him, he became quiet and very serious. He was always a good fire team leader, but now became nearly sullen in his attitude. No more kidding or horsing around.

On November 27, we boarded some of "Rocky" Williams' 6×6 trucks and were taken over the Toktong Pass into Yudam-ni on the west side of the Chosin Reservoir. We arrived after dark and disembarked in the valley to spend the night, in reserve. I am sure it got colder later on, but this night still sticks in my mind as the coldest I encountered. This was the night the Chinese chose to eliminate the 1st Marine Division. Parts of Baker Company were called to reinforce the lines on the hill to our east. The rest of us remained in Yudam-ni.

On November 28, Baker Company was sent up Hill 1240 to relieve Dog Company of the 7th Regiment who had been hit extremely hard the night before. As we reached the top, Dog/7 was still in the foxholes and we hit the deck between them. Unfortunately for us, the Chinese had the ridge we were on zeroed in by a 60mm mortar and we began receiving heavy mortar fire.

With all the men on the ridge, both Dog Company in the holes, and Baker Company around them, the mortar seemed to hit someone each time it came in. Several good Marines got theirs right there. After a while, Dog Company moved out and the mortars quit.

As soon as our fire team was assigned its area, Ben and I started to dig our foxhole, but our entrenching tools just curled up when they hit the frozen ground, they were useless. I spotted a small World War I-type pick on a dead Chinese, so I took it and carried it on through the rest of the campaign. It was difficult even with that pick to dig in the frozen ground, but after about six or seven inches down the digging got easier, as we got through the frozen ground. Ben and I dug a real good hole. It was bottle-shaped, small at the top and bigger under the ground, We figured that it would be harder for the mortar to hit a foxhole designed like that. Ben and I spent a rather uneventful night in our new foxhole.

The next day, we were transferred one foxhole south of my beautiful, safe one. My new foxhole was about eight inches deep and seven feet long. Boy, what a target for a mortar! I bitched a lot about this transfer which was sure to get me killed. Cpl Cruz took my place in the beautiful, safe hole Ben and I had dug.

I had zeroed my M-1 in on the ridgeline about 200 yards to our front when we first arrived and could hit pretty much anything at that distance. When it started getting daylight the next morning I saw some Chinese carrying ammo to the bunker on the ridge. Being a good Marine, I got a couple of them, but nobody else fired.

The enemy had moved a machine gun into that bunker during the night and it opened up on me. There was no room for my gear in my shallow foxhole, so they shot hell out of all of it. All of my rations were shot up, everything I couldn't get in the hole with me was shot up, then the mortar from somewhere over the hill started sending its message.

I was in deep trouble! The first mortar shell sent Ben back for coffee, then a later one went right in my beautiful foxhole on top of Cpl Cruz. He was right, he would not make it back from Korea alive. His premonition had been fulfilled. I didn't bitch about being moved out of my foxhole, anymore. The Marines had lost a good man. I cannot explain how he knew it was going to happen, but he did.

—Emmett—

# Magnificent Rear Echelon Support!

## Corporal Emmett Shelton, Jr.

Down the mountain, through the Chinese, came what was left of a Division of Marines. We had been fighting, scratching, kicking and biting for their very existence for more than a week. Food was scarce up there and always frozen beyond being edible. Marines are always hungry, but these were extra hungry.

Our clothing, while being the best our Corp could offer at the time, was inadequate. Our rayon wind-proof trousers were not fire-proof and most of them had big holes burned in them, many had more holes than trousers. The filth inherent with our profession of living in holes in the ground, standing around sooty fires trying to thaw rations and get a little body warmth, and the fact that we had not shaved for more than a week, made us less than sharp looking. Every man had dirt and blood on his clothing, either his own blood or that of his buddies who he had tried to help. All of us had the strain of the last few weeks etched on our dirty faces, but down off that mountain we came.

Chow line (Sydman)

As we neared the bottom, the temperature rose and with its rising, the pain from our frostbite increased, measurably. We noticed our smell. We were no longer dodging bullets, so we finally realized we had not eaten for a long time.

As we reached friendly lines, an army unit was lined up at their mess tent for a warm meal. Our starving Marines saw our opportunity, but we did not have any mess gear, except our homemade spoons we had made. Several did not have a spoon so they hobbled over to the nearby trash dump and commandeered cans which we attacked with our handy-dandy can openers, cutting away the top nearly all the way and bending it over to form a handle. Our scroungy bunch lined up behind the army troops for chow. The army Mess Sergeant, seeing what was transpiring, ordered his men out of the line, saying, "These Marines need to eat worse than you men do, so make room for them."

**GOD BLESS YOU MAGNIFICENT REAR ECHELON SUPPORT!**

*—Emmett—*

# Down off Hill 1240

*The Marine Officer's Guide*

When the Communist Chinese threw 270,000 troops into the Korean War, numerous U.N. divisions were overrun. Eight Chinese divisions engaged the 1st Marine Division. In the face of "General Winter" and overwhelming numerical superiority, the Division concentrated promptly, rescued and evacuated surviving remnants of adjacent, less ready Army formations, and commenced one of the greatest marches of American history, from Chosin Reservoir to the sea.

As Puller says, "Retreat, Hell! We're attacking in a different direction!"
                                                            —*Major General Oliver Smith*

Sixteen days later, having brought down its dead, saved its equipment, and rescued three Army battalions, the 1st Marine Division—supported by the 1st Marine Wing—reached the sea with high morale and in fighting order.

The 1st Division had shattered the Chinese Communist Forces 9th Army Group, killed at least 25,000 Chinese, and wounded more than 12,500.

# USMC Historical Diary for the Period December 1 through 15, 1950 ~~SECRET~~ Declassified

**Dec. 1** The 5th Marines reinforced was in company with the 7th Marines operating under a Joint Operations Order and conducting a withdrawal from YUDAM-NI to HAGARU-RI. This withdrawal was directed as a result of fast deteriorating situation across the United Nations front in northern Korea and the overwhelming numbers of enemy Chinese Communist Forces surrounding the regiments. The operations which followed were of unusual military significance as they represented a combination of military attack strategies and were conducted simultaneously during movement from YUADM-NI to HAGARU-RI to KOTO-RI.

The movement from YUDAM-NI to HAGARU-RI is 18 miles over rugged mountain pass controlled by the enemy. Marines were required repeatedly to clear enemy road blocks to protect the vehicle column of two regimental combat teams. Sharp enemy action and the sub-zero weather took a considerate toll, especially on infantrymen who were consistently under enemy pressure.

B Company continued a move to Hagaru-Ri (Bridgeman)

**Dec. 2** Non-essential gear was destroyed. Dead were buried. All vehicles were loaded to carry stretchers for casualties. Movement over the pass toward HAGARU-RI began at 2000.

After moving two miles toward the pass, approximately 100 more casualties of the 3rd Battalion of the 5th Marines and the 3rd Battalion of the 7th Marines, were picked up and loaded on the trucks. Snow fell and many of the patients were in poor condition due to the cold. Weather was extremely cold 15 below at night.

Personnel report for the 5th Regiment for the period 1800 Nov. 30 to 1800 Dec. 2: 62 killed in action, two died of wounds, 19 missing in action, 148 wounded in action, 118 non-battle casualties.

**Dec. 3** Another 100 casualties were loaded on passing vehicles near the top of the pass while many walking wounded accompanied the column. Most of the casualties came from F Company, 7th Marines, which was isolated in position for several days. Troops consistently had a shortage of hand grenades and mortar and small-arms ammunition. Approximately 900 casualties were evacuated by the convoy. About 80 percent of the patients had frostbite. About half had battle wounds in addition to frostbite. In spite of the conditions, leading elements of the regiment arrived in HAGARU-RI at 2000 in the bitter cold.

**Dec. 4** The column continued to move into HAGARU-RI with last elements arriving at 1700. A total of 1,026 patients were evacuated during the day by air. Rations, fuel and ammunition supplies were replenished.

**Dec. 5** The regiment took the day to prepare for the move to KOTO-RI. Patients were assessed and only the most serious 1,300 were airlifted. Rations, ammunition and clothing were issued to all units and loaded on trucks. Protestant and Catholic services were held. All surplus equipment and supplies were destroyed.

**Dec. 6** The 5th Marines began the move to KOTO-RI in a slowly advancing column about dark. Attacks on the column forward slowed the move and only about one mile was made all night. Fuel supplies were air dropped. Weather was bitterly cold and the 5th Marines fought a heavily contested rear guard action all night.

**Dec. 7** Forward units arrived in KOTO-RI at 1400 after the 3rd Battalion cleared several enemy roadblocks. Hot coffee and one pyramidal tent for warm-out was provided to each battalion. The weather remained sub-zero cold with several inches of snow. The men slept in the open for the most part. Many disabled vehicles and dead Marines, army personnel and British Commandos were found. They were the remains from previous convoys. All the dead allied troops discovered were picked up.

**Dec. 8** The last units arrived at 0030. The regiment was resupplied with two days' rations and ammunition. Casualties were evacuated by air from the KOTO-RI airstrip which was hastily extended for bigger aircraft. A mass funeral for 117 dead was conducted. Weather remained very cold with a low temperature of minus 10.

**Dec. 9** The regiment got an air drop of 110 gallons of fuel and planned the move down the pass to HUNGNAM. Air evacuations continued. Personnel report for the Regiment for the week of 3-9: 32 killed in action, eight died of wounds, 205 wounded in action, 45 missing in action, 416 non-battle casualties. Weather was very cold and windy. Lows below zero.

**Dec. 10** The 5th Marines moved in convoy from KOTO-RI to HUNGNAM. The enemy brought the convoy under heavy fire at the top of the pass as successive elements went over. Airstrikes and tank fire helped to neutralize the resistance. Light resistance was encountered after dark near SUDONG-NI but was quickly overcome with no casualties. Weather was very cold and windy but much milder at the foot of the pass. At MAJON-DONG trucks were waiting and moved personnel into a bivouac area already set up with tents, stoves, galley with hot food, water.

**Dec. 11** The 1st Battalion, which was bringing up the rear of the convoy, finally reached MAJON-DONG at 1530. All other personnel spent the day resting, reading mail from the U.S. and preparing to go aboard ships. Replacement clothing was issued. Church services performed. The weather was clear and cold at night, but mild in day. The ground thawed and the entire camp was ankle deep in mud.

**Dec. 12** The 5th Marines loaded personnel on the USS *Randall* beginning at 1430. [This is the same ship the Baker Bandits had taken from Inchon to Wonsan in early October.] Regimental Aid Stations discovered and evacuated several hundred frostbite cases and some respiratory cases directly to hospital ships. Most of these cases refused evacuation until they reached the final objective. Hot food and showers were available on the USS *Randall*. Troop spaces were very crowded and many slept on the decks. Church services were held onboard. The *Randall* was rated for 2,500 but held about 4,200 that day.

**Dec. 13** Personnel loading continued and continuing until 0020. The USS *Randall* sailed for PUSAN in mid-afternoon.

**Dec. 14** USS *Randall* and 5th Marines arrive in PUSAN and unload equipment. Personnel remain aboard ship.

**Dec. 15** Marines were offloaded to Landing Ships to move to MASAN. The 2nd Battalion moved by rail.

**Dec. 16** Most troops had arrived in the bivouac area near MASAN by nightfall Dec 16 and were billeted in available tents. A dispatch was received that all personnel be vaccinated again against typhus when available. The feet of all personnel were thoroughly examined for a final check for frostbite. The criterion for evacuation was second-degree blisters or clinical evidence that blisters had been present. The numbers of additional evacuated: 1st battalion 68; 2nd battalion 40; 3rd battalion 11; Other 14. Total 133.

We recovered our dead (USMC)

# And We Started Back

## Lieutenant "Bud" Kohler

About 0920 on December 1, 1950, we began our withdrawal from Hill 1240. All other elements of the 5th and 7th Marines had started to move back across floor of the valley of Yudam-Ni to the high ground. B Company was to fight the rear guard action for the column.

Staff Sergeant Charles Schmidt, who took over the 1st Platoon after Lieutenant Austin "Swede" Jenson was Killed in Action, began by moving his platoon down the hill and across the valley. Then I sent my machine-gun section down, then Lieutenant Ed Morris started moving his platoon back. They took <u>every</u> <u>article</u> of any value down the hill to the company command post with them! Not one single weapon, none of our wounded or dead, not a belt or blanket was left for the Chinese! After Ed had gone down, I began to move my own men out. It was a very

difficult and dangerous maneuver because the enemy snipers came right in behind us and fired like crazy. I waited until my last man had started down, then I followed.

By George, come to think of it, I must have been the last Marine to begin the withdrawal! A dubious distinction. I might have been the last to <u>start</u> down, but by the time we reached the B Company command post at the bottom of Hill 1240 I was, at least, in the middle of the platoon.

By the time I got to the bottom the Skipper, Lieutenant John Hancock, and the 1st Master Sergeant Phil Dierickx, the "Ole Top", had started a fire to burn all the gear we couldn't carry. Gunnery Sergeant Wright tossed a case of hand grenades on top of the fire, just before he left, it worked!

Staff Sergeant Charles Schmidt assumed command of the 1st Platoon (Palatas)

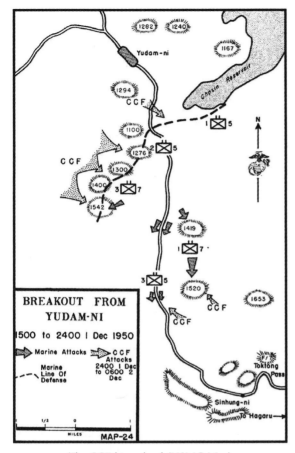

BREAKOUT FROM
YUDAM-NI

1500 to 2400 1 Dec 1950

Marine Attacks

Marine
Line Of
Defense

CCF
Attacks
2400 1 Dec
to 0600 2
Dec

MAP-24

The CCF hit us hard (USMC Map)

The rest of the company had started across the valley floor and were being fired on from the positions we had just left. We tried to call artillery fire on the hill, but the radio went out. Lieutenant Mike Palatas had moved his machine guns onto the creek bed in the center of the valley. They began strafing the ridge and the enemy quieted down a little. The company continued to move South and we "leap-frogged" the machine guns, letting one gun move at a time while the others fired at the enemy that swarmed all over the ridge.

It seems miraculous that with the bullets flying faster and more frequent than the snow flakes, we were able to make it to the safety of the 2nd Battalion's defense perimeter having only one man wounded and <u>none</u> killed. I prayed every step of the way.

It might be well to mention here that it was mighty cold up on the ridge. Snow was about ankle deep and the wind was terrific. On the valley floor below us, temperatures were recorded at -8 degrees F. We had sleeping bags with us, or at least some of us did. At night we put our legs into the bag, and left our boots on of course. We sat up in our holes and managed to get perhaps two hours sleep at the best.

We moved behind the high ground across the river after blowing the bridges we had crossed, and formed in an assembly area in some Korean houses and shacks that were available. C Company was on the high ground just above us and had engaged the enemy in a nasty firefight. The 2nd Battalion, 5th Marines were shooting up a storm on the high ground to our left, while the artillery fired continuously

Can't stop for snow—war goes on (Bridgman)

at the enemy who tried to rush us from the front or from the positions we just withdrew from. On up the canyon we heard constant firing, our own and that of the enemy.

We managed to scrounge some food from the artillery positions and heated it in one of the enemy houses. It tasted good—but I suddenly stopped eating long enough to realize just what was taking place. Here we were, unconcerned as could be, eating and talking while around us a terrific battle was raging, and we were about overrun at several points. An occasional mortar shell landed a few yards from us, and stray bullets slammed through the building we were in, but we remained quite unconcerned about anything but the food we were eating.

We kept waiting for word to move on down the road. The 7th Marines were pounding at the road block—the biggest one—between our position at Yudam-ni and Hagaru-ri. We waited until 3am when Lieutenant Hancock received a call for help from C Company. He ordered me to move my platoon to the high ground. I shouted to the platoon, and before the echo had died, they were on the road, machine-gun section attached! As we climbed the hill in the darkness we were fired on from the rear. I was leading the platoon and the man behind me fell wounded. A bullet went through the stock of his rifle and lodged in his leg. He went back to the sick bay under his own power. The few enemy troops that fired at us were quickly destroyed by our men. They were just a few that had infiltrated the C Company positions.

We moved up to the crest of the hill and reinforced the C Company area in their weaker points. By now I didn't have much of a platoon left, but C Company didn't have much of a company left either. We held up well until nearly dawn when Sergeant Rabcheck of the C Company machine-gun section thought he spotted about 400 of the enemy crossing the ice towards us. Actually they were only about 100, and the mortar fire I called for sank all that it didn't kill. When I went back to tell Sgt Rabcheck of our success, I found him lying just outside his hole with a bullet wound in the forehead. Some Private told me, "He's dead, OK Lieutenant, and it was quick."

At dawn, the enemy fire slackened and those very beautiful Marine Corsairs came in sweet and low. What a welcomed sight! With napalm, .50 cal., bombs and rockets they plastered the remainder of the attacking force. I could see the enemy running all over the hill we had left the day before, and managed to have an airstrike called on that hill. Results were "very effective!"

About 8am, after most of the shooting was over, I decided to heat up a can of C-rations I had in my pocket. I built a small fire on the reverse slope of the hill, then inspected my platoon and was delighted to learn that we had only one wounded and no dead. I returned to the can of chow—and was shot at by a sniper just as I reached for the can. I dove into the nearest hole and waited about five minutes. I could see the bubbles coming out of the top of the can, so I tried again, this time the bullets from the snipers "burp gun" kicked snow all over my legs, so I got a long pole and tried to pull it in to me, that failed too. I approached the can at least half dozen times before deciding that hunger pangs were less painful than bullet wounds. I still get hungry when I think of that lovely can of food I had to leave for the Koreans.

We moved down from the hill and joined the rest of B Company about 10am. Then we went down on the road and marched behind the motorized convoy. Many of our wounded were removed by helicopter before we began the withdrawal, but many, many more were strapped to the radiators of Jeeps along side the dead. The worst cases rode on stretchers whenever possible.

A few hundred yards down the road, we ran into a road block that was set up between us and the attacking 7th Marines by our ingenious little enemy troops. They seemed to pop up out of nowhere! C and B Companies moved to the left of the road, up around the road block in an attempt to outflank them. As we climbed the hill a sniper fired at us from very long range with a machine gun. The two companies, completely exhausted from the preceding days, the present climb and the cold, paid little attention, but continued to march up the mountain side in single file. The bullets were going over our heads at first, then he got the range and shot the belt off a man in front of me, put a couple of slugs between my legs and one into the leg of a man behind me. Corpsman "Doc" Pechak patched him up and he slid back down the hill to the convoy.

We moved on around the road block and C Company took over the lead, launching an attack to clear what was left of the enemy. The one Marine dead we found on the crest of the mountain was taken back down to the convoy, the hundreds of Chinese dead were left. Ed Kennison (my runner after Patton was wounded) picked up a pair of binoculars with the hammer & sickle on them, but threw them away because they were useless.

About midnight, we decided to move down to join the convoy again. Rather, we were ordered down. In the darkness we became separated and I found myself to be the only officer in the "lost patrol." It was too dark to follow tracks for certainty, and of course we did not dare use a light. If I had a dime for every fall

I took that night, and a penny for every twig that hit my helmet, my eyes and my face, I could retire wealthy. Funny how the mind works during such occasions. I knew that it was my imagination, but then I wasn't too sure. It seemed that every twig that brushed against my helmet or my coat sounded like a bullet going by. It added to the agony. I finally managed to get the patrol down to the road where we met the rest of the company. We fell in with the 18-mile convoy of trucks, Jeeps, tanks, and men.

We were almost completely exhausted by this time and it seemed that we couldn't go on much further. I'm sure I would have given up if I hadn't known that those brave kids behind me were depending on me to lead the way and be an example for them.

The convoy crept along for a few yards, then stopped. It was bitter cold, about −10 degrees F. Our feet perspired on the hike down the mountain, and now the perspiration froze in those damned water-proof shoe packs. My feet were numb at first, then they ached. The troops dropped onto the icy road and fell asleep. I walked up and down the convoy kicking them, cursing them and making them stand up and move around. Sgt Lischeski and I took turns. I'd lie down at the head of our platoon as Ski walked the length kicking people in the feet and making them stand. When he got back he'd kick me and I'd take over the "Kick Ass" job while Ski got a few minutes rest until I got back to kick him awake, etc. Not Standard Operating Procedure, but it worked! The men in my platoon made it except for a few whose feet were too badly frozen to walk and had the corpsman's OK to ride a truck. Some of the boys in other units did drop off to sleep, however, and some of them never woke up. They froze where they dropped!

All night we continued the march. I said the rosary over and over and prayed

Clarence Godeard from Oklahoma was evacuated for frozen feet (AP Photo)

constantly. I thought of Fran and our car, our apartment, our luxurious life at home. The thoughts of those wonderful weeks we had together before the Marines sent me to Korea. I begged Our Lord and Blessed Mother to guide me back to her, safely.

At dawn, we moved back up the ridgeline again. It seemed impossible that any one of those exhausted men could move up another mountain, but they did, and carried machine guns and mortars with them. I prayed for the strength to lead them up—I could never have carried the load some of them did, I begged for strength to make it carrying only a rifle.

When we reached the crest of the hill the 1st Platoon was hit by fire from still higher ground, on the side away from the convoy. Our mission was to act as flank guards for the convoy on the road, and after looking the situation over Lieutenant John Hancock and I decided that the hill we were on masked the fire of the enemy's rock fortress from the road, so we would bypass them. We moved along the forward slope with the company in a "V" formation. Suddenly we realized that the rock fortress was on our left flank while we were in completely open ground with no cover available. We held our breath and continued to march—and the enemy did not fire a shot at us! My only explanation is the constant prayers I uttered, and I presume that I was not alone in uttering such prayers. By late afternoon, we had moved on back to the road, followed it for a few hundred yards, and then back onto a windy frozen knob where we were to set up a defense perimeter until A Company relieved us. I placed my platoon and we drew rations from the convoy. They dug holes and my runner "Ken" dug a spot for us in the center—rear of the platoon line. After a hot can Ken & I huddled together and slept like babes until we were ordered down about 10pm. I hope my platoon kept a man from each hole on watch—I'll never know because I simply passed out there in the hole with my runner.

We spent all of that night and the next day on the road, walking a few steps and stopping. The men were too tired to even gripe about it. They continued to try to lie down and sleep, and I continued to stop them from it, although I was mighty tempted to try myself. I lost a couple more men with frostbite that day. Feet had to be black to make them eligible to drop out! Cruel measures, but we needed the manpower in the line companies.

That night was one of the worst I've spent. The worst in fact. My feet felt like they would drop off at any moment. I changed my socks and inner soles daily, put the wet ones under my clothing, wrapped around my waist to dry. The socks were white with frost and the inner soles frozen to the bottom of my shoe packs.

The snipers stopped shooting at dark, but occasionally some enemy would rush close up to the road and toss a couple of hand grenades into the motorized convoy. We were so miserable with the cold that unless someone next to us was hit, we paid no attention.

At about 10am we arrived at the outskirts of Hagaru-ri, what a welcome sight! In a defensive perimeter outside the city, to the north was a battalion of Royal Marines. They handed us cigarettes, candy and finally someone gave us water! The only water we'd had before this was melted snow—or snow we ate. How delicious a canteen cup full of pure flowing water can taste can be known only after

Hagaru (Palatas)

deprivation such as we had endured.

On entering Hagaru-ri, Lieutenant Hancock pulled his green "Piss Cutter" with a silver bar out of his pack, ordered everyone to stand tall, and we <u>marched</u> into the assembly area singing the Marines Hymn! <u>**WHAT A MAN!**</u>

Hagaru-ri is a typical, dirty little oriental town. It had been almost entirely evacuated when we marched (or staggered) through. Outside the (city) we came to our campsite. Real tents, and only 18 men to a six-man tent. We fed the men hot chow and then turned them loose on the ration dump that was going to be blown up when we left. The troops went wild over great quantities of <u>Tootsie</u> <u>Rolls</u> and various cans of fruit juice. On the high ground to our front, our right and our left, perimeter defenses were maintained by other battalions. We ate hearty and then dropped off to sleep, unaware of the firefights raging on the high ground all around us. The next day we rested, ate and scrounged up extra clean clothes. Again that night we slept a good 14 hours. The 1st Battalion, 5th Marines were assigned to the perimeter defense, the following day.

December 6 was a quiet day, too quiet perhaps. Occasionally our artillery dropped a few rounds over the ridge, and a lone Corsair could be seen bombing or releasing its rockets on targets of opportunity, but the day was exceptionally quiet. A Company was on the high ground across the river to our left, C Company was in the low ground to our front, tied in with A Company and B Company was in reserve just standing by. The high ground on our right was being held by another battalion, the 2nd Battalion, I believe.

We had planned to leave at dark, but at dark the battalion on our right became engaged in a terrific firefight with the Chinese forces. Our artillery had already pulled out, so we had no support from them. Our 4.2" mortar ammo was getting very low. It was a dark, snowy night and we could get no air support. I was thinking about all these things when the enemy started shooting faster, and at the same time a bugle call sounded to our front and C Company was attacked by a tremendous force. Mortar fire started dropping in our B Company area. They "walked" mortar rounds (81mm U.S. mortars by the way) right up the road until one round landed right beside my oochie. I was in the oochie with about six

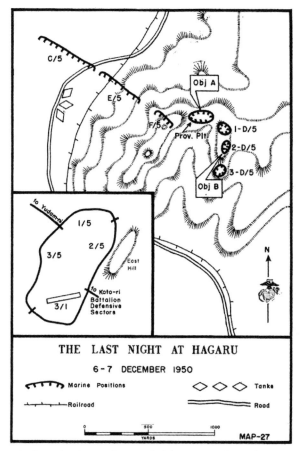

THE LAST NIGHT AT HAGARU

6 - 7 DECEMBER 1950

Marine Positions      Tanks

Railroad      Road

0    500    1000
YARDS

MAP-27

We planned to Hagaru leave at dark but we were hit with mortar fire (USMC Map)

men from my platoon at the time. It was a nice little oochie too—made by forming a semi-circle with empty oil drums and covering the top and the front with ponchos to break the wind. The mortar shell blasted through the drums and hit one man in the legs. Paint chips from the can hit my face and left ten little cuts that were sore, but not at all serious. "Doc" and I stayed in the oochie to help the wounded man, but I ordered the rest of the platoon to disperse.

We stood around and stamped our feet for a while to keep warm, then started hugging the deck as C Company was getting heavier fire and bullets were slamming into the ground and the few trees around us. Suddenly, A Company over on our left began firing. We then got the word that two full regiments were attacking our battalion and A Company had been overrun, but was still holding the high ground. Lt John Hancock barked at the Company and the Baker Bandits were en route to aid Able Company.

Of all the close calls we had, this little episode was most terrifying to me. We had no air support, and no artillery. Our heavy mortar ammo was just about gone. Our two battalions of 5th Marines (the 3rd Battalion had gone on south with the 7th Marines) were weakened greatly from casualties—companies were no more than half strength—and the two battalions were under attack by four full-strength Chinese army regiments! They started the attack on the right, then fire grew in intensity and the enemy grew in numbers and it seemed inevitable that we would be surrounded. As usual, I prayed all the way up the A Company

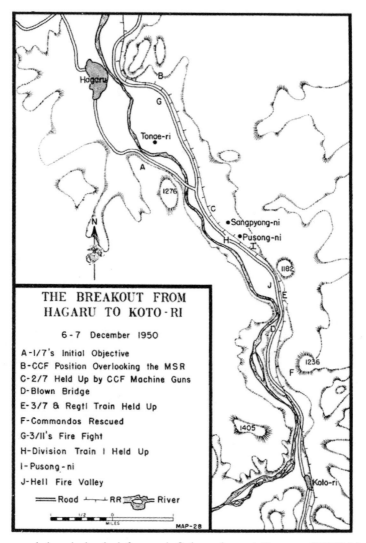

It was so dark we had to look for muzzle flashes to locate A Company (USMC Map)

hill where we contacted by Lieutenant Orrin Shelton, Commanding Officer of A Company. He told us that his company's left flank had been overrun. John Hancock sent my platoon to reinforce the left flank, while the 1st Platoon moved to aid the right flank and the 3rd moved into the middle of the line. Our 60mm mortars were set up about 25 yards in the rear of the line.

It was so dark that the only way I could locate the line position of A Company's left flank was to look at the muzzle flashes from their rifles and machine guns. I hopped into a hole with a Marine and asked him who was in charge and where he was. In the hole was Staff Sergeant Lawson who said, "Boy, Lieutenant! Am I glad to see you! Collins is in charge, he's in the third hole down. These Chinese ain't hurtin' us none, they just keep comin' faster n' we can shoot 'em down."

As I moved up to talk to Lt Collins I heard him say, "Who are you!" Just as I was about to answer, I realized that he was talking to another man who was standing between us. The other man answered by firing a burst from a "Tommy Gun" which tore a hole in Collins's sleeve. Collins dropped him with his .45. We bent over the man and to be sure, there was a very dead enemy soldier!

Collins attempted to show me where his lines were, so I yelled for "Ski" (Sgt Lischeski) to bring up the platoon. As I placed them in the lines, several men asked for extra ammunition, so I sent for some and then scouted out a ditch that could house our wounded. While I was in the ditch, helping the corpsman move one of our wounded, an A Company Marine ran back where we were, thinking that he was deserting the lines, I was about to "chew him out" when he said, "I'm out of ammo, got any?" I told him extra ammo was on the way and he said, "OK—I'll be back." With that he dropped his rifle, grabbed a hand full of grenades and ran back to the lines! It was men like that who deserve the medals—but he won't get one. It's all just in the line of duty.

Apparently the Chinese thought our flank was weak, they had managed to push a squad through the lines before Baker-2 arrived. Consequently, they made an all-out push right down the middle of the area held by B-2 and A-2. Mortars were fired into our positions by the direct-lay method, and they poured rifle grenades into our positions. Chinese Communist Forces (C.C.F.) grenadiers charged in yelling and throwing. For the first time we fixed bayonets. I was in one of the holes then, and all of us were firing as fast as we could, not bothering to aim because they were all around us, and besides it was too dark. Occasionally, we could hear a man or two breathing hard in front of our hole, then we would toss a grenade. We were firing at troops not more than <u>twenty feet</u> away many times. One or two of the boys found out why I ordered them to fix bayonets.

Finally dawn broke, and in the grey I could see the C.C.F.—or what was left of them—had started to withdraw. Mortars still falling occasionally, but the real barrage had let up. I trooped the line, getting out of my hole just long enough to see Private Sturtevant take a rifle grenade in the chest. He died a few minutes later as I read a "Prayer for a Dying Comrade" from Msgr. Sheen's *Shield of Faith*. When returned to the lines I could see more clearly, Staff Sergeant Lawson lay dead in his foxhole. Several of the dead Marines were in the area, but literally hundreds of dead Chinese were strewn all over the lines.

By this time it was light enough for our aircraft, and those beautiful Corsairs came in again. Then the Chinese forces really started to run and my boys stood straight up in their holes to fire at them as they ran. I can imagine how proud the regimental commander was to know that his two weakened battalions had repulsed <u>four</u> full-sized regiments by sheer guts and determination. I was certainly proud of my men!

Baker-2 came down shortly after dawn with only three less than we started up with. We were tired, but still cocky. As we passed the C Company area, we could see hundreds of Chinese dead actually piled up—in some places three and four deep. They must have killed nearly as many as we did, but not at such close range. I had found three dead chinks on the parapet of my foxhole at dawn—along with three grenades which for some reason had failed to explode. Why?—I am convinced that there is only one answer! For the same reason that I managed to escape so many other close ones, Faith!

It was about 9am when we started down the road from Hagaru-ri to Koto-ri. As we made the turn, B Company moved from the road to the rail road tracks. It was there that I found out what the 7th Marines had been shooting at. The tracks were loaded with the burned bodies of hundreds of Chinese. Napalm tanks and bomb fragments were strewn all over the area. The stench was awful. Further down the track I found headless, handless corpse of a Marine. Apparently he had been holding his hands over his face when he was hit by a large shell.

We continued to march down the tracks, then up on the higher ground to act as flank guards for the motorized convoy once more. Occasionally, an automatic weapon fired at us, but they usually ceased firing when we returned fire on them. They were fired from very long range—on tops of the surrounding mountains. Our planes spotted them every now and then and strafed and bombed their positions.

This sort of movement kept up most of the day until we came to a small farm with several buildings. I sent one squad in to search it out as the others were set up to protect our flanks. Sgt Hanes and his first squad found three enemy soldiers, killed one and captured two. They also found quite an arsenal of Russian, U.S. and Japanese weapons and ammo.

The cold and bitter hike continued until we arrived at Koto-ri about midnight. There we met some army troops as well as some of the 1st Marine Regiment who had fought their way up to join us. Koto-ri was quite a fortress in itself. Most of the troops found tents to sleep in, but Baker Company slept out on the ground. I stretched my parka out on the ground with my sleeping bag on top. I put my socks and inner soles inside the bag with me, and rolled over on my side and slept like a baby. At dawn I awoke to find about three inches of snow all over me and my gear. After bumming a cup of coffee from the army, I moved out with the rest of the company at 0800. We started up a mountain immediately out of

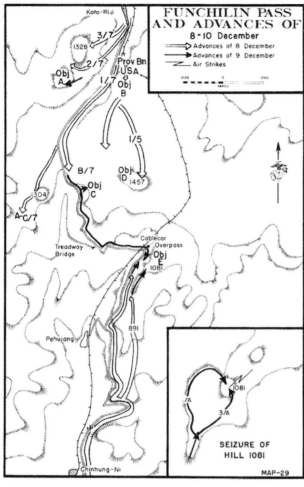

The snow was knee deep, the wind was howling at 23 degrees, and the C.F.C. had blown the bridge (USMC Map)

Koto-ri. C Company was in the lead at first, then B Company took over. As we neared the crest and the hardest part of the climb, Lieutenant Hancock ordered my platoon up to act as the point. I sent Sergent Yesenko and his squad ahead to break the trail. I placed myself in with the first fire team. The snow was about knee deep and still coming down—and there was a very heavy fog just to make it worse. Finally we reached the crest of the hill and our objective, "Objective Dog" according to the regimental withdrawal plan. I placed my platoon on the forward slope in a defensive position and told them to take a breather. The wind was howling and, although we didn't know the temperature on top of the mountain, it was 23 degrees below zero on the road!

I contacted the Skipper and he informed me that we would probably be there all night as this was the top of the pass, and the C.F.C had blown out a bridge ahead of us. The boys groaned and cursed when I told them to dig in for the night, but they did it. We built fires from slices of cardboard used to wrap our C-rations because the only available wood on the mountain top was too green to burn. "Ski" and I managed to melt a canteen cup full of snow and brew up a concoction "Ski" had the nerve to call coffee. Ken had no sleeping bag, so we put him between "Ski" and me, who had wrapped our legs in our bags. We were too cold to sleep, but we did rest a little that night.

At dawn, C Company got into a little firefight, but nothing too serious. They had a couple of wounded and no dead. That was the extent of our enemy contact for the day, however, we could see the Corsairs flying way down below us, strafing and bombing positions on the opposite side of the road. It seemed odd to look down and see airplanes flying—way, way down below.

We spent the day stomping our feet and changing our socks in an effort to prevent serious frostbite. My feet looked bad, big white spots and a few blisters, but Ken's were turning black. We spent that night there too, but were encouraged to learn that the engineers were making progress on the bridge.

We had no rations that day, but we managed to build a few small fires, enough to melt snow for coffee at least. I found a few of my men burning the handles of their entrenching tools and didn't even attempt to stop them—just told them not to get any such ideas about the stocks of their rifles.

About 10am the following day Lieutenant Bill Kerrigan came up the hill with a crew of his mess men and a sled load of rations. He told me about Bob Snyder's being hit back at Yudam-ni and more scuttlebutt about the enemy situation at Hungnam. We gorged ourselves on the rations, and we again attempted to heat them, but the firewood on Objective Dog was all gone. Plastic spoons are far too fragile to use on frozen meat and beans I found. I opened the can lengthwise and ate them as one would eat a candy bar.

It snowed hard again on that day, but I could delay a bowel movement no longer. Never shall I forget the shock of squatting too low in the snow bank, nor the horrible feeling of pulling up my long drawers full of snow! How we missed the luxuries of flush toilets and hot water!

That night, about 8pm I heard one of my sentries challenge a man who answered "Lieutenant Clapper, D Company, 1st Marines." Sure enough, it was our relief and it was Lt Clapper from the Dearborn Reserve Unit—and acting as his platoon sergeant who should I find, but my old beer drinkin' buddy from the Detroit Reserves, Gunnery Sergeant Woods! Of all places to meet, we met on the highest, coldest and windiest mountain in all Korea. It was a warm greeting at least.

The B and C Companies started down the mountain, almost immediately after we were relieved. We joined the motorized convoy and marched down the road. It was quite a thrill even in the darkness—drops of over 1,000 feet on our right and cliffs over 1,000 feet on our left. Our own artillery and mortars, which by then were way ahead of us, kept dropping rounds on likely avenues of approach, and continued to harass the enemy. At dawn we found several of our own vehicles that had been hit by an enemy ambush. In one truck, two young boys were huddled together in death—apparently trying to escape through a door that was wedged into the cliff. It was a pitiful sight. There were many pitiful sights along that road. Hundreds of half-frozen Korean civilians huddled together along the roadside trying to keep warm. I felt sorry for them, but I would have felt more sorry for them had there not been so many husky young men in their midst who were running to safety along with the old men, the women and children.

About noon we reached the outskirts of Majon-dong and found hundreds of soldiers who were very kind to us. They passed out <u>Tootie Rolls</u> by the box full and gave us C-rations and water. A train was waiting for us—just open dirty box cars, but they were full of fruit juices and candy—gratis from our army buddies. Guess we were a motley-looking crew by then and they felt sorry for us.

We arrived at Hungnam about 4pm and had a good meal—this was on December 11, I remember. Prior to that we made no attempt to guess what day it was. We paid no attention to time or dates, we just noticed that it was dark, or it was light. It was day, or it was night. The hour, the day or the month seemed very unimportant.

After a good night's sleep at Hungnam, we boarded the USS *General Randall.* What a wonderful sight she was! I had a beautiful room, heated, with a real bed and clean, white sheets—and a genuine flush toilet. I immediately took of my clothes and hopped into the shower—my first since October 28—and nearly drowned myself. Then I glanced in the mirror and was scared half out of my wits at the number of bones visible through my skin. Later on I found the sick bay and weighed in at 154! The least I've ever weighed by far—my best weight being 175.

The galley was open and they served ham—on plates and coffee—in cups, in a warm room on real tables with chairs to sit in! It seems silly, but we noticed every

North Korean refugees evacuate (USMC)

detail that is usually taken for granted. Just being in a warm room and having a place to sit down seemed like the most luxurious thing in the world at that time.

North Koreans were evacuating en masse from Hungnam on anything that would float.

Well, that's it. It might be interesting to note the uniform of the day for Marines up there at the "Frozen Chosin" however, so here it is:

- One or two suits of G.I. double-barreled long-john underwear.
- One high-necked wool sweater.
- One flannel shirt.
- One dungaree blouse.
- One field jacket with hood.
- One parka with hood.
- One pair of wool green trousers.
- One pair of water resistant trousers.
- One pair of mittens.
- Two pairs of heavy wool socks.
- One pair of inner soles.
- One pair of shoe packs.
- One steel helmet, and of course
- Our weapons and belts.

It doesn't seem possible that a person could get cold when dressed like that, but we did! By the way, I had 18 men left in my platoon when we arrived at Masan for a rest, and ten of them were evacuated for frostbite! My platoon was about average for the two regiments.

*—Bud—*

# You Never Know

## Corporal Emmett Shelton, Jr.

The time was December 1950 and Baker Company had just returned to the roadway in the valley and the slender column of Marine vehicles in route from Yudam-ni to Hung-nam. They had just been ordered down off their assignment on the ridges on the left flank, where their job had been to keep the Chinese enemy snipers and mortars out of range of the precious vehicles carrying the dead and wounded Marines and what little equipment and food the division still had.

Baker Company's turn had come to rejoin the column for a short rest period. The Chinese desperately wanted to wipe out the 1st Marine Division and with that in mind they had placed road blocks at every location they thought they could defend.

The column of trucks stood still most of the time and only inched forward when another road block was cleared. A good Marine could have walked much faster than the column was traveling.

The temperature was hovering near 25 degrees below zero, the north wind was making the Marines' parka tails flap and riverlets of wind blown snow skittered past their feet on that ice-covered two-rut road.

At this temperature, there is no getting warm, a person seeks shelter or freezes, but the infantry of Baker Company had no shelter. They stood and stomped their feet. Woe be it unto anyone who sat down, because their leaders knew they would freeze solid if they stopped, so they stood and stomped.

Right in front of where Baker Company rejoined the column was a little ¾-ton truck with a metal walk-in top on it, the kind that was usually thought of as a communications truck.

One of the Bandits opened the back door only to see that it was full of Marines sitting along each side. After a lot of shouting to close that door, it was closed to the Bandits. Inside looked like heaven to a freezing Marine, out of the cold wind and in relative safety from the snipers and mortars which were always after the column. In what seemed like a very few minutes a mortar round came from nowhere and hit that truck right on its top. The round did not go off upon impact with the top, but went right on through the thin top and exploded when it impacted the floor. The back door flew open and smoke poured out.

Baker Company Corpsman Ray Christman rushed forward and entered the ill-fated vehicle, only to find that it was too late. Those Marines would never suffer cold again.

Safety is relative, those who thought they had it perished, while those of us who envied them survived. You Just Never Know!

*—Emmett—*

# D-2-7 A Story of Marines

## Lieutenant Goldie J. "Dutch" Givens

I was in Dog Company 7th Marines on Hill 1240 and Easy Company 7th was on Hill 1282.

On November 27, Dog Company was out on combat patrol. We had left that morning at 0500 to pick up stragglers from the North Korean Army. We were about 2,000 yards in front of Hills 1240 and 1282. When we caught these stragglers, we broke the stocks off their rifles and sent them back to Easy Company on Hill 1282. I was the point fire team leader.

We patrolled all day and up until 1400 and had taken several North Korean prisoners. We knew they were North Koreans because they wore the blue uniforms. Dog Company was the first to draw blood from the Chinese at Sudong and the railhead pass back on November 1 to 9, so we knew the difference between Chinese and North Koreans. The Chinese broke off the attack on November 9 and we did not see them again until November 27.

The battle for the Chosin reservoir really started out on this combat patrol on November 27. We started picking up small-arms fire at about 1400 hours. Captain Hull backed us up for an assault. We didn't know it, but we were taking on a whole Chinese army. My fire team had the extreme right flank. We had something like a pill box holding us up and our company was yelling that the right flank was holding things up. We were under heavy enemy fire and I had all new men in my fire team because after the battle at Sudong, Frank Brennan's squad had only three men left, Cpl Frank Brennan, Cpl Tugupa and myself. The replacements came in just about November 25. We were under heavy fire from this pill box. Don't ask me how they dug it in 35-degrees-below-zero weather, I don't know, but they did. This pill box covered the whole right side of the hill.

I had five rifle grenades with me and I broke out one of them. I fired it and it wobbled right through the slot in the pill box. I shouted, "Come on guys, this is our break, let's get it." When we got there, there were three dead Chinese (with brown uniforms on). I said, "Oh God. We're fighting the Chinese again. Pass the word!"

In a few minutes here came Lieutenant E. H. Suburger, who was our old platoon leader. At that time, I did not know we had lost our platoon leader. Lt Suburger said, "Damn it Dutch, break it off and get your Point out and head right straight to Hill 1240. We have run into the Chinese army." I said, "Bull shit. There are not that many Chinese out here." Lt Suburger replied, "Damn it, do what I say! We had 60 or 70 men lost in that assault. Lieutenant Thompson has been Killed in Action and Lieutenant Mullaner was shot up bad."

When we started back, believe me we ran those 1,500 to 2,000 yards. We were shot at all the way back to Hill 1240. It was getting dark when we got back. This was from about 1400 hours on. Charlie-1-5 got into the same battle 16 or 17 hours later.

We watched the 1st Battalion, 5th Marines come into Yudam-ni by trucks with the headlights on at about 1900 hours. Dog and Easy Companies 7th Marines had already lost Hills 1240 and 1282 by this time.

The 5th Marines were damn lucky that when they turned around near the artillery, they did not have Thompson Subs sticking in the back of their trucks, because at that time we, Dog Company, had so many Chinese after us. We had the 235th and 236th C.C.F. Chinese Regiments of the 124 C.C.F. Army.

Dog and Easy Companies were only about 300 yards from the artillery when we counterattacked. At that time, Dog Company only had 30 or 40 men left out of 260. "Yes," I said, "We retreated, and if you call it anything else—you are lying to yourself."

I had picked up the radio on the way out when the operator got Killed in Action and called regimental headquarters since we had no battalion commander. Captain Hull told them our situation which at that time was impossible. Regimental gave Capt. Hull an order to take back the hill. He told them he didn't think he could because Dog Company only had 30 or 40 men left. Someone broke into their conversation and said, "I don't give a damn how many men you have left, take it back." Capt. Hull replied with, "Yes Sir!" I'll never forget that the rest of my life.

Captain Hull turned to Lt Suburger and said "Ed, start turning them around. We have to take back Hill 1240." Lt Suburger turned around to me and said "Dutch, start turning them around."

Now, you talk about a mess, we had one. We finally get lined out to go back. If you remember on November 27, 1950, the sky had cleared and we had a full moon, but the moon would go behind the clouds and stay for awhile. We were going back when the moon went behind the clouds, we were about halfway up—and a flare popped. Bob Lance and I were closest to the enemy at the time. Man we had our hands full. We both just started firing. I said, "Head for that razor back ridge." The enemy headed there too! You're talking about point blank fire, we beat them off in a fight that must have lasted an hour. All we occupied on Hill 1240 was this small part and they were shooting down on us. I got caught right there with four of the meanest officers in the Marine Corps. Capt. Hull, Lt Suburger, Bob Lance, Charlie Strunk and me. Bob got hit in his back and Charlie got hit in his hand and Capt. Hull got hit two times that night and morning of the 28th he got hit at about 0300 or 0400 in a grenade battle. I got hit about 0100 on the morning of the 28th. We only had 16 men left in D-2-7. Easy Company only had 27 men left, but we did the impossible for 16 hours. Dog and Easy never knew where the other was half the time.

When we looked off Hill 1282 and Hill 1240 in front of us is about a mile of open terrain. When we first started the battle after we returned from the combat patrol we realized that Lt Suburger was right, we did have a Chinese army in front of us. Dog Company threw two flares in the air and as far as you could see there was nothing but Chinese coming our way. I had been down south and at Sudong. I told Lt Suburger at that time, "Damn it 'Mister' Suburger, I have never seen so many Chinese, it makes you want to run!" He said, "Where are you going to run to? They're after our ass, and our ass, only." I thought to myself, "man this is where we want them, out in the open." I told my fire team, "Machine guns will start cutting in on them at about 300 to 500 yards. You must pick up what they miss, if you don't those Chinese will be living with us."

They closed to within about 500 yards and I said, "Damn it machine guns start cutting them up." But, the machine guns were frozen up! It was 35 degrees below zero with a wind chill factor of 65 below zero. Our Browning Automatic Rifles didn't work either because of the cold, so now all we had was M-1 machine guns and grenades, plus, I had never seen a mortar hit or a artillery shell hit.

I can never explain what took place. We had a Jeep down there, we set it on fire. The Chinese were coming through there like flies. We just kept on stacking them up. I could not believe what I was seeing, the Jeep was giving us quite a bit of light, we also had a full moon and they enemy was wearing white clothing. There wasn't that much snow on the ground yet. It was like a shooting gallery.

They were stopped there, but they had overrun Easy and Dog Companies. The only part that was holding was Frank Brennan's squad and Lieutenant Suburger's platoon. Suburger passed the word on what was to take place. I said, "Where next!" The Chinese had us right there.

Captain Hull passed the word to pick up and get out of there. We didn't just get up and walk out. We had to shoot our way out. I mean Chinese were all over the place. Bob Lance was all I had left in my fire team. I asked Bob later on, "How come every time I turned around, I ran into you?" He said, "Frank told me when it gets rough stick with 'Dutch' and I wasn't going to let you out of my sight." I have to say this about Bob Lance, I would rather have his rifle with me than against me. Same way with Charlie Strunk, neither one would back off from anything. Lt Suburger and Capt. Hull are the same way.

The 5th Marines can thank God for the remaining 16 men of Dog Company and the 27 men of Easy Company for keeping the Chinese off them long enough for them to get out of there. But, we must also thank God that they made it safely from the east side of the reservoir to join us on the west side or the 7th Marines might have been wiped out.

I know what happened to Dog Company, we were overwhelmed by the Chinese. It was my first time to be overrun and when they get in with you, you grab your best hold and hang on.

Number one, you don't know where you are. Number two, you don't know where you are going. The only advantage I had was I had been down to the road with Gunny Jones to get supplies. I never thought I would ever come down it in the dark. It's no fun being shot down on.

Medal of Honor recipient Robert S. Kennemore in Easy Company didn't have a machine gun working, Dog Company had it, but at that time we didn't know it until the green tracers started hitting the top of Hill 1240. They had already made three or four assaults on us there and we beat them off. They ran 16 assaults on us that night. So you could see from dead Chinese laying around that we did our job.

When C-1-5 got there, all they had to do was to walk to the top of the hill. If you also remember, I am the one who stood up and told your lieutenant to get down because we had just beaten off an attack five minutes before. We weren't worried about the dead, we were worried about the living. I am the wise-ass person who told him to look around, he could see Dog Company. Sixteen of us left, so as you can see why we only had that little piece of ground left. It wasn't our choice, it was all we had left.

This is just part of our story, just like your report on Hill 1240. Dog Company 7th Marines got back to Pohang with only five men. We are not proud of that, but that is the way things happened in the 2nd Battalion of the 7th. The battalion had only two officers left, Lieutenant E. H. Suburger and Lieutenant Vey, Easy Company, and they both got hit on December 3, bringing that tank out. Semper Fi,

*—Dutch—*

# D-2-7 off Hill 1282

## Corporal Emmett Shelton, Jr

*The following is based on a story printed in the 1985 Chosin Few Magazine.*

When the Korean War started, John Yancey was a 32-year-old family man, the proprietor of a Little Rock liquor store he had built up between the wars. At the age of 24, Yancey had been awarded a Navy Cross medal and a battlefield commission as testament to his coolness under fire at Guadalcanal.

He volunteered to fight again in Korea, more out of a yearning for action than anything else. In that sense, 1st Lieutenant John Yancey, commanding "Easy" Company's 1st Platoon, was typical of many Pacific War veterans who had stayed in the reserves in the late 1940s. They were called to the colors from good jobs and fledgling businesses in the summer of 1950.

But John Yancey was a certified hero and the impulse to stand and fight was still very much with him.

On the night of November 27–28, 1950, the second round of Chinese probes unfolded directly in front of Yancey's platoon. The probes were light and the Chinese were content to draw fire to learn the whereabouts of the rifle pits and supporting machine guns.

Yancey was not overly perturbed by the probes. He had ordered his gunners to hold fire to avoid giving away their positions.

The unearthly silence was replaced by the cadence tread of thousands of sneaker-shod feet crunching down upon the thin film of snow. In the distance, above the sound of the crunching, Yancey and his men could discern the rhythmic chant of a single voice. Straining his hearing to the limit, the former raider heard the words, "Nobody lives forever. You die!" repeated over and over in heavily-accented English.

Yancey cranked the handle of his sound-powered telephone and was answered in a whisper by the company executive, 1st Lieutenant Ray Ball. "Ray, they're building up for an attack. Get the 81s and give us some light, and then lay in on the bridge and work back toward us."

"There's a shortage of 81s," Ball revealed. "We can't give you many."

Yancey's platoon waited while the shadowy mass of Chinese peasant-soldiers stalked nearer. But for the crunching of feet on the snow, the only sound was that lone Chinese voice: "Nobody lives forever. You die!"

Index fingers lightly traced outlines of triggers and trigger guards. Moments passed, and those fingers toyed with the first pull, then tensed and froze before squeezing through the final pull. It was midnight.

The first trip-flares burst, giving the illusion that the Chinese were motionless silhouettes. The picture that was burned into the memory of Yancey's Marines was unprecedented, horrifying.

The Chinese ranks stretched endlessly, it seemed. Each was a precise 15 yards from the one in front, as far as the eye could see. Leading the mass of white-clad infantry was a lone officer who yelled over and over, "Nobody lives forever. You die!"

Yancey leaped to his feet and hurled a challenge at the Chinese officer, but his voice was lost in the din of Chinese chants and bleats of whistles, bugles and shepherds' horns.

"Lay it on, Ray," Yancey blurted into the phone to the company executive. He dropped the receiver and fired a full clip from his carbine at the Chinese officer leading the attack.

As the Marine line erupted in gunfire, mortar fire rained down on the Chinese. But the Marines' supply of mortar ammunition was limited, and the fire quickly abated. Certain that Yancey's platoon was bearing the brunt of the attack, Captain Walt Phillips sprang from his command post and sprinted forward to take charge.

He found Yancey and his platoon sergeant leaping from hole to hole, shouting encouragement and distributing his spare ammunition. Yancey could barely breathe because a grenade splinter had penetrated the bridge of his nose and his eye had popped out of its socket. He pushed it back in and his report was delivered amid much spitting of the blood that trickled down his throat. While Yancey moved one way, Phillips moved the other, shouting encouragement, seeing to the evacuation of wounded, and calling up meager reinforcements from the company command post area. Though hit by bullets in an arm and a leg, Phillips continued to stand his ground, an example to his troops.

First Lieutenant Bill Schreier, the company mortar officer, was directing his crews amid exploding hand grenades and mortar rounds, when he glanced up to see a half-dozen infantrymen with the People's Liberation Army coming right at him. He snapped his carbine up and fired, momentarily stopping the attackers until the simultaneous explosions of numerous grenades forced him to duck.

Schreier next saw about 20 Chinese heading his way. His fire had little effect, so he trundled uphill to the company command post where he found the wounded company commander.

Phillips and Schreier spent the next several minutes attempting to form a line around the company command post. There were no more than ten Marines in the vicinity, and there was no cover. White forms were moving through the area. Grenades were bursting in batches, like firecrackers.

Schreier had the impression that Chinese grenadiers were dragging baskets of concussion grenades, stopping now and again to hurl whole clusters of them. He felt a sting in his left leg as he steadily fired his carbine at the grenadiers, but he had no time to check for a wound. Two or three grenades exploded practically on top of the mortar officer, and Schreier was wounded in the arm, wrist and chest.

The Chinese attack faltered, and then receded. In time, it was nearly quiet, but for the desultory discharge of weapons as frightened men from both sides fired at targets, real and imagined. The marines on the line reported that hundreds of dead and dying Chinese had been stacked up within 10 feet of Yancey's line, and throughout the perimeter.

Walt Phillips phoned the commander of the 7th at the first opportunity. "We broke up the first attack, sir, but we've taken a lot of casualties. We need some help."

The 1st Battalion, 5th Marines' encampment in the shadow of Hill 1282, was ordered to bail out the companies on Hills 1282 and 1240. The only officer of the 5th who had ever been on Hill 1282 was 2nd Lieutenant Nick Trapnell, a professional Marine who had been leading his platoon in constant action since joining Able Company as a replacement on the Inchon–Seoul highway.

While establishing an outpost line between his battalion command post and the hill mass late that afternoon, Trapnell had been shown the awesome terrain by Capt. Phillips, with whom he had shared some pre-war service. Phillips took pains to call Trapnell's attention to the numerous Chinese on distant ridges.

The night's action began for Trapnell when one of his fire team leaders crashed into the platoon's command post screaming, "They're coming! They're coming! There are thousands of 'em!" Terrified at the prospect of being caught on low ground in the dark, Trapnell immediately called in the fire team outposts he had strung across the open ground and reformed his platoon on higher ground.

Closest to Hill 1282, Trapnell's platoon was the first unit ordered to aid Easy Company. The 35-man platoon was probably smaller than the losses Easy Company had already sustained.

The trek up the back of Hill 1282 was frightening, strange, and confusing. Tracers passed overhead, but the reinforcements did not hear the sound until they were virtually on top of the besieged summit. Unsure of the way, unsure if Easy Company still existed, Trapnell's platoon stumbled upward, calling in vain "Eas-ee Compan-ee! Eas-ee Compan-ee-?"

John Yancey was speaking with the right flank platoon leader, 1st Lieutenant Leonard Clements, trying to coordinate a defense, when the Chinese approached through the darkness.

Before either man could react, a large hole appeared in the front of Clements's helmet. Yancey and Clements, and their wives, were the best of friends. At the time, I thought it was obvious that the round through Clements's forehead was fatal. However, Clements had been knocked unconscious and was not badly injured. The bullet had glanced off his head at an oblique angle and had spun about harmlessly in the helmet's liner.

The 1st Battalion, 235th PLA Regiment, tore back into "Easy" Company's line after a 30-minute respite. Hard one-two punches beat at one flank, then the other. Marines were deafened by the discharge of bullets and the close-in bursts of their own and Chinese grenades. The line was thinned as more and more Marines were killed or disabled.

Yancey was wounded again when a grenade fragment blew a hole in the roof of his mouth. Walt Phillips was cut down by machine-gun fire just as he thrust a bayoneted rifle into the frozen earth. "This is Easy Company, and we hold here!" he roared an instant before the fatal burst hurled him to the ground.

First Lieutenant Ray Ball, the company executive officer, too badly injured to assume command of the company, propped himself up in a rifleman's sitting position beside his foxhole and fired his carbine with telling effect as his life's blood froze in expanding puddles beside him. In time, he fainted away and later died.

Nick Trapnell's platoon of "Able" Company, 5th, found its way to an Easy Company unit, 1st Lieutenant Bob Bey's 3rd Platoon. Lieutenant Bey had no idea as to the dire straits his company was in. Bey suggested that Trapnell's thin platoon push off to the right to cover the open ground between Hills 1282 and 1240. Trapnell had not nearly enough men for the job, but he gamely led his riflemen into the void, dropping them off two at a time until he was alone on the dangling flank.

The next platoon of Able Company, 5th, up Hill 1282 came in directly behind the engaged portion of Easy Company, 7th, and was cannibalized to flesh out Yancey's and Clements embattled platoons.

The first news of the company's predicament reached Bob Bey when a squad leader and four riflemen from Yancey's platoon tumbled off the summit almost into the arms of Bey's platoon sergeant, Staff Sergeant Daniel Murphy.

When Murphy first heard about the fight higher up, he rushed to Bey, repeated the gruesome tale, and requested permission to take every man he could find to help. Out of touch, unable to even hear the sounds of the furious battle because of strange breaks in the ground, Bey felt that he could spare no more than one squad and the platoon's corpsman, who volunteered to go along.

It wasn't much: Murphy, the corpsman, 12 riflemen, the five 1st Platoon stragglers.

Breasting the summit, Murphy's group slammed into the gaggle of Chinese which had just broken through at the center of the Marine line. The tiny group of Americans clawed their way over the beaten ground, overran the company command post, and re-formed while the corpsman went to work on the wounded.

Walt Phillips was dead. Ray Ball was dead. Leonard Clements appeared to be dead. Bill Schreier was down with shrapnel in his wrist and a lung. The young officer commanding the reinforcing platoon from Able Company, 5th, was severely injured. No one knew where John Yancey was, "Easy" Company's senior NCOs were also missing. It was all up to Daniel Murphy.

Bellowing for attention, the platoon sergeant rallied isolated Marines to his position by the command post. He redeployed those who came to him, moved a machine gun to better advantage, and prepared for the worst.

It was not long in coming. Masses of Chinese loomed out of the darkness and slammed into the Marines. Murphy doled out the last of the grenades and began dismantling rifle clips to eke out the last of the .30-caliber rifle ammunition.

On the far side of the gap, John Yancey counted nine men who could still fight beside him. Hoping to instill some confidence in beaten men, Yancey gurgled the battle cry he had learned as a Marine Raider: "GUNG HO!" It means "Work Together," and it is spoken in the Cantonese mother tongue of most of the men who were then trampling victoriously across the summit of Hill 1282.

"GUNG HO!"

Ten weary, wounded Marines lifted themselves to their feet, fixed bayonets, shuffled forward, their reedy battle cry cutting through the shrill night wind, their bayonets silhouetted in the firelight.

"GUNG HO!"

John Yancey went to his knees as a shadowy Chinese soldier fired a Thompson submachine gun into his face. The amazed platoon leader crawled blindly up the blood-bespattered hillside.

The thin Marine line faltered, dissolved.

It was by merest coincidence that elements of Charlie Company, 5th, a reserve unit from Salt Lake City, reached the summit of Hill 1282 as the last gasp counterattack by element of Easy Company, 7th, were being turned aside by the Chinese victors of the night-long mauling match.

One platoon of Charlie Company had been dispatched at midnight to help Dog 7th hold Hill 1240. The remainder of the support company was sent in the traces of two Able Company platoons that had begun their ascent of Hill 1282 much earlier.

The bobtailed company hurriedly picked its way across the broken moonscape, stopping stragglers and wounded Easy Company Marines to ask directions and learn more about the nature of the fighting.

It was tedious work, and it took Charlie Company two hours to get within range of the killing ground at the summit. The point man, Captain Jack Jones, knew he had arrived when he was "greeted" by a long burst of machine-gun fire.

Jones made contact with Staff Sergeant Murphy about 100 yards below the summit of the hill. By that time, Murphy's small group of riflemen had been pushed onto a spur to the right of what had been the company's main line. Farther on was 2nd Lieutenant Nick Trapnell's unengaged platoon.

Murphy was attempting to re-form about 20 Easy Company Marines for a stand across the center of the spur. He told Capt. Jones that other Marines were on the far side of the summit, possibly with survivors of the Able platoon which had followed Trapnell's up from the valley floor hours before.

The main body of Charlie Company could not have been operating under worse conditions. None of the men had seen the ground in daylight, and not one knew the effect supporting fire might have upon friendly troops who might be hiding or holding isolated positions indeterminate distances beyond an enemy force of unknown size.

Charlie Company had taken casualties from heavy grazing fire on the approaches to the summit, and the darkness had thrown the organization into a state of mild disorganization.

Time slipped away. Captain Jones deployed his two platoons, the company 60mm mortar squad was sited, and firm communications were established with 81mm mortar platoon in the valley. Word was received that friendly aircraft were on the way, but they would not be on station until first light. Capt. Jones decided to wait until he could see what he was doing.

Sunrise was an omen. As Charlie Company waited pensively, Marine F4U Corsair pilots strafed the Chinese-held portions of the summit with 20mm cannon fire and Corsairs and AD Skyraiders dropped 500-pound bombs and napalm. Nick Trapnell's Able Company platoon, guarding the rear approaches, was treated to an incredible display of airmanship.

As the last of the attack aircraft pulled up and away, Capt. Jones lead Charlie Company against a company of the 1st Battalion, 235 PLA Regiment. Fifty Chinese armed with machine guns and hand grenades stood to receive the assault, forcing the attacking Marines to charge uphill into the face of a murderous fire.

The Marines closed and fought a brutal hand-to-hand struggle. The 1st Battalion, 235th PLA Regiment, had been ground to dust during the night. The 50 enemy soldiers holding the summit were all that remained, and they were blown to the winds by Charlie Company, 5th Marines, and Easy Company, 7th Marines under SSgt Murphy.

The last fresh platoon of Able Company, 5th Marines, arrived up the rear slope to complete the job and pry through the rubble to sort out the dead and wounded.

1st Lieutenant John Yancey emerged from the "dead." He was bleeding from untreated shrapnel wounds across the bridge of his nose and the roof of his mouth. His jaw had been shattered by a .45-caliber bullet, and one eye was whirling crazily in its socket.

The former Marine Raider formally requested relief from the first officer he could find. Then, quitting his last battle, John Yancey led the 35 walking-wounded Marines who were Easy Company slowly down the defile toward the valley.

—Emmett—

# Captured at Chosin—Three Years a POW

## Sergeant Don Griffith

*As told on May 21, 1988, by Don Griffith (F-2-5) at a MidStates Reunion of the Chosin Few at Fort Wayne, IN. Thanks to Fred Ellis for sending it to me.*

*—Emmett—*

I wouldn't take a million dollars for the experience I went through, but I would not go through it again for a million dollars, either. I was taken at Chosin and spent three years as a Chinese POW.

On the night of December 1 '50 at about 2200, we were just above Yudam-Ni on the west side of the Chosin Reservoir. We were told that we were going to be moving out at midnight. I was a sergeant and a squad leader so I told my people to dig in for now, it was the rule over there. We dug in, unfortunately, it didn't save lives because we were overrun.

About 0230, the Chinese bugles started blowing, the whistles started sounding and the yelling and screaming started. It was like a herd of cattle coming right at us.

We had no machine gun attached because on that night we were planning to move out, but we never did. As things would happen, even my M-1 had a broken firing pin. I didn't have any fire power except two grenades. I managed to disable my M-1 by pulling the trigger housing out and threw it away. I threw my two grenades at the enemy. In response, an enemy grenade hit right in front of my hole. It struck me in the face with shrapnel, blinding my right eye, cutting my nose, and wounding me in the leg.

At that time, I had a young American Indian Marine in the foxhole with me. I made a habit of staying in the foxhole with a different member of my squad each night. That way, I would get to better know my men. I turned to this young Marine and said "Romero, go back to battalion and tell them what is happening."

After Romero left, my bloody wounds started to freeze and I started to make a lot of noise breathing. I had my helmet on and my fur-lined parka hood up over the helmet. I was lying there and the Chinese were overrunning our unit. This one Chinese soldier jumped down in my hole and gave me a rifle butt. I thought "Oh Lord, the next one is going to give me the bayonet." When the next one jumped down in the hole, I jumped up and I don't know who was scared worse. He let out a scream and about 15 of them grabbed me. The first thing they wanted was my fur-lined parka, which they took.

Believe it or not, the young Indian Marine, after losing his left index finger and thumb and being bayoneted in the neck, made it back to battalion and told them what was going on. They called in airstrikes, much to my woe, because the Chinese had captured me by that time and were removing me from the hill. When all the airstrikes and bombing were taking place I was on the backside of the hill with the Chinese.

There were two brothers, who had just come into the unit and I tried to split them up but we didn't have time before this attack. They were both from Cleveland, Ohio, and both were captured, the Dowling Brothers. They both died as prisoners, one was 17 and the other 18. They were good Marines and never faltered, not one bit.

After I was captured, the Chinese marched us for three days and nights straight. Three or four Chinese would march us so far and they would get relief from fresh troops. They took shifts but we marched straight through moving northward.

During this march, I was bleeding a great deal from my wounds. They offered us no food, water or medical attention. The only way we could get any moisture was to fall in the snow and put it in our mouth. If they caught us, they hit the snow out of our hands. It took us about one week to march to a place called Death Valley. It was seven mud huts. All the captured UN troops who were wounded were held in this POW camp. The Dowling brothers were not wounded so they continued to another camp. I stayed in Death Valley.

I was put in a hut with several Marines. Unfortunately, so many of our younger troops would get a fatal disease "Give-It-Up-Itis." It was horrible. We would plead with those affected, almost shake them to death, we slapped their faces to bring them to their senses. They would refuse to eat. They became so weak they couldn't move. Their hands and feet froze. I kept telling this one Marine to rub his feet to keep up the circulation, he didn't. One day he asked me "Sarge, would you please help me take off my snowpacs?" I unlaced them for him and, as I pulled off one snowpac, I pulled off his foot at the ankle. His feet were frozen and gangrene had set in. In spite of this, the Marine survived, just by his own will to live. It was not due to medicine or doctoring, the Chinese offered none.

Due to the many atrocities and cruelties I saw in North Korea, I could **NEVER** condone any goodness towards the North Koreans or Chinese during my lifetime!

Being a POW certainly made me a better person. I don't take anything for granted. I don't take a sitting down for granted, I don't take food for granted, or even electricity. Unless you go without for a period of time, you don't realize what a marvel they are.

When we had to go to the toilet, we would yell out the door, "TOBEYEN." One night I yelled "TOBEYEN," no answer, so I yelled a little louder, no answer. I thought, the guard must be sleeping, "I'm leaving." I started walking and didn't look back. I must have walked seven miles. As it started to get light, I saw a Korean house with a shed. I went into the shed. I was wearing a Chinese coat. I found some baggy pants the Koreans wore and put them on over my dungarees to disguise me. I got under some straw for warmth.

The Korean farmer came out to the shed and woke me up moving around. I stayed put until he went back in the house. After a while, I approached the house and opened the door. I signed him I was hungry but he looked really scared. He took me in and said something to his son. I didn't pay any attention. Then, he rolled me a funnel-shaped cigarette. What I didn't know was his son went for the Chinese soldiers.

Next I knew, the Chinese soldiers were outside and threw in a couple of grenades to get my attention, and they sure did! What else could I do but go outside. The soldiers took my snowpacs and marched me seven miles back to Death Valley in January in my socks.

They paraded me in front of the other POWs to make sure they knew I was recaptured. This little Korean officer, who looked to be about 16, had a fancy machine pistol with a wooden holster. He motioned for me to walk up the side of the mountain. I started up and he shoots. The bullet passed over my head, and he called me back down. He sent me back up and he shoots over my head, again. I came back down and he started hitting me in the face. He reopened all of my wounds. I thought "if I yell in pain a little maybe that will appease him" so I started yelling and that is what he wanted.

His troops were there and he was belittling me in front of them. When I figured out that he wanted me to shout out in pain to make him look good, I obliged. After he was through beating and degrading me he had me thrown into the pig pen. In the pig pen was an army lad from Chicago. He had been in the pen for about a week, he was driven insane in that place. He lasted about two days after that. One morning when I woke up, rigor mortis had set in on his body. He had died during the night, a brave man. So here I am all alone with the pigs and believe me it is not only the loneliness that hurts, but it's good to have other bodies around and believe me, it wasn't for making love. It's trying to keep warm by huddling together. After a while I was reunited with the other POWs. I guess I had served my time in the pig pen hell.

They moved us from Death Valley to Chongsong Camp. Chongsong had some semblance of being a POW camp, Death Valley didn't. All that Death Valley was, was a place for people to die. I would venture to say that out of the hundreds that were held there, only a few of us were yet alive. At Chongsong, they at first did not separate the officers and NCOs from the other troops. Later, they did start separating when they started their indoctrination on Communism.

They had a pretty good indoctrination with instructors who had graduated from UCLA. These instructors could use English very well including slang. Their big bang was to downgrade Truman, MacArthur and other politicians and the United States in general. We had to read their literature and write essays on it. We thought a lot about how we were going to get around this. Those in our hut did not want any affiliation with the communists; we hated them and didn't want to get involved with them.

What we did to avoid making statements against the United States, which they demanded, we would write the disclaimer, "according to our text" so and so. That way we were not saying or affirming it, the text was.

They finally allowed us to write home. My mother didn't even know that I was a Prisoner of War for the past 16 months. When she found out, she didn't know if I was still alive or dead. They allowed us to write home until, well, we could have written home at any time. I wrote five or six letters home before they made us start using the return address and the return address was "In Care of The Chinese People's Army Against American Aggression." We refused to write home using that address. Not all POWs refused and some did use this return address.

After a while, they had seen it was futile trying to convert us to Communism, so they dropped this program. Instead they sent us out on work details and everyone was supposed to bring back a large amount of wood each day, some of us did and it helped us physically. We started to build out bodies back up again until the winter time, then it was tough up in the mountains. Sliding and slipping, carrying a log on your shoulder.

When we were first captured, they gave us what we called "bug dust" to eat. It was many different grains or flours, kind of brown. They added water to it and shaped it into a ball. Each of us got a 2½-inch ball twice daily. It created some problems like constipation, but we welcomed that when we already had dysentery and diarrhea. Once in a while, we'd find a piece of peanut and that was something we really relished because it had flavor. Most of the food they fed us had no flavor, it had no seasoning, no salt, no pepper etc. That's another thing that we Americans have learned to take for granted, until it's gone!

Once in a while, we'd pass by an old farm field where Koreans raised hot peppers and we'd see an old hot pepper dried up on the vine. We'd reach over and grab it and if we crumbled it into our sorghum or whatever we were going to eat, it would give it some flavor.

After we got to Chongsong, our diet changed somewhat. We got sorghum grain. It looks something like corn except it is smaller. The grain is purple. When steamed it's a lot like rice, but purple. It's pretty, but it has no taste, very little food does. The rice that we did get was full of weevils, stones and everything else, but it was a change. We did get pork at Christmas. Everybody got a little square patty about like so (1" square). That was about the first meat other than, I did eat some liver from a dog.

Health conditions were horrible. Dysentery and diarrhea headed the list, night blindness, malnutrition, beriberi and of course problems with frozen feet and frozen fingers were also a real problem. One Marine that I knew whose finger had been frozen had part of the bone above the joint (2nd) was exposed and kept catching on everything, really getting in his way. One day, we were allowed to use an axe to cut wood and I saw him put that finger on a stump and chop it off at the knuckle.

There was one guy in our camp who had had dental experience in the army. It seemed to become a vocation to him. He got hold of an old toothbrush and he filed it down to the handle. He would use the handle and a wooden mallet to knock out some bad teeth for the guys.

I had a chunk of shrapnel in my right calf and it was becoming infected so this navy corpsman in our camp did a fantastic job with a C-Ration can opener and a piece of copper wire. He was able to lance the wound, probe with the copper wire and remove the shrapnel. Had he not done it, I probably would have died because of the infection. He was a real gentleman!

As peace talks started, things started to become a little better. They started feeding us a little bit. We could always tell when the peace talks were bad, they started cutting down on the food, again. When the talks improved, the food improved.

First, we had the "sick and wounded" release, then Christmas really put the frosting on the cake for me. We had been going on work details up this one valley. We noticed they had some ammo dumps up there. When we found out that some of the sergeants were going to be released with the sick and wounded, we drew maps up for them showing where these dumps were. Of course, they had to memorize these facts because he could not carry anything like that out. You know what? In about a week after their release American planes came in and flew right over our camp. They used our camp as a spotting pole and flew down the valley and bombed those ammo dumps. We were out there cheering, screaming, yelling and jumping up and down knowing that our plan had worked and that we had done something against those damn Chinese. They were very upset and mad.

We had been getting scuttlebutt about the peace talks and the possibility of a POW release. The POW question was one of the things holding up the talks. I had prepared myself, physically, that if things did NOT come to a head with our being released, I was going to take off, again.

You all recall the monsoons we had in Korea? It would rain for 30 days straight and when it would happen the Yalu River would just churn, so I made my mind up that when this happened, I was going to climb onto one of those free-floating logs and ride it as far as it went. From there, I was going to try to make it out to the coast, but fortunately, the peace talks concluded and we were released.

We thought things were going to be simple from that point on, but we had to walk, I guess it was about 30 miles to a rail head. That was a pretty good haul for us, but we did it. Then we loaded into box cars and we were taken to Panmunjom.

The Chinese were only releasing so many each day. What really confused me was the ones they were releasing had all these beautiful new clothes and shoes. The POWs were ripping off and throwing them away, I couldn't figure it out?

When I reached Freedom Village a Marine Colonel grabbed me and said, "Sergeant, you are out of uniform," and he put a dungaree cap on my head. That little bit of the Marines made me feel very proud! He said, "What do you want"? I said, "Gosh, I don't know." He said, "You can have anything you want to eat." I said, "I'd like to have some tomato juice and some ice cream. I'd also like to have some meat, but I don't know if my stomach can take it." So he took us in and they fed us.

They took us through a battery of examinations and we got a shower. OH BOY, you don't know how that felt! There's nothing like a good shower when you haven't had one for 33 months. We got clean clothes, a haircut, and shave. Those things are things we really all take for granted, until you don't have them.

After I returned to the States, I spent nearly 25 years with Nationwide Insurance as a supervisor and tried to instill in the people under me that, if you are going to do a job, do it good! If you don't, you'll only have to go back and do it again.

I've read as many books as I could on what happened after the night that I was captured and I have nothing but pride and admiration for us Marines, navy and army personnel. I know what you went through and I marvel at what you did.

Cold is cold. When you are walking along and it is so cold that Jack Pine on the side of the mountain explodes because of the freezing sap—it sounds like a rifle shot and everybody is diving—that's cold. People freezing to death in a sleeping bag, that's cold, we all saw that. When you have people forget to put their snowpacs inside their sleeping bag with them and they can't get them on in the morning because they have frozen so solid together, that's cold. When your rations are so cold you have them in the fire to melt and by the time you get them out of the fire and up to your mouth, they've frozen again, that's cold.

I wish that there was some way that our story could be told so that more people could hear what really happened and what hell we went through. We've got to get our story out, we do! I'll say this—I LOVE YOU ALL—MY BROTHER MARINES!

*—Don—*

# Close Call on Hill 1240

## Charles R. Lyles

Baker Company was ordered down off Hill 1240, east of Yudam-ni and most of the company slid its way down that icy slope, promptly. Company command stayed to call in an airstrike on the over-eager Chinese. The B Company Commanding Officer, Lieutenant John Hancock called in the strike to go overhead and drop a short distance past his men.

Charlie Lyles, our communications expert (Palatas)

I was Lieutenant Hancock's radio operator and, as the planes came in, he turned over on his back to watch the action. As the napalm bomb was released, it came right at me and the small group of Marines. I shouted, "Damn Lieutenant, you almost got me killed!" I then turned and covered up my head ready to take what came.

The bomb passed right over their heads and struck the east slope where it was aimed. Lt Hancock could be heard all over the hill chastising me severely for my panic. Those wonderful fly-boys had delivered the goods again!

—*Charlie*—

# The Reservoir

## Chuck Hall, 1989

They came ashore at Wonsan,
And headed up the road
Battle-hardened warriors,
In the art of lock and load

By Christmas it's all over,
"Mac" had said it's so
But these Marines weren't buying,
The weather *looked* like snow

Funchllin Pass and Koto-ri,
Names they'd learn so well
Heading toward the great unknown,
On the M.S.R. to Hell

Slowing down their forward pace,
As caution reared its head
'Twas better safe than sorry,
And better live than dead

They built a strip at Hagaru,
To fly the wounded out
And dug in deep at Toktong Pass,
For them there'd be no rout

The Arctic cold had bit them.
As they marched toward Yudam-ni
Their fate had been decided,
By a foe they could not see

Hiding in the frozen hills,
Chinese poised for attack
Striking swiftly so not one,
Would walk the long road back

But these Marines were hardy,
And fought both long and well
Fighting down to Hagaru,
They served their hitch in Hell

The pass had been kept open,
By "Barber" and his crew
But not without a bloody cost,
His men were down to few

The regiments joined together,
And smashed toward Koto-ri
No power on Earth could stop them,
As they headed toward the sea

More battles would come after,
As they did in days before
But the ordeal of the Chosin,
Will live forever more

# "Baker Three" and Hill 1240

## Lieutenant Ed Morris, Platoon Leader of Baker Three

After a hectic night in the valley at Yudam-ni on November 27, 1950, Baker Company was ordered to relieve D-2-7 on Hill 1240 the morning of the 28th.

Baker Three, the 3rd Rifle Platoon, was given the mission of passing through Dog Company 7th and continuing the attack to seize the high ground to their front. Dog Company had been shot up pretty bad the night before and was in no position to render us any assistance in the way of a base of fire.

Baker Three passed through and proceeded into a saddle between Dog Company and the objective. As we got into the saddle, we came under heavy fire from the objective; small-arms and mortar fire.

We continued to advance and got within grenade range of the enemy position. We kept "playing catch" with grenades, but finally they had us pinned down.

I reported back to our company commander, Lieutenant Hancock via radio, that we were pinned down and could not advance; or go anywhere for that matter!! It so happened that there were some F4Us (Corsair fighters) on station and Baker Six wanted to know if I could use an airstrike?

Men of the B-1-5 ready for combat (USMC)

The only problem was, I had no forward air controller (FAC) with me or in position to control the strike. It was decided that I would relay the information via our SRC-536 radio on the strike, to Baker Six and the FAC in that location would pass the information to the pilots.

The first pass of the aircraft was a dry run, which was fortunate because they were on us! We had no air panels at the time to mark our front lines. I asked them to move the strike a little further in a northerly direction. They did and the next run, which was a strafing run, was right on target.

The following runs of rockets, napalm and strafing, by two aircraft, relieved the pressure on Baker Three and at Lt Hancock's order we fell back to the forward slope and assumed defensive positions.

The night of November 28 amounted to a few probes by the enemy and some mortar fire, but no serious problems arose.

During the day of the 28th, we attempted to register 105s on the Chinese position, however, the howitzers were too close and their trajectory was such that they couldn't come in that close. We received one round in my position, trying to bring them in.

The 4.2-inch mortars came into play then, and with no problem, they registered and named the concentration "Baker Three" so I could call for it any time I felt the need.

During that night, they fired H&I missions all night long on the Chinese positions. I thought it was great and I'm sure there was a lot of sleep lost on the other side!!

The day of November 29, Lieutenant Austin "Swede" Jenson's 1st Platoon launched an attack on the same position, with Baker Three providing the base of fire. They met with the same intense fire and grenades that my platoon had met with the day before and they were also unable to seize the objective. Unfortunately, Lieutenant Austin "Swede" Jenson was Killed in Action.

Following the 1st Platoon's attack, the Chinese forces launched a counterattack, but we were able to hold our ground. I estimated about 80 to100 enemy in the attack and I saw very few able to get back over to their hill and safety, we really hurt them. We never did take that enemy position and I would have liked to have seen how they were dug in there.

When we were ordered to pull off Hill 1240, Baker Three arranged a few surprises for the Chinese. We knew that as soon as we pulled back they would take over our positions, so we constructed a few booby traps. We left empty C Ration boxes with a frag grenade inside with the pin pulled. Heaven help any guy that opened that ration box! The spoon flying at him wasn't one he could eat with! Semper Fidelis,

—Ed—

# Leader Lost in Chosin

## Cliff Duncan

Lieutenant John Hancock was vividly remembered by all, his leadership and stance while under fire. I personally I recalled the following. On November 27, 1950, Baker Company had moved with the battalion by foot and truck around to our position in the center of "Nightmare Alley." We had been delayed and were almost the last to arrive due to darkness. The 1st Platoon was the Point and my squad, the 1st Squad was the point of the platoon.

We did not dig in due to the frozen ground and darkness, but set up a 50 percent watch and proceeded to sack-out.

I was asleep when the Chinese commenced the first attack. I quickly got my shoepacs on and started to try to figure out what we should do. The fire was intense, there was no cover, so I decided I would request permission to pull back. I crawled back to the command post and found Lt Hancock discussing the situation with other officers. They were shouting to be heard over the incoming fire. I requested permission to pull back. Lt Hancock looked at me and said, "Pull back to where?" With that I returned to the squad and was fortunate to not lose a man that night.

The last time I saw Lieutenant Hancock was at the base of Hill 1240 on November 29 after the following events.

The 1st Platoon was then commanded by Lieutenant Austin "Swede" Jenson, a real gentleman and a fine officer. Lt Jenson had only been with the company a few weeks and on this day with the platoon down to either 33 or 34 men we had been selected to lead the primary assault on a bunker just above us.

The word was passed by Lt Jenson that there were about 50 Chinese in a bunker and that we should be able to handle them. There had been several airstrikes earlier that morning on that bunker. We were told to drop everything except our weapons, grenades, and bandoliers.

As the platoon started the assault uphill, Lt Jenson was in the front and center of the platoon, and to my immediate left. The bunker was no more than 35 yards away when suddenly the Chinese started pouring out the end closest to the downhill side. Lieutenant Jenson yelled, "COME ON MEN, YOU CAN'T GET THEM LAYING ON THE DECK!" With that he stood up, moved forward only a few steps, and then took a fatal round in the head.

The Chinese continued coming out of the bunker, both front and rear, firing was intense, when suddenly we found Chinese behind us downhill.

Four Chinese directly below me were tapping their potato masher grenades on the rocks and throwing them at us. I was hit and stunned by the grenades, but was able to walk out of the immediate firing area and move down the hill towards the aid station.

As I approached the bottom of the hill, Lieutenant Hancock was standing there with a worried look on his face. He asked me, "What is happening on the hill?" He had lost radio contact with everyone. I reported that I had passed 2nd Platoon coming down and had asked for their help in assisting the 1st Platoon, which was in great danger of being overrun by far more than 50 reported Chinese.

Lieutenant Hancock then said, "You did your duty, now go see the corpsman." That was the last time I saw him, standing there with his green winter dress cover on, looking intently up the hill.

*—Cliff—*

# Evacuated from Chosin

## Corporal Emmett Shelton, Jr.

Korea

Dec 20, 1950

Dear Dad,

I have been evacuated to an Aid Station for a case of frostbite feet. They are not too bad but they evacuate anyone who has any possibility of catching trench foot. They want to prevent it. They say we may not go back into our company while it is still cold. I hope we don't because my feet would freeze and that would be no fun.

I don't think my feet are too bad. I can't wear shoes but I can limp along short distances. No combat for a while.

It did not take long for me to get really battle weary. At times when we didn't get rations or they were too frozen to eat, we were being shot at, we were cold and disgusted—I felt like crying. Lots of my buddies died or were badly wounded. I didn't think any of us would get out of that place. The other Marines felt the same.

I want you to know that I have suddenly realized what you and mother have given me all my life and when I think of how much trouble I have caused you, I am ashamed. And I want you to know that I love and miss the whole family very much and am looking forward to the day when we will once more be together.

Now about my Chevy. I know that you have never had a car like that but I want that one taken care of. Grease it at least once every two weeks. Wash it at least once a week or the paint will fade and need Simonizing. Let Mike look at it if anything goes wrong, he'll fix it for you. Oh, and use Humble Esso only in it. That car doesn't even have a squeak and it will last me five to six years if it is taken care of. I hope you do.

I was feeling pretty bad and under the weather after coming all the way down to Pusan. I saw a Protestant Church advertisement so I went. I came out of there feeling 100% better. It was surprising what something like that can do. I know that God was with me up in the Korean mountains or I would not have gotten out.

Mother wanted to know if I had killed anyone yet. If she still wants to know, tell her we all have. I have lots to tell my family when I get home. We can't say them in a letter because they don't want us to start a panic back home.

I better quit now and go eat. Again, I say I miss and love you very much.

Your Son,
*—Emmett—*

# We Were Marines

## Private William G. Irwin

We were pulled out of one battle and taken back to Pusan where we boarded ships. We didn't know it at the time, but we were about to be part of an amphibious landing at a place called Inchon. They told us later it was a huge success. We went on to liberate the city of Seoul and on across the 38th Parallel. Of course, that didn't last long, either.

We were soon pulled out of the battle lines again and taken back aboard ship. This time, we were going into North Korea. When we landed at Wonsan, North Korea, it was already getting cold. It wasn't bad though. After all… we were Marines! We could handle a little cold weather.

Thanksgiving Day was an experience. HOT FOOD! At least it started out that way. Does it get cold in Korea? That's like asking if it gets hot in Korea. It can go from one extreme to another in a very short time. We were about to experience that first hand.

There was a lot of scuttlebutt (rumor) about going all the way to the Yalu River, wherever that was. Somewhere north of us was all we knew. There was also talk about the Chinese entering the war, but it was just talk… wasn't it? A couple of days after Thanksgiving someone brought in a prisoner dressed in a uniform we hadn't seen before. It was a dirty white thing made out of some kind of padded material. He had been carrying a "Burp Gun." Could he be Chinese?

By this time we had reached the Chosin Reservoir and realized that we were indeed fighting the Chinese Army. We found ourselves surrounded,

Hot chow in the field for Thanksgiving—we will never forget (Sydman)

and literally fighting for our very lives. We found out much later that we had pretty much been written off. We were told the Chinese had specific orders to annihilate the 1st Marine Division. Well, that was much easier said than done. After all… We were MARINES! So we began to fight our way out.

Sometime around December 1, we had been fighting on Hill 1240. How do people remember the numbers of all of those hills? We were just fighting to stay alive and watch out for one another. I think we were all more afraid of letting our buddies down than we were of being killed ourselves.

Just after one especially fierce firefight in the night, along toward morning the enemy had withdrawn. Since we were low on ammo, I had gone down to a little ammo dump to get some more. About the same time I got there, another Marine arrived. Neither of us knew who the other was. We were gathering up ammo when we looked and saw what seemed like all the Chinese in the world coming across a little clearing right at us. There was nowhere to go, so we had to fight for our lives. I remember thinking, "This is it! There is no way we're going to get out of this alive." So we began shooting and throwing grenades. It couldn't have lasted very long, but it seemed like an eternity. Several times that morning I said, "Lord help us!" And He did.

They were trying to go up the back side of the hill we had just come down. Our company was up there fighting for their lives, too. So we had no choice but to continue to fight. After all… we were Marines! At one point it looked as though we were confronted on three sides and I said, "Man, this looks like Custer's Last Stand!" The other guy said, "Yeah, look at all them cotton pickin' Indians!" And we both laughed at the top of our voices. The Chinese must have thought we had lost our minds… laughing at a time like that. It's strange what men find to laugh about in times of great stress.

Periodically, one or the other of us would say, "Here come some more Indians!" And we laughed some more. I'm sure both of us saved the other's life that morning. Several times there were grenades thrown at us that we picked up and threw back.

As dawn came, someone called in an airstrike and the enemy left in a hurry. We didn't waste any time either and gathered up our ammo and ran up that hill as fast as we could go. I think it was that same day that our company moved out.

How did we live through that morning? Let me tell you what I believe with all my heart. I believe God must have had plans for two young Marines who were sure they were going to die that day. We were still a long way from getting out of that mess. A lot of our friends didn't make it, but—After all… we were Marines! And we weren't about to give up.

—*Bill*—

# Baker Company Leaves Yudam-Ni

## Master Sergeant Phil "Ole Top" Dierickx

Lieutenant John Hancock, Commanding Officer of B-1-5, received orders to disengage with the enemy. He was told that all gear that could be used by the Chinese be delivered to the bottom of the hill.

Gunny Sergeant Edward Wright and Master Sergeant Phil "Ole Top" Dierickx, piled up the gear in a heap as troops filed by. Anything that could not be removed by truck was discarded—parkas, boots, etc. When the area was policed and the rest of the company had crossed the bridge, these officers booby-trapped the pile with grenades, etc. The Chinese had started over the top of the hill, but the Gunny sent them scurrying off with a few well-placed shots from the 03 rifle he always carried. Rushing to complete the job before the engineers blew the bridge, the two finally set fire to the pile and took off for the bridge, 2,000 meters away.

They hit the deck as soon as they got over the bridge, and just in time, as the engineers blasted it to pieces. Before rejoining the rest of the company the Gunny took a moment to look back as the Chinese arrived at the fiery pile and watched them try to put it out and pull items from the flames, but were gratified to see them forced back as the entire mass went up in a series of explosions.

*—Phil—*

# A Plausible Scenario

## Lieutenant Mike Palatas

Somewhere in the fertile countryside of southern China an aging warrior of the Chinese "Chosin Few," puffs on his long-stem tobacco pipe and sips rice wine while staring staring at the wall of his humble one-room adobe. There hangs a brass bugle, tarnished from age and the lack of care. The old man's eyes become misty as he reminisces about his days as a youth in the Chinese People's Army and his fighting U.S. Marines in Korea during the harsh winter of 1950.

He was a 16-year-old rifleman then and he was outposted on Hill 1240 just east of Yudam-Ni. He fought hand to hand with a stubborn small force that refused to yield and kept coming on determined to take his position. His hands and face still bear the scars resulting from napalm burns received when a Marine F4U Corsair dropped a large canister of the sticky gel on his position. He was not evacuated however.

A couple of days later he and members of his platoon were astonished to see their enemy break contact in an orderly withdrawal. When the din of battle became sporadic and all but ceased, he and his cohorts scavenged the area. From a pile of still-smoldering sleeping bags and 782 gear, he retrieved a bugle (an unusual find) and he kept this souvenir of battle through all the years. The bugle was charred by the flames and its tassel was partly burned off, but what remained was still attached to it. In all this time, he has never been able to decipher the writing crudely scratched into the horn. It read, "PFC Felix PALMER B-1-5"! The bugle had belonged to our company bugler and was last blown to signal our Baker Bandits.

—*M.V.P.*—

# B-1-5 Casualties and Medals at Chosin

## Killed in Action

*November 28–December 13, 1950. Confirmed through Korean War Project*

| | | |
|---|---|---|
| PFC William A. Boudin, from Utica, New York | KIA | 28NOV50 |
| CPL Allen M. Bowman, from Covington, Indiana | KIA | 28NOV50 |
| CPL Richard S. Cruz, from Long Beach, Calif. | KIA | 28NOV50 |
| CPL Robert L. Dobbs, from Kansas City, Kansas | KIA | 28NOV50 |
| PFC Robert J. Fisher, from Worcester, Mass. | KIA | 28NOV50 |
| PFC George Giedosh, from Harleigh, Md. | KIA | 28NOV50 |
| PFC Eugene D. Tangeman, from Omaha, Neb. | KIA | 28NOV50 |
| PFC Donald W. Forbes, from Nevada, Iowa | KIA | 29NOV50 |
| 2LT Austin Jenson, from Coolidge, Texas | KIA | 29NOV50 |
| SGT Wayne H. McCuskey, from Holyoke, Minn. | KIA | 29NOV50 |
| PFC Herbert F. Morgan, from Akron, Ohio | KIA | 29NOV50 |
| PFC Bobby J. Chandler, from Stockton, Calif. | KIA | 7DEC50 |
| PFC Charles A. McAndrews, from Chicago, Ill. | KIA | 7DEC50 |
| PFC Roger V. Sturtevant, from Groton, Mass. | KIA | 7DEC50 |
| CPL William A. Ward Jr., from Portland, Oregon | KIA | 7DEC50 |
| PFC Donald L. Coleman, from Richmond Va. | KIA | 8DEC50 |
| PFC Leon E. Patchon, from Anoka, Minnesota | DOW | 12DEC50 |

The following awards from Chosin were taken from the book *Red Blood... Purple Hearts* published by our supporter, Joe Saluzzi:

Staff Sergeant Kennemore MEDAL OF HONOR
Private Gallagher NAVY CROSS
Captain Jack R. Jones NAVY CROSS.

Staff Sergeant Murphy NAVY CROSS
First Lieutenant Smith NAVY CROSS
Second Lieutenant Austin Jenson NAVY CROSS (posthumously)

First Lieutenant Yancey was awarded a GOLD STAR in lieu of a second NAVY CROSS. He had received his first NAVY CROSS in the battle of the Lunga River, Guadalcanal, November 30, 1942.

## Medal of Honor

Staff Sergeant Robert Kennemore

Staff Sergeant Robert Sidney Kennemore, United States Marine Corps, for conspicuous gallantry and intrepidity at the risk of his life above and beyond the call of duty on November 27 and 28, 1950, as leader of a machine-gun section in Company E, Second Battalion, Seventh Marines, 1st Marine Division, in action against enemy aggressor forces north of Yudam-ni near the Chosin Reservoir, North Korea. With the company's defensive perimeter overrun by a numerically superior hostile force during a savage night attack north of Yudam-ni and his platoon commander seriously wounded, Staff Sergeant Kennemore unhesitatingly assumed command, quickly reorganized the unit and directed the men in consolidating the position. When an enemy grenade landed in the midst of a machine-gun squad, he bravely placed his foot on the missile and, in the face of almost certain death, personally absorbed the full force of the explosion to prevent injury to his fellow Marines. By his indomitable courage, outstanding leadership and selfless efforts in behalf of his comrades, Staff Sergeant Kennemore was greatly instrumental in driving the enemy from the area and upheld the highest traditions of the U.S. Naval Service.

Medals are awarded at the Bean Patch (Palatas)

# Navy Cross

Austin "Swede" Jenson (Posthumously)

Following the success of an adjacent platoon in repelling a vicious assault by the enemy, many of whom withdrew in disorder to a heavily fortified key position to the front of friendly lines, Second Lieutenant Jenson promptly assumed the responsibility of attempting to storm and seize the stronghold. Spearheading the attack, he advanced to within forty yards of the area before the enemy pinned down his unit under a blistering automatic weapons and small-arms barrage. Ordering his men to cover him, he crawled forward alone under the intense fire to reconnoiter a tactical route of approach and, after locating a defiladed area to the left flank of his platoon, directed a forward movement, at the same time delivering accurate fire into the pillbox with his carbine. When the enemy again attacked from concealed foxholes at the base of the stronghold, seriously endangering his troops, he boldly stood upright to draw the fire to himself, thus distracting the enemy's attention and, firing upon the hostile force, disorganized them sufficiently to enable his platoon to proceed.

Stouthearted and indomitable, Second Lieutenant Jenson accounted for many dead and wounded while firing from his exposed position before he himself was fatally struck down.

Second Lieutenant Jenson was posthumously awarded the **NAVY CROSS.**

# The Bean Patch: Late December 1950

## Chuck Hall

*Dedicated to the men of the 1st Provisional*
*Marine Brigade, Pusan Perimeter, Korea, 1950.*

The anchor dropped at "Pusan,"
The "Brigade" had come ashore
At a place called The Bean Patch,
And a different kind of war.

The Old Breed and the New Breed,
Would fight now side by side
The training was all over,
They were here to turn the tide.

With "Task Force Keene" a forming,
They joined the new-found fight
To route guerrillas from the hills,
And put them all to flight.

They finished up their mission,
They headed back once more
Bean Patch looking mo' like home
Than it ever did before.

Then up front to the "Naktong,"
To a Hill named "Obong-ni"
They stopped the "North Koreans,"
From marching to the sea.

The Bean Patch beckoned once again,
As they headed south once more
To get and train replacements,
And teach them ways of war.

They came to love that "Bean Patch,"
As if it were their own
A place of rest and safety,
Where no foe dared to roam.

But nothing lasts forever,
So they saddled up once more
To the "Clover-Leaf" at "Naktong"
And another taste of war.

When the dust had fully settled,
They pulled back for a rest
They drank some beer and packed their gear,
For a landing in the west.

The Bean Patch is thought of fondly,
By those who made it back
They speak about their comrades,
And the place that cut them slack.

# Bean Patch at Masan: December 1950

## Lieutenant Mike Palatas

We owe a lot of credit to those Marines responsible for establishing our camp at Masan. Though it was primitive (most of the infantry still had to sleep on the ground), for us, after the Chosin ordeal, it was the Holiday Inn or Sheraton Masan.

The Division Motor Transport would work around the clock to take the troops from the docks to our new, but temporary, home. When we arrived, most of the tents to accommodate us were already set up. Replacements had a lot to do with this too. It wasn't easy getting wooden tent pegs into the hard frozen ground.

Engineers and Seabees were busy getting at least one electrical light for each company in our battalion and our wire men went right to work laying lines for the battalion's switchboard network. Also, our battalion mess cooks knew no break and got right on with the task at hand of feeding hot meals. We had three types of tents in Baker Company—our "CP" was a pyramidal—this was big enough to sleep six in cots. Some of the troops were assigned to these type tents, others to the squad tent which was double in size. Officers and Staff NCOs would get cots which were scrounged by Sergeant Shoemaker. Sleeping on the ground wasn't anything new for us—it was standard, only now, we were under canvas and not being sniped at, or mortared. Placing the mummy bag between two bean rows made a rather cozy bed—better than being propped against a tree on a hillside or in some wet rice paddy!

Sergeant Shoemaker, our "supply" NCO or, better, "Property Sergeant" worked overtime to get and distribute replacement sleeping bags and other equipment which was "lost" in the Chosin Campaign.

Our Top Sargent, "Ole Top" Phil Dierickx, told the Lieutenant Hancock that we best

B-1-5 C.O. John Hancock handed out stockings for Christmas (Palatas)

make the end pyramidal tent our command post. He too had his work cut out for him. There were letters of condolence to write, fitness reports were still a requirement for officers and NCOs, the unit diary was a daily time-consuming task, recommendations for awards and much more were required.

Now, the mail caught up with us and our mail clerk had a job sorting out a mountain of mailbags. There was some first-class mail which came by air via FPO San Francisco. The bulk was the lesser mail of newspapers and packages from home, but too often the goodies, sent from Mom or a girlfriend, were covered with mildew and mold. Nonetheless, mail call was a highlight of the day. There were the "Dear Johns" and other sad news from back home too, and these served to lower the morale of the recipients. Good news would come also—our Skipper, Lt Hancock, was elated to learn that he was the proud father of a boy. (But he would not live to see his newborn son!)

I believe it was Sergeant Wolfe who showed Sergeant Shoemaker how to make an instant hole suitable for the four-holer folding toilet, procured from battalion. They somehow obtained a "Bee Hive" shape charge and with a loud "FIRE IN THE HOLE," we had our head. Noteworthy the EE-8 phone jangled in the command post and it was battalion wanting to know what had happened when the charge went off. (They had to explain to Colonel Murray.) It gave our troops a knee-jerk reaction too! Our "Pee" tubes at the end of the company street were easier to install and "Shoe" had to spread "lime" around these daily to keep down the stench. Thus we had our open-air 4-holer and the urinals, but we had no washing facilities. We resorted to the helmet, as usual, for a bath and to shave.

Each tent had a small pot-belly stove resting on the ground and it was fired by diesel fuel. It gave off either too much or too little heat because of its temperamental carburetor. Even on low setting, it wouldn't last through the night on the five-gallon jerry can of fuel. Our company command post tent even had a door courtesy of our Supply Sergeant Willie Shoemaker. Some of us will never forget one mail call when Sergeant Mayer received a package from one of his girlfriends. With his calloused and grubby hands he tore off the paper, opened the shoe box and inside was a loaf of bread. He tore this open (it was dry and hard) and inside was a 5th of whiskey! We all had a laugh at that. Not only was it an illegal shipment, the troops weren't allowed to have hard liquor "in-the-field"—beer was OK though.

Comfort on the battlefield but no privacy (Yolinsky)

—*M.V.P.*—

# Lt Hancock Kicked Private Jeremiah out of Baker Company

## Corporal William Dove

The first time I met Lt Hancock was around January 5, 1951, at the Bean Patch. Prior to that date, I had been safe at Sasebo, Japan while Baker Company was fighting, dying, and suffering in the reservoir. I was waiting to turn 18 years of age so I could return to my company.

At this base, one of the smart Marines came up with a brilliant idea. It was so good in fact a lot of us followed suit. He took his dungarees to a Japanese tailor shop and had them altered into an Ike jacket complete with sewed-in military creases. I had proudly stenciled on the back of mine "Bill Dove" and "South Carolina" below it. This is how a buddy of mine, Roy Fairchild and I were dressed when we entered the Bean Patch to rejoin our companies. We thought we were the sharpest things in Korea. We even had creases sewed into our trousers.

When I entered Baker Company's command post, I was met by a sergeant who was escorting me to my platoon when a loud voice rang out, "Bring that Marine in here!" I quickly entered, stood at attention and said, "PFC Dove reporting as ordered Sir." Lieutenant Hancock looked me up and down, and then said,

"Has the Marine Corps changed the dress code and I didn't get the word?" I proudly replied, "No Sir, I had this done in Japan." He replied, "I have a good mind to make you the last Ammo Carrier in the machine-gun section." He then ordered the sergeant to get me properly dressed. They surveyed all of my clothing except my leggings.

Not too long after this, a big time movie director by the name of

Baker Company's command post (Schryver)

John Ford selected Baker Company to take some film. As we entered this village, which had some of the houses on fire, each Marine had the opportunity to look directly into the camera as we rounded a curve in the road.

Not long after this, we entered another village on the way to the north towards the outskirts of this village, I observed a flock of white bantam chickens running wild. Being from the country, I had to have one. I broke out of the column and got a rooster hemmed up in the corner of a fence. I quickly picked him up and put him under my parka. I then rejoined the column. Being partial to biblical names, I named him PFC Jeremiah.

During the next week or so, Jeremiah became one of the best kept secrets in the Korean War. My luck would soon make a drastic change and another butt-chewing from Lt Hancock was forthcoming.

If I remember correctly, it was around February 1, 1951 when we entered the reserve area, which was on flat ground. As we began to set up our pup tents, I knew I had a problem. The only thing I could do was tie him to a bush and hope for the best. The following day, my worst nightmare came to pass.

I observed the sergeant and the lieutenant, winter issue piss cutter, shiny silver bar and all making a random check of the tent area. In the modern military, they have rank sewed into the uniform, but in our time this was not the case. The officers stood out like a sore thumb and made them easy targets for the enemy. As he came closer and I said to myself, please Lord don't let him come this way. I believe they wrote that song "If I had no bad luck, I'd have no luck at all" after me because he came directly towards my tent. He then noticed Jeremiah tied to a bush. I knew I was in deep trouble! He said, "Dove, please tell me what a chicken is doing in this camp?" With a pitiful look on my face, I replied, "That's Jeremiah, sir, my pet chicken." He replied, "The Marine Corps don't have pet chickens. The next time I lay eyes on you, that chicken better be history!" I talked some guys at Motor Transport into taking him.

I've had many roosters since that time and have named them all biblical names. None would ever take place of PFC Jeremiah. For a short period of time, he was a member of a select few, Baker Company, 1st Battalion, 5th Marine Regiment.

*—Bill—*

# Daily Routine and CO's Time

## Lieutenant Mike Palatas

Lieutenant Hancock was in daily contact with battalion either through a staff meeting with Lieutenant Col. Stevens, or by EE-8 telephone. At one of our earlier conferences, word was given to allow the troops as much free time and "space" as possible. The priority of time would be devoted to upkeep of individual weapons, however, there would be no liberty call. This was because of our tactical situation, the need to get ourselves rehabilitated and besides, there was no place to go. The towns of Pusan and Masan were already overcrowded with refugees and off-limits to us.

Lieutenant Hancock wanted to keep B Company men feeling that they were in the loop. Shortly after each night, we would go to the Lt's tent for a briefing about the day's news. Afterwards, the men would stay and talk, joke and even sing hymns and folk songs. Some of our favorites were "Life is Like a Mountain Railroad" and "This World is Not My Home."

## Life is Like a Mountain Railway

Life is like a mountain railroad
With an engineer so brave
We must make this run successful
From the cradle to the grave

As you roll across the trestle
Spanning Jordan's swelling tide
You behold the union depot
Into which your train will glide

Watch the curves, the fills the tunnels
Never falter, never fail
Keep your hand upon the throttle
And your eye upon the rail

There you'll meet the superintendent
God the Father, God the Son
With a hearty, joyous greeting
Weary pilgrim, welcome home

Oh, blessed Savior, thou wilt guide us
'Til we reach that blissful shore
Where the angels wait to join us
In God's grace forever more

Oh, blessed Savior, thou wilt guide us
'Til we reach that blissful shore
Where the angels wait to join us
In God's grace forever more

"Skipper" Lt Hancock holds a daily de-briefing (Palatas)

What we saw of Korean civilians consisted mostly of the young and old—no in-between. The able-bodied youths were pressed into the ROK (Republic of Korea) army or Marines. We began to receive replacements and our Top Sergeant "Ole Top" Dierickx would make their assignments according to the needs of the platoon or section. The new people had to be integrated mentally and physically. Speaking of integrated, up to this time, we had no black Marines in B Company, however, we would gain one in our ranks later, in March. Changes also were made within our Platoons—veteran riflemen of the Pusan Perimeter, Inchon, Seoul and Chosin were now going up the promotion ladder as fire team leaders, squad leaders and platoon leaders (with or without a stripe).

We were always short an officer or two. Sergeants Schmidt and Lischeski would continue as capable platoon leaders. Lieutenant Ed Morris of the 3rd Platoon still led a charmed life and kept a low silhouette—he was the only officer left in B Company's rifle platoons to stay with the unit since arriving as a member of the Brigade. I think Ed was the last officer of the "Brigade" to be rotated. Gunner Bob Clement was evacuated along the line (at Hagaru-ri as I recall) and eventually Lieutenant Schryver would replace him as 60mm Mortar Section Commander. Our executive officer, Lieutenant Cronin, would still come and go, working with commanders.

Our routine included test firing our weapons at a designated "range" in the side of the hills just to our south. Sergeant Versage, the Battalion Armor, would be on hand to make needed repairs to our .30-cal and our 60mm mortars.

Our spirits were high, all of us knowing that we survived quite an ordeal. But even before the year ended, rumors originating from our machine-gun platoon began circulating that we were soon moving out! There was always the scuttlebutt—"rumors" spread by mischievous individuals, intentionally!

Yes, we even had "office hours" on a few of our Bandits. Art Markey already spoke of his. Another was the case of one of the machine gunners I won't name—he did a no-no along side his tent and it didn't sit too well with Lieutenant Hancock. He felt that it was no example for an non-commissioned officer. The man was reduced in rank by one stripe, but given a suspension of the sentence for six months. There were occasional accidental discharges of weapons and these, at the best, would bring a reduction in rank.

Corpsman "Doc" Christman (Palatas)

A run-away tent stove also would bring some excitement to our bivouac, the soot in the chimney pipe would build up, then ignite with a whoosh and the thin pipe would become red hot—sometimes the tent would go up in a flash. At night when it happened on our battalion area, it was a spectacular display of sparks.

The activity of "Rocky" Williams and his men was to get his motor transport in order. They would cannibalize some vehicles to make others operable. The two army Jeeps he "procured" at Hungnam had to be repainted and renumbered to look like Marine Jeeps. "Rocky" and his men made sure they had their full table of equipment at all times regardless of the procurement methods. They even painted a white cross on one Jeep and presented it to our Battalion Chaplain even though he didn't rate a Jeep. It gave him a portable alter and a way to carry his "sacramental" wine. I always wondered why "Rocky" didn't like strangers hanging around his motor pool?

I would be remiss not to mention the continued role of our corpsmen. There were still enough scrapes and bruises to keep them constantly busy. Colds were a number one item for one to go on the binnacle list (sick list) and get light duty and an OK chit to miss morning formation. "Doc" Christman was sympathetic in this respect. On occasion they could come up with "medicinal" brandy in those little bottles. Our corpsmen were always there when we needed them most and they were great morale builders. They had our deepest respect—always.

We had at least one pay call while in the Bean Patch. The "Ole Top" would handle the pay roster which showed just how much money one had coming. The individual could indicate how much he wanted and it was usually very little. Most men let their money ride "on-the-books," since there were so few ways to use it. One popular way for some was the card game... our officers would usually look the other way when stumbling into a tent where a game was in progress.

Our chaplain not only provided spiritual guidance and moral support, but he was a source of good paperbacks, so there was ample reading material just for the asking. He was also a great help when someone had problems arise at home and the man needed counseling or help with emergency leave. Our Regimental Red Cross man would help in such cases, also.

As our Christmas season came to a close at Masan, the corpsmen had the "straight scoop," we would soon be moving to a place called Pohang for some special operations—the "Guerrilla Hunt."

—*M.V.P.*—

# Christmas in the Bean Patch

## Lieutenant Frank McDonald

The Marines hated to say goodbye to the warm ships, good food, and showers we so much enjoyed on the "cruise" down from Hungnam to Pusan. We then moved by truck to Masan where a campsite had been established. I was still with Weapons Company at that time, but the whole Division moved back to Masan. The Marines who had survived the Chosin Reservoir battles were, to a man, thin, run down, tired, and in many cases suffering from dysentery caused by multiple factors.

After getting the camp organized and comfortable, the routine became chow, shots for dysentery, volley ball, receiving replacements, and training. Weapons were serviced or repaired and fired. It was either at Masan or at Pohang where we set up a firing range to make sure the replacements knew the battle sight settings for individual weapons, M-1s and Carbines.

We received a lot of packages from home, which were generously shared by the Marines within their units. These packages were a real treat for all: mostly rich foods, nuts, candies, fruit cake, canned turkey, and chocolate, all of it with a Christmas tone. One young Marine, Thad Laird, had his family send him jars full of olives. I was given to understand that the fluid covering the olives in the jars was a touch of vermouth and the rest gin. Marine ingenuity at its best!

Frank McDonald, 1st Platoon B-1-5 (Palatas)

To get back and maintain physical fitness, we played a lot of volley ball. The Weapons Company Machine Gun Platoon, won our Battalion Championship, and then got beat in the finals by a team, of high-ranking officers from 2nd Battalion, 5th Marines. It's a hard thing to go up on the net using "jungle rules" when your opponent is a lieutenant colonel or a major. Chow lines were always full, and the Marines were always going back for seconds. Marines would snack on the Christmas food packages between meals. We were really run down. On a personal note, I was really sick with dysentery, and was within a short time to be evacuated to Japan if the shots did not take effect. Fortunately, I started to get better at the last moment. I did not want to leave my weapons company.

There was liberty in Masan, but not much to do. The local brands of whiskey could be poisonous and mostly were avoided. We had beer rations issues. Religious services were very much a part of our Christmas. There are few atheists in foxholes, and even fewer after surviving the Chosin. As exhaustion was overcome, the spirits of all the Marines rose and a great camaraderie arose, even stronger than before, within and among the units within the battalion. It was a good time to be in the 1st Battalion, 5th Marines, in the best Marine Division ever!

The machine-gun platoon of weapons company finally got its water-cooled heavy machine guns. We started training with them, and training replacements at the same time. I remember at this time how much Gunnery Sergeant Steve Mihalik, Staff Sergeant Carl Evans and Sergeant Robert Fairbanks were worth their weight in gold in training activities. Few platoon leaders were ever served better than I was with these men.

One final note, I found myself looking forward to meeting the Chinese, again. It was not so much an eagerness for combat as it was a desire to hurt them badly, as badly as we could. We did hurt them on the Chosin plateau, but I wanted to be part of a battle where our battalion, and the whole division, would utterly beat them, beat the hell out of them, beyond any hope of recovery. We would come close to that in "Operation *Killer*."

Those were my thoughts as we left Masan in late January aboard Japanese landing ships for Pohang.

—*Frank*—

# Our Christmas Dinner

## Lieutenant Dave Gally

On Christmas Day, 1951, the 1st Battalion, 5th Marines, was on a mountain 884 looking north across the valley of the Nam-Gang (Nam River). This area is northeast of the "Punch Bowl" near the place where the Soyang-Gang turned west. By this time I was in H&S Company learning to be the Battalion S-2. The command post was near and the rear of the mountain top but I don't recall the position of Baker Company. Early Christmas morning, a field tent, kitchen, cooks, steel trays, and food were flown by chopper to a flat area near the top. Snow began falling around 11:00am when hot Christmas dinner service commenced. We were served in the tent, but sat on boulders, or the ground to eat. Big fluffy snow flakes were falling on the food as we ate. In a few minutes we were scraping snow off to find the food and eat before it froze. The food cooled anyway, but we ate most of it. It was a great improvement over C-rations. Fortunately, it was a quiet day. The North Koreans seemed to show respect and no guns were fired by either side.

*—Dave—*

Murray's Christmas card (Palatas)

# Christmas at the Bean Patch 1950

## Lieutenant Mike Palatas

It was Christmas morning in Company B area, and there was no reveille. At mid-morning, Gunny Wright sounded off for B Company to fall in and he waited to take roll call as the sluggish troops formed, wondering what gives. He had to resort to voice command, because we no longer had our bugle to blow the normal calls—the bugle was reluctantly tossed onto a trash heap after we came off Hill 1240 at Yudam-ni. Also, naturally, everyone was reported present by the platoon and section leaders, because, where else would they be?

The Battalion Chaplain gave each company a Christmas tree (from Lord knows where) and ours was set up in the company "street" in front of the command post tent. It had some makeshift decorations on it, put there by the "Ole Top" (Dierickx) and our property sergeant (Shoemaker).

As the company was formed, our Skipper, in his green fore 'n aft cap and the "Ole Top" Dierickx took positions at the tree. Not in a Santa Claus suit, but in field jackets and scarf. Next to the tree there were three big boxes, the type that clothing and boots come in. These were filled with woolen socks, olive drab, which in turn were filled with fruits and candy, from the galley and PX sundry packets, put together by Sergeant Shoemaker and his helpers. The Gunny had the troops file by and the Skipper handed each one a filled stocking with a wish of "Merry Christmas." The rest of the day was "Holiday Routine" meaning free time to yourself.

The battalion cooks and mess men put on a great feast, also and it wasn't all that bad sitting in the open field, balancing our loaded mess gear. We had turkey, ham, sweet potatoes, cranberry sauce, a mix of candy, and some cigars. Then too, the cooks made coffee available throughout the day. During chow, we were visited by our battalion commanding officer and a couple of staff members. They extended their best wishes also.

—*M.V.P.*—

# That Special Jeep!

## Corporal Emmett Shelton, Jr.

It was muddy as hell when we got to the "Bean Patch." Lots of us were in pain from wounds and frostbite and I had my share of the frostbite! When you move to a warmer climate and your extremities start to thaw out, the pain is nearly overpowering. I was pacing up and down the mud street by our company area when I noticed a chaplain giving communion on the hood of a Jeep. I limped on over and partook of this and felt as if a great weight had been lifted from my shoulders. I was only 19 years old, and I had just seen more dead people in 10 days than most will see in a lifetime.

In retrospect, this Jeep must have been the one "Rocky" donated to the Chaplain and Mike mentioned, you just never know how something you do in good faith may positively influence others?

*—Emmett—*

# Bandits Regain Strength at the Bean Patch

## Lieutenant Mike Palatas

Our stay at the "Bean Patch" was a time of healing for the entire 1st Marine Division and especially for the rifle regiments. Our B Company area was just a small part of the division's assembly area. We were not much over 200 men strong whereas the division and its supporting units totaled 22,000. Within the three rifle regiments, there were 27 rifle companies total. But, we knew of only one—B Company, "The Embattled Baker Bandits" as Lieutenant Hancock, our commanding officer, would say.

Our replacements fleshed out our Table of Organization, dramatically. Our "Top" can be credited for his continued effort with battalion personnel to ensure our proper share. We still fell short of the recommended seven officers and 235 enlisted men. Ed Morris continued as our leader of the 3rd Platoon. The 1st and 2nd Platoons were led by non-comms, Schmidt and Lischesky. Lt Schryver would have the Mortar Section and I would lead the Machine Gun Platoon and the executive officer duties. Our enlisted replacements were standouts. An old salt could definitely identify a recent joiner by his new clothing, boots, and equipment.

Our weaponry was looking good too—clean and gleaming with a light coat of oil. It included 81 carbines, 18 pistols (45s), 27 Browning automatic rifles and 120 rifles, and .30-cal. M-1. Our crew-served weapons included six light machine guns and three 60mm mortars. Each of us knew the value of keeping these weapons clean and operable—it was a matter of life and death. Our pistols were carried by the gunners and assistant gunners of the Machine Gunners and Mortars. Personal weapons were not allowed. Officers were armed with carbines and would carry 45 rounds of ammunition for it—two magazines in the pouch over the end of the stock and one in the weapon. Other items of our trade would include: K-bar knives, Hamilton wrist watch down to the rank of Sergeant, bayonets, rifle grenade launcher, entrenching tool, compass, first aid kit, and map case.

*—M.V.P.—*

# Leaving Masan—Early January 1951

## Lieutenant Mike Palatas

Our last hot meal in the Bean Patch at Masan would be noon chow and it consisted of B-rations (next larger than the famous C-rations). We ate them at the stand-up tables in the open field.

Our tents were already down and rolled the best our men could. Willie Shoemaker, our Property Sergeant, would oversee the breaking of our part of the camp and police the area. Local villagers were already on the perimeter waiting for us to depart to begin their "salvaging."

Our basic loads of gear were neatly arrayed in each platoon area and small fires began to creep up. Broken tent pegs, make-shift chairs and tables, were the primary fuel. Men were dismantling the alter/chapel. It would all end up in the fires.

We were all in our parkas or field jackets and wore our helmets. The heat of the fires warmed our hands. The fires also warmed us psychologically. Sergeant Wolfe always stood out because of his height. But now, it was his parka. It was over-sized and came down to his ankles. He was like a walking sleeping bag.

The bulky tents were dragged to pick-up points and loaded on 6×6 trucks and came with us on our move. It took at least four men to load one tent into the truck . It was done with lots of grunts and groans and four-letter words.

Our corpsman "Doc" Ray Christman tended to the last-minute sick calls. His field jacket pockets were budging with casualty tags, tape, and a cure-all ointment in each pocket.

Around 1400, on a gray January afternoon in Korea, our company moved into our departure area. Gunny Wright called the words to "saddle up." B Company was back to action.

—*M.V.P.*—

# Guerilla Hunts Begin—Our Time of Loss January–February 1951

## The Roll Call of the Dead

### Chuck Hall

The battlefield is silent,
Where comrades fought and bled
The drums are beating slowly,
The roll call of the dead

The names I still remember,
Called out one by one
Resting now forever,
Beneath the setting sun

Emblazoned in my memory,
The blood that ran so red
The Captain slowly reading,
The roll call of the dead

Their lives had ended quickly,
Cut down in their prime
Young now and forever,
Until the end of time.

We go back out tomorrow,
The Captain slowly said
We still have yet to finish,
The roll call of the dead.

# Pohang, Korea—Mid-January '51

## Lieutenant Mike Palatas

From midwinter to the middle of spring of 1951, there would be many changes experienced by all, especially in the area of personnel. Rotation would begin in earnest. The lot, however, for the rifleman, would change little.

We would experience new, but capable leadership in all areas affecting us. We would confront a new type of enemy—the guerrilla, and for a while, we would suffer more casualties in our pursuits from rear actions/accidents than we had at this point. It would be more grueling operating in the steep mountainous countryside—there would be not an ounce of fat in B Company.

Sergeant Heacock replaced the Ole Top (Palatas)

Our battalion commander would rotate to Camp Pendleton. His replacement would be a newly promoted lieutenant colonel from 3rd Battalion. Our recently promoted Regimental Commander, Colonel Ray Murray would rotate and be replaced by Colonel Hayward.

Even the division command group would change hands. Our own Master Sergeant "Ole Top" Phil Dierickx, who was always ready with a smile, would be replaced by 1st Sergeant Heacock. He sported a menacing black mustache and seldom smiled. Long-legged Gunny Wright would take his turn stateside and his replacement was short-legged Gunny Long.

In April we joined our first black, a wide-eyed private in the heavily ethnic ranks of B Company. That in itself, would be a milestone in the long "white" history

of B-1-5. We would see a new and
important role for the helicopter in
re-supply and casualty evacuation.
We would also encounter re-supply
on foot, by large numbers of Korean
laborers hired by our S-4.

The "water buffalo" (Schryver)

Three of our rated seven officers
would be killed and some newly
joined 2nd lieutenants would be
wounded and evacuated soon after
joining. Lieutenant Ed Morris and
Lieutenant Nick Schryver would leave us, too. Our leadership would garner at
least four Navy Cross awards. A share of our non-commissioned officers would
eventually be commissioned as 2nd lieutenants in the states and their skills put
to use in training new replacements for the prolonged actions in Korea.

Back to Pohang. We were just setting in at our camp somewhere on the
periphery of Pohang near an airstrip. Our battalion command post wasn't much
more than 500 yards away from our company area and the galley was in the
process of being made operational. There were more than enough volunteers to
serve as mess men, but to put a "Bandit" on mess duty was like putting the fox
in the hen house. Behind us now was the volley ball upset, which occurred on
the 3rd day.

Each day, including our day of arrival, we were directed to provide our share
of the working parties to battalion. Most of those were for manual labor needed
in establishing the battalion supply dump and the restocking and redistribution
of clothing, equipment, ammo and other essentials. A shower unit was set up for
the regiment's use by division engineers at a nearby water point and if the heater
unit remained in operation and the pumps worked to fill the large rubberized
tubs, we might soon get a shower. The water point would also provide water for
drinking and bathing in the company area. The water was made potable through
filtering equipment on trailers operated by the engineers. A "water buffalo" trailer
would be parked in our company area. Also, a laundry unit was set up near
the showers and dirty clothes would be exchanged. Best of all, it was rumored
that division was establishing a bakery and soon we would get fresh bread and,
occasionally, donuts.

Replacement personnel still trickled in and two of these stick in my mind.
The first was a private, very large in stature, and he must have come into the
Marines on a physical waiver. He was well over 6 foot tall. On arrival, he tried
to convince our "Top" Phil Dierickx that he was told by in the "rear" that he
was not to let go of his special-sized and tailored clothing in his "Willie Peter"
bag because regular issue stuff wouldn't fit him. The "Ole Top" Sergeant, with his

2nd Lieutenant Harvey Nolan (Dally)

usual political knack and tact convinced Private Kerrigan that his "stuff" would be safe in Sergeant Shoemaker's care.

The second standout replacement was a newly commissioned 2nd Lieutenant Harvey Nolan, who was brought to the company command post by Jeep driver Pendergast. Lieutenant Cronin was the first to greet him and welcome him aboard.

Lieutenant Cronin sought out Lieutenant Hancock and with minimum courtesies told Harvey he was happy to have him and that he would take over the 2nd rifle Platoon from its acting platoon leader Sergeant Lischeski.

Harvey Nolan looked his best. He was clean shaven except for a neatly trimmed mustache. As Lieutenant Cronin introduced him to the rest of us officers, I was impressed by his eagerness and meticulous appearance in pressed twill dungarees, canvas leggings and shined boots. About the time Lieutenant Nolan arrived, two Koreans, under the watchful eye of Sergeant Shoemaker, were putting the finishing touches on a hinged doorway at the company's command post pyramidal tent. That door, with its acetate window gave us a real uptown look. When they finished, Shoemaker made sure Lieutenant Hancock was first to use it. To me it was an omen that we'd be moving out soon—and so it was!

"Hacked off," "P____d off" and "Teed off," the expletives all imply the same and were common vernacular in our day. "Hacked off" is what some old navy salt would use; "P____d off" a term often used in our machine-gun platoon to indicate one's mental state; "Teed off" a more genteel expletive heard amongst the officers. Except for Ike Fenton, it meant to address a golf ball and give it a good swat. Any one of these, however, is what the Bandits would have been, had they known the real reason we left the Bean Patch at Masan for Pohang.

On January 4, 1951, the enemy caused the U.S. Army to move 25 miles south of Seoul. Knowing this, our Marine veterans of Inchon–Seoul would have harbored those unflattering, dark thoughts of our army brethren for losing Seoul for the second time in about six months!

Now, on our second day in the Pohang area, the 1st Battalion's company officers and acting platoon leaders were assembled in one of the squad-sized mess tents. The sides of the tent were rolled up and secured to allow some light in. The smoking lamp was out.

Our Operations Officer, a major, entered and called "Attention." Behind him was our battalion commander, then next was Colonel Murray. It was rare for us to see our battalion commander, let alone to be in the presence of Colonel Murray, our regimental commanding officer.

Purple heart recipients, January 5, 1951, Pohang (Schryver)

At this rare gathering, this Marine couldn't help but note the uniforms worn by our regimental "Six." He wore army boots, the type with the upper portion being a leather add-on which served somewhat as leggings. His boots were well shined though! More obvious was his outer wear of an army trench coat. This was an overcoat with a button-in liner for cold weather and in its unique hem was a button-secured arrangement that, when undone, would drop down to wrap around the calf—a forerunner of today's "garters." To complete his outfit he wore the short-billed army rain-proof cap with his new "eagle" rank insignia on the front and "eagles" adorned the epaulets of his army trench coat. In spite of his "army" appearance, he was still our beloved and respected "Big Six."

The mood at this meeting was a somber one. After introductions by our commanders with words of what a fine job our men had done, the army intelligence officer from corps headquarters gave us the low down on recent events along the front and told us about our new mission—The Guerrilla Hunt.

He said, in a southern drawl, that the mountains and valleys to our north were strongholds to remnant North Korean and some Chinese elements. We were to enter their domain, seek out these isolated groups and destroy them and any equipment and keep them from harassing our Main Supply Routes (MSR) and rear logistics facilities.

The following day we were back in business. Our S-2 began issuing the 1:50,000 scale maps with names such as Pohang-dong, Kusan-dong, and Sinny Yong. Battalion Supply, Daly, began distribution of C-rations, heat tabs, and other essentials. First, we would provide small unit-sized patrols led by non-commissioned officers (NCOs). They would be foot patrols or sometimes motorized. Sometimes the patrols would assist engineers to probe roadways for mines, other times, the Battalion Motor Transport Section would truck a patrol to a drop-off point and make a pick-up at a later time. Rocky Williams would coordinate these Motor Transport moves and provide trucks with sandbag-lined beds as protection for the troops in the event of a mine detonation, which often did occur.

These patrols would be a major test of leadership for our younger NCOs. In size, they would range from fire team to squad. They would be without mortar or machine-gun support attached, but might be augmented by an scout from Battalion and a Korean serving as interpreter. Primarily, they were reconnaissance in nature—to seek intelligence data. Some were daylight and some would extend several days. The routes were set up by the Battalion Intelligence officer. The multiple-day patrol would often spend nights in a village hut. The interpreter would arrange this with a village elder, a "Papa-san" who wore white clothes and a black horse-hair hat, a symbol of respect. Our small-unit patrolling was short-lived because we would soon move back to company-sized patrols.

We would lose a squad-sized patrol unit to Missing in Action and later declared Killed in Action. Another, 2nd Platoon patrol, would have to abort because one of its men, Kerrigan, became a casualty and it took all the men to carry him back.

—*M.V.P.*—

# The Longest Night

## Private Bill Dove

Like in any war zone, the ordinary Marine grunt does not know where he is going, when he is going to get there, or when he is coming back. He is trained to dig in, attack, or saddle up. This was true on one cold winter day in either January or February of 1951 as we began our push to the north. I always did hate the "Point," but we were told that—the Chinese always let the Point get through and attacked the main body. While on the Point, I always wondered if the enemy knew this?

Anyway, I was one of the chosen few that day to get assigned to the Point. While advancing, we were about one-half mile in front of the main column in the valley floor when we came upon three mountain ranges. There was one valley on the left, one to the right, and one straight ahead, we elected to go straight.

This was a bad mistake, because after about 30 minutes, we looked back and our main column was nowhere in sight! To make matters worse, we had no radio. It was as if the Lord had come and taken everything, but us. We decided to climb to higher ground to get a better view. The only thing that we observed was a deserted village about two miles away in a valley.

We proceeded toward the village and indeed it was deserted. Nightfall was soon to set in, so we decided to spend the night in the village and make our way back at daybreak.

It was as quiet as death as darkness set in, except for the occasional sound of artillery in the distance. We broke out our sleeping bags and got ready for a cold night's sleep, when the first guy on watch made a welcome discovery. There was a stack of wood next to the hut. There was also a hole in the foundation to heat the hut. You simply put the wood into the hole and lit it. The fire heats the clay floor and the heat rises and you have a heated hut.

Everything was going well until a line of torches was observed coming down the hill about a half-mile away! We made a quick exit heading south towards sounds of the artillery.

We dug in on top of a hill about two miles from the village to await daybreak. As daybreak came, we made our way southward with no water or rations. We came across a mountain stream where three dead Chinese lay. We kept to the high ground, sending out a scout to prevent any surprise attack as we made our journey.

We ran across a small village with about 10 huts. As we entered the village, we were met by women, children, and an elderly man with a tall black hat like Abraham Lincoln.

Two bandits and a villager share their perspectives (Palatas)

After checking the village to make sure we were safe, we approached the elderly man and said "Chop-Chop." He nodded that he understood and several children built a fire under a wash pot (like mama used to wash clothes in) and added water. He pointed to the side of a hut, and as Lord is my witness there hung two dried-out octopuses.

He broke one up into pieces and put it into the pot along with rice and other ingredients. About an hour later, we ate this dish like a bunch of hogs. After eating, we nodded our head "thanks" and continued our march. Shortly thereafter, we made contact with our lines. Needless to say, we were happy to be well fed and back with our Brothers!

*—Bill—*

# A Little Baby Was Saved

## Sergeant Albert Bellanger

I think it was around April or May of 1951 when early one morning the 2nd Platoon was to leave the MSR and scout a hill that was shielding us from a enemy position and to see how far we could go before they noticed us. The fog was close to the ground, so we moved along pretty well until I heard a cuckoo bird call across an open field on our right. I stopped the platoon and asked for the interpreter to come forward. No need of that, for he was always in my back pocket. I could not get him to keep any distance from me (I don't like a crowd). Anyway, I asked him what he thought the noise like a cuckoo bird was, and his statement was, "It was a cuckoo bird." After I tried to explain to him that cuckoo birds live in wooden clocks and he was a North Korean spy and getting close to death, he finally convinced me it was a real live cuckoo bird.

We moved on again and rounded the end of this hill, on our left, which put us right in front of the North Korean lines, less than 100 yards up the hill, now on the right, still covered by fog, we could hear the enemy talking and banging their mess gear together so they had not spotted us as yet.

Off the path about 15 yards was a house which we promptly scouted and entered to find a complete family of Koreans living there. They included Grandpa, Grandmamma, elderly men and women, children from baby to teenaged girls and some in their 20s. We had to move them out of the house which was no easy task and started moving them towards the rear on the path we came in on, but grandpa didn't want to leave without his cow, so that took a little more persuasion. Finally we started the column toward the rear and when we had gone about 300 yards and were once again out of the Koreans' sight the interpreter came to me and said, "Mamasan had hidden a baby under the porch."

I forget who went back with me, but I think it was my radioman, Carroll, Cpl Yocum and two other men. When we got back to the house, the fog was just beginning to lift, but luck (as some call it) was still with us. The first board in the porch we looked under, we found the baby. We scooped it up and were moving out of there on the double. The North Koreans finally spotted us and began dropping mortars on us, but we made it around the base of the hill and out of their sight.

We had to hurry and get the people back to the MSR. The only problem with that was the men in the platoon all wanted to carry the young girls and no volunteers to carry the old women and men, so we could double time out of there. I finally got that straightened out and we made it safely back to the MSR, where trucks were waiting to take the civilians out. Just another day's work done by some of the corps' finest men from B-1-5.

*—Al—*

# Pohang Guerrilla Hunt— January–February 1951

## Lieutenant Mike Palatas

We began the "Pohang Guerrilla Hunt" in the middle of January of '51 following our brief respite after our Chosin Reservoir break-out.

In the Pohang area, we began this new phase of combat, guerrilla hunts, with small-sized patrols venturing into the mountainous backdrop off the Main Supply Route (MSR). Otherwise, the area was pretty quiet and somewhat secure.

On January 31, 1951, Sergeant Yesenko and his squad-sized patrol set out on patrol but were somehow taken prisoners by the Chinese. We later heard they met with violent execution-type deaths at the hands of irregulars in the hills probably not too far from our encampment near the Pohang airstrip.

After a short time, we returned to our "company-sized" patrols for safety deeper into the mountains, northwest of Pohang. Lieutenant Hancock's incredible ability to "read" and interpret the Korean maps served us well in the rough wooded countryside where only foot and animal trails existed.

On February 7, 1951, after two such guerilla hunt patrols, our Skipper Lieutenant John Hancock was killed by automatic weapons fire as he directed an attack on the remote village of Morak. Some type of casualty had become almost a daily experience, even amongst our newly joined replacements.

Second Lieutenant Frank McDonald would join us from the Battalion Heavy Weapons Platoon. He would relieve Tsgt C. M. Schmidt, who did a superb job as leader at Hill 1240

Lieutenant Wright and machine gun platoon ready for a guerilla hunt (Gally)

B-1-5 on the guerilla hunt (Palatas)

Yudam-Ni after Lieutenant Swede Jenson was Killed in Action at Chosin.

At the same time, we of B-1-5 were consolidating our isolated and remote position at the Ha-Hoe-Dong road junction, U.S. Army units were under severe attack far to our north, just below the 38th parallel. At the town of Hong-Song over 2,000 enemy and U.S. casualties were suffered.

Unaware and unconcerned of this, we were digging in for our night defense. Lieutenant McDonald's 1st Rifle Platoon would be hit this night and casualties would be taken. One of these was Private Bob Knause, a member of the 4th Replacement Draft which joined "B" Company on January 12, 1951.

The 1st Platoon was in the lead when we were ambushed at Ha-Hoe-Dong in a Valentine's Day surprise.

We made it to Sinny Yong on February 17, 1951 and waited for word to saddle up and move out. The weather was below freezing at night and to make a head call at the open air, folding and portable four-holers, you peel through the four layers of cold-weather gear to get to the business at hand. You cringe at the thought of sitting on a 30-degree cold seat in the bare. Most of us will not have had a change of underwear or clothes since leaving Pohang, a month ago. Each man has a strong aroma.

On February 20, 1951, we prepared for a night move by 6×6 through the mountains to Wonju. Sometime during the night, while most of us slept, we came to a crawl. Just ahead, but not yet seen, was a sharp curve in the road. These roads were all gravel or sometimes just dirt and mud. When we reached the curve, a pallor of dust hung in the air. The truck driver ahead had negotiated the turn too sharply and the left-side wheels dropped over the embankment causing the truck to roll. The Jeep had its lights facing the darkness downhill and not far down a 6×6 rested on its top. Marines were scrambling downhill to render assistance. A piercing plea came through the darkness as one of the men pinned under the truck begged to be put out of his misery. Two died and nine were evacuated due to injuries.

*– M. V.P.–*

# Baker Company Patrol Is Captured

February 1, 1951 USMC Historical Diary ~~SECRET~~ declassified

**Feb. 1** On this date intelligence sources reported that the enemy (North Korean guerrillas) were moving generally toward PALGONG-SAN raiding villages for food and other needs. Up to this time no concentrations of more than 300 had been observed by 5th Marines' patrols. Efforts were being made by the enemy to capture or destroy our patrols. <u>One 11-man patrol of B" Company failed to return from a four-day reconnaissance on January 31 and are still missing on this date</u>. Prisoners interrogated were untrained and unaware of their unit's mission. They reported that only 13 men out of a platoon of 50 ever had fired a rifle and that half of the platoon had been conscripted since Nov 15, '50. Civilian police reported that the enemy in the regiment's patrol sector actually were bandits with no formal liaison with regular North Korean troops north of AN-DONG, Their combat efficiency was considered low and it was believed that their operations would be limited to harassment and "Hit and Run" tactics.

# Baker Company's Only Captured Squad

## Corporal H. J. "Syd" Sydnam

On January 29, 1951, 3rd Squad, 2nd Platoon, Baker Company was captured. Rumors said they were taken prisoner of war and later Killed in Action.

Sergeant Thomas Yesenko, Corporal Douglas S. Finley, Jr., Corporal Roy L. West, Private Michael C. Grubisish, Private Donald W. Donnell, Private Lee E. Dutcher, Private Alfred Lawrence, Jr., Private Charles W. Melvold, Private Paul E. Warren and Private George W. Rae were those assigned to that squad.

My squad, the 2nd Squad, was lead by Sergeant Billy R. Hidy and my fire team consisted of Private Roberts and Private "Ted" Skeals, who was later Killed in Action on Hill 313 in April.

Our two squads were sent out to different sectors from Pohang-dong during the "Great Guerrilla Hunt." Our orders were to "make contact with the enemy, observe his distribution, morale, equipment, resources and deployment and report back." We were issued a fair amount of "Wan" to pay for food and lodging and trucked to our areas. In our area, we had no problem making contact as the village was under siege.

Sgt Thomas Yesenko (Wray)

Sergeant Hidy chose discretion and we holed up in a local "hotel" to await a break in the action. There we became quite friendly with a commander of the South Korean police and if my notes are correct, he was Commander Shim and we were at Kusan-dong. PFC Charles Nail, of Gainsville, Florida, was one of the squad and he taught Shim to sing and strum a Carbine sling to "That Good Ol' Mountain Dew." Often after that we encountered Shim and serenaded each other back and forth!

When the shooting cooled we took to the field to do our job. The first night out we holed up in a tiny village and spent some Wan for the "food and shelter." We played cards and some went to sleep.

Sergeant Hidy had "a bad feeling" and had us quietly "saddle up" and tip-toe out into the road back to Kusan-dong. We were underway only a short time when all hell broke loose behind us and a sort of pursuit developed, but no shooting. We did a VERY quick march back to our known safe area at the above hotel. It was very spooky all the way and the hackles were definitely up!

The next day, we got the word that Sergeant Yesenko's squad was missing and our mission went into abortion. I have always felt that the villagers set up both squads, but Hidy was just enough in tune to trust his vibes and hike us out of there before our "hosts" could jump us. I spent a good deal of

Cpl Douglas Finley, Jr., of Yesenko's squad (Wray)

time, especially during the Guerrilla Hunt, under Sergeant Hidy and Lieutenant Harvey Nolan and though they put me "in harm's way" with great frequency, I learned to trust my "antenna" at all times. I was brought up as a hunting farm boy who played "cowboys and Indians" and knew how to shoot and duck, but Harvey and Billy helped me hone it to the point that I exited Korea with bullet holes only in my clothes!

I just wanted to write a bit of a memory thing for our only captured squad from one of the guys who might have been in their shoes.

*—Syd—*

# More on Yesenko's Captured Squad

## Sergeant Waldo Wolfe

There really is no mystery to the Yesenko patrol and the fate of its members. What we initially heard shortly after their disappearance eventually came back to us even sadder than originally laid out. Lieutenant Hancock had extreme confidence in Yesenko to operate at night, and they were very successful, but, a combination of over-confidence and a turn of bad luck caught up to them, unfortunately.

They thought they had a "safe" ville to hide out in during the day, and that was where they ran out of luck. They were captured, and supposedly were being led away toward POW status "up north."

Somewhere along the line, I think they realized they were going toward their execution. Supposedly, Corporal West attempted to lead a breakaway, which did

Cpl Roy West of Yesenko's squad (Wray)

Gunnery Sgt Waldo Wolfe (Palatas)

not succeed. He was rewarded by being bayoneted while the rest were forced to watch. Two of the villagers who were accompanying this charade were then directed to bury him off the beaten path, while the rest of the unit, squad members, guerrillas, and villagers, continued deeper into the wooded area, never to be seen again.

Supposedly, the only two "survivors" of this escapade were those two villagers who returned to their ville and dummied up, that is, until some time later, when Sergeant "Red Dog" Keller and his company of green-clad Korean Police got into the act in trying to locate and determine their fate. It was a short time after Lieutenant Hancock got killed, that "Red Dog" and his police supposedly wormed all of the above story from those two surviving villagers. I know "Red Dog" fairly well, and he knew that Yesenko and I sometimes fox-holed together. I do remember how heavy he emphasized the hearsay aspect of what he told me.

—*Waldo*—

# Men of the Lost Patrol

## Lieutenant Frank McDonald

The story about the Yesenko's squad, with the photo in the right-hand column of the front page of the June–July 1998 issue of *The Guidon* is certainly Roy West. I knew him from Baker Co. even when I was still with Weapons Co. He was a very aggressive and independent-minded Marine, and I was surprised and very saddened when I heard the news about Yesenko's squad. West was the type of Marine you would want with you in a firefight. I did not know Thomas Yesenko well, but I was surprised and anguished to think that West, who was an "attack mode" Marine, would have allowed himself, and his group, to be caught. He was a little wild, but he was trustworthy when trust counted. It was a great tragedy, and we live to remember some very good men who were brutally executed. I also knew Douglas Finley from that squad. Why I knew those two and not Thomas Yesenko is a puzzle. Thank God for Sgt Billy Hidy's intelligence, and then you anguish over how it could have turned out better for Thomas Yesenko, Roy West, Douglas Finley and the rest of the squad.

*—Frank—*

# B-1-5 Casualties—January 31, 1951

## Missing in Action—Killed in Action

*Confirmed through Korean War Project*

SGT Thomas Yesenko, from South Fork, Penn.  MIA-KIA 31JAN51
CPL Douglas S. Finley, Jr., from West Monroe, La.  MIA-KIA 31JAN51
CPL Roy L. West, from Dansville, Mich.  MIA-KIA 31JAN51
PFC Michael C. Grubisish, from Peoria, Ill.  MIA-KIA 31JAN51
PFC Donald W. Donnell, from Oakland, Calif.  MIA-KIA 31JAN51
PFC Lee E. Dutcher, from Hastings, Neb.  MIA-KIA 31JAN51
PFC Alfred Lawrence, Jr., from Norfolk, Va.  MIA-KIA 31JAN51
PFC Charles W. Melvold, from Henning, Minn.  MIA-KIA 31JAN51
PFC Paul E. Warren, from Oakland, Calif.  MIA-KIA 31JAN51
PFC George W. Rae, from Roundup, Mont.  MIA-KIA 31JAN51

## The Lost Patrol

In late January 1951, patrols from the 1st Battalion, 5th Marines, were assigned to search out North Korean guerrillas operating in the area north and east of Taegu. The operations were part of the Pohang Guerrilla Hunt. On January 31, 1951, the 1st Battalion picked up six patrols, but one B Company Patrol 8 consisting of 11 men was overdue. By February 1, 1951, the 5th Marines reported that "one 11-man patrol of B Company that failed to return from a four-day reconnaissance on January 31, 1951 was still missing on this date."

Based on information obtained from civilians, the patrol was captured intact on January 30, 1951, near Jiha-Dong. "According to a civilian woman who was reported to have witnessed the patrol's capture, the Marines walked into a North Korean ambush on a trail and surrendered when trapped." The Marines and an accompanying Korean National policeman were taken Prisoners of War and later executed. Some reports indicate the executions occurred shortly after capture, but other reports cite February 20, 1951. Remains were found by Korean policemen in the vicinity of Ihwa-Dong on or about March 7, 1951. A total of 26 Korean and American remains were recovered. The unidentified American remains were taken to the Tanggok Cemetery for identification, and were assigned X-File designations. Subsequently these remains were identified and returned to the United States for burial. From research, it appears these Marines were never identified officially as Prisoners of War. (*Korean War Project*)

# The Day C.O. Lt Hancock Is Killed

## February 7, 1951 USMC Historical Diary ~~SECRET~~ Declassified

**Feb. 7.** At 1025, A Company jumped off in the attack with the 1st platoon attacking northeast toward the southern slope of Hill 582 and the 2nd platoon attacking northeast toward the APKOK TEMPLE, TA 8303. An airstrike was requested at TA 8403-T where the enemy was observed. B Company continued across the northeast slope of 582. One platoon of A Company which was advancing up the southern slope of Hill 582 reported enemy on the reverse slope of the hill that they were firing into the rear of B Company. The airstrike was called for could not be conducted on Hill 582 due to the short distance between A and B Companies and at 1215 the airstrike was conducted on the village of YUSA, TA 8804-G. At 1310, B Company was preparing to move out and envelope the town of CHORAK, TA 8404-F. AT 1230, At 1230, A Company reported that it was placing Hill 582 under heavy mortar and machine-gun fire and that one platoon would assault the hill.

B Company continued to advance to TA 8404-F. Fire was received on their front and right flank. By 1410, the 1st platoon had advanced against scattered resistance to TA 8302-G overlooking the temple, but was ordered to return to company CP. <u>At 1415 B Company Commander was killed and Executive Officer assumed command</u>; the company could not advance due to heavy fire from Hill 385 at 1530 and by 1600, B Company's advance was still being held up by heavy enemy automatic weapons and small-arms fire. At 1630 the battalion commander ordered B Company to draw back to the positions they held the previous night…

# Another B Company Disaster

## Charles Lyles

Just one week after Sergeant Yesenko's squad went Missing in Action, another disaster befell the Baker Bandits.

Most of us remember Lieutenant Hancock as our Company Executive and Company Commander through the battle of the Chosin Reservoir. After the Chosin Reservoir was over, B Company was back to chasing guerrillas in late January 1951. Fighting was down south and one of our squads, Yesenko's, was sent on an overnight patrol. When they did not return, the rest of the company went looking for them.

Baker Company chased the guerrillas for some time, but it may have been a trap. By February 7, 1951, some of the guerrillas were on ground higher than the company. We went into the Apkok Temple area. It was spooky. There was an old temple but way back there in the woods were giant boulders with ancient carvings of Buddha. I felt like there were people watching.

We turned a corner in the path and Lt Hancock and I were showered with bullets from the higher ground and the lieutenant dropped with mortal head and chest wounds. My radio saved me, but was no longer operational so I shucked it and went for cover. When I rejoined the company, I wanted them to retrieve Lt Hancock but they insisted that I go after the damaged radio. Gunny Ed Wright and I retrieved the radio and checked on Lt Hancock's body. Later, the lieutenant's body was brought down the mountain. It was a very sad day.

—*Charlie*—

B Company Commanding Officer, Lt Hancock (Palatas)

# Our Skipper Is Killed

## Lieutenant Nick Schryver

In February 1951, B Company was involved in a "search and destroy" mission, looking for guerrillas. Our objective was a village at the end of a long valley and an old temple, Apkok Temple. It was believed the village was a guerrilla base. B Company was to attack down the valley from the east, and A Company was to move in from the south, a sort of pincer attack. Speed was essential; therefore Lieutenant Hancock had us moving at "flank speed" along the road leading to the objective. Guerrillas opened fire on the column from the ridge on our right flank. Return fire quieted the guerrillas, so Lieutenant Hancock again put the company in high gear towards the objective.

The company arrived at the saddle which was to be the "line of departure" into the assault. Lieutenant Hancock went forward to make a reconnaissance. As the Mortar Section Leader, I was with him, as were others in the command group. My job was to plan the mortar fire support.

I recall that upon arriving at the saddle, I looked back at the high ground from which the guerrillas had previously opened fire. I realized that, even though we had quieted them a short while ago, they were still around and should they decide to return, they had an excellent field of fire into our position. So, I selected a foxhole left over from some previous operation as the place where I would seek shelter should we come under fire.

Lieutenant Hancock and the rest of us then got busy with the task at hand. Then it happened, automatic-weapons fire came in like hail. I dove for my previously selected shelter. As I was thus engaged, I saw puffs of dust therein and realized that this foxhole was a lousy selection, so I just kept somersaulting until I was over the saddle and out of the line of fire. From his position, Lieutenant Hancock yelled for me to get the mortars busy. I gave him a "Wilco!" Since I could not observe from my position, I had to run back and dive into the cut where the road went through the saddle. Another volley came and I believe this was the volley that found Lieutenant Hancock. Rifle and mortar fire again quieted the guerrillas, but too late for a mighty fine Marine officer and Company Commander!

Lieutenant Hancock was the only casualty. The mission continued, life went on, and that's the way it was and is in the infantry.

*—Nick—*

# Our Skipper's Last Patrol

## Lieutenant Mike Palatas

An overcast winter day and no shadows! The Bandits of B-1-5, onboard trucks courtesy of Rocky Williams, our Motor Transport Chief. Our men are huddled against each other on the wooden benches which line each side of the 6×6 and the truck bed is sandbagged for some protection against land mines.

You men of the "Brigade" remember Hill 105, north of Seoul and what happens when a land mine lifts a vehicle!? The canvas covers are not on the trucks, so even though the distance we ride is not too great, our men will be exposed to a wind chill factor. Each truck will have at least one case of sniffles and a lot of coughing. We couldn't wear enough clothing; for example, heavy wool socks (maybe two pair), long johns, trousers overlaid by wind-proof trousers. It might take a minute or two to get to the basics of making a side-of-the-trail head call. For upper body it was long johns, woolen shirt, red cross sweater, then the field jacket w/hood, we all looked alike.

Our mission was to seek out and destroy any guerrilla elements we encounter. Our truck convoy would go west through the town of Yon-chon which is on the East–West Main Supply Route (MSR) out of Pohang to Taegue. Yon-chon is in a broad open valley, not a big town, more like a village. The road continues west to the big town of Taegue, but we would turn north on a narrow road and follow the rail line through the town of Sinny Yong, where B-1-5 would soon have its command post. We would go about eight miles more then get out of the trucks. The road continues north to the town of Uihung. The entire area is now mountainous and tree-covered. Some peaks are over 700 meters. Access to the interior (eastward) is mainly by foot trails over ridges or single-lane oxcart trail along the valley floor. Our point of departure on this patrol will be just south of Ha-Hoe-Dong, only a junction in the road. This road junction, Ha-Hoe-Dong or Hwasudong would, in about a week's time, set out a "Welcome Committee" and draw blood on the next Bandit patrol.

When we got out of the trucks, we lined the roadside while Lieutenant Hancock, Lieutenant Morris and T/Sgt Schmidt reviewed their maps. Lt Hancock directed

Lt Morris to lead out and the point began the uphill climb. We moved in column formation and our Korean interpreter went with Lt Morris.

Lieutenant Nolan and the 2nd Rifle Platoon were detached to battalion headquarters where they would provide command post security. Thus, we were operating with two rifle platoons, the entire machine gun platoon and our 16-man 60mm mortar section.

By about February 5, 1951, we were about 10 miles into the boonies, without any contact, and at a place named Sokchong. We occupied a low hill in the center of a valley where a lane branches north and west. We took this direction toward the village of Chorak, less than two miles' distance.

The area was heavily wooded with pine trees. From our Observation Post (OP) on the top of the hill we saw, with binoculars, the road cut where it crosses the saddle and drops over the other side into the village of Chorak. We did not make it that far, however. We "jumped off" on the morning of February 6, 1951, as best I recall. Lieutenant Hancock directed Lieutenant Morris and his 3rd Platoon to follow the ridge on the right of the narrow valley. T/Sgt Schmidt and his 1st Platoon took the ridge on the left side. The rest of B Company followed the single lane trail leading to the road cut in the saddle. No sooner had the 1st Platoon jumped off, it had a brief exchange of rifle fire in the dense woods. We must have been under surveillance all the time we were on the hill. After the exchange, the enemy fell back and our move forward continued at a slow pace on both sides of the valley.

The Lead Team proceeded up the trail: Lieutenant Hancock, Lieutenant Palatas, Gunnery Sergeant Wright, Top/Sgt Dierickx, Charles Lyles (radioman), the headquarters group, which included Lieutenant Randolph and his forward observation team from the 11th Marines, and the 60mm mortar section with Lieutenant Schryver. It became ominous and forbidding almost immediately. We knew we were in "contact" and now, several trees had been felled across the trail. Next, half the lane on the hillside had been dug out and debris thrown down the slope. It would be impassable to a Jeep.

We continued in silence and could hear our platoons on the right and left moving a bit ahead of our lead. They had tough going through the wooded slopes and had limited visibility. We made it to the road cut and saddle sometime around noon. The rifle platoons were above us on the right and left and their lead elements (Point) were a bit ahead. Their visibility was still limited.

The bulk of the headquarters' group was left in the road cut and Lieutenant Hancock moved onto the saddle for better observation downward toward Chorak. There was an old Buddhist temple in the area. There were huge boulders with ancient carvings. We felt we were being watched. From this vantage point, those of us in the Observation Post group could see the enemy not far ahead crossing in front of us through an open area. We had a machine gun section set up and began firing at these targets.

Lieutenant Schryver's mortar men were already setting up in the defilade behind us and his F.O. was already in position observing and ready to call in fires. Our observation post group did all the firing since we had the best observation. The enemy that managed to escape our fires, moved out of sight to our right. They eventually got to the higher ground above our 3rd Platoon. We were still bringing fire on those in front of us. Then the enemy, unseen by us and above us, rained automatic fire into those of us in the saddle.

Lieutenant Hancock was between me and Lieutenant Randolph, our Artillary Fire Officer. The initial burst of enemy machine-gun fire was traumatic, close, and echoed in the valley. The natural instinct is to take cover. I was a few feet from the cut in the trail and slid down the embankment about 12 feet high and out of the line of fire. Our "Top" was here in the cut. Shortly, from the Observation Post above I heard the screaming voice of Charlie Lyles say, "TELL BAKER 'FIVE' HE'S NOW BAKER 'SIX'!" I knew that Lieutenant Hancock had been hit. We lost our Company Commander! He died instantly from that burst.

I had Charlie Lyles radio the 1st and 3rd Platoons to halt forward movement and to take higher ground then notified our Battalion Commander of our situation. I gave them our coordinates and battalion sent a Jeep for evacuation of our casualties.

We held our positions until the Jeep arrived at the 1st roadblock. I watched the Jeep depart and at the same time, was told by radio that Lieutenant Nolan and the 2nd Platoon were on their way back to us. I was told to hold where we were and await further orders.

Shortly, Major Olsen came on the radio to say that A Company with Scout "Red Dog" Keller were approaching us from somewhere to the northwest. We never made contact.

I was shortly directed to occupy our position of the night before. As our lead element arrived at the hill, a firefight ensued from guerrillas already on the hill. With that exchange of fire, the enemy withdrew. We occupied our previous positions and now were joined by Lt Nolan, his 2nd Platoon and two tanks!

They came up the valley from Ha-Hoe-Dong. Our Battalion

Radio men 2Lt Randolph and Sgt Watson, south of Chorak (Palatas)

Commander apparently set up his Command Group in the valley not far to our west. We perimetered our hill and I emplaced the two tanks to best advantage. It was late afternoon and the sound of digging in could be heard. Just prior to darkness, I heard the cough of an enemy mortar from behind our position (south). The round whistled over our heads and "splashed" in front of our position. "Bandits" needed no prodding to dig in now. The mortar coughed again and the round whistled and "splashed" to our rear—we were bracketed—a mortarman's dream! Next his F.O.'s command would be to fire for effect, but nothing more happened

Night fell moonless and pitch black. Our wireman has us "wired" in with sound-powered phones, one to each platoon and to the mortar section. The machine gunners are attached to the rifle platoons. I had Gunnery Sergeant Wright pass the word to maintain a 50 percent alert tonight. There would be no fires and the smoking lamp was out. Charlie Lyles would pass out the password and countersign for challenging.

At about 9pm the tanker sergeant called asking permission to start his engines to "charge" his batteries. I told Lyles to deny his request. Not long after, the tank sergeant reported activity to his front. A moment later, his .30-caliber machine gun was in action, but there was no return fire. A light snow fell during the night.

In the morning I went off the hill to the tanks below to check on what happened. There was no body count, but they did find an enemy pack about fifty yards to their front.

Back up on the hill top, one of the Bandits informed me of movement in the saddle where we were the day before. Sure enough, two forms were in the saddle and began to move down the trail towards us. I passed the word to T/ Sgt Schmidt to hold his fire and take the men prisoner when they came into our perimeter.

Our battalion commanding officer now called on the radio and directed me to bring Baker Company westward down the valley and at a point, wait for a motor convoy, then entruck for a move to Sinny Yong, via Ha-Hoe-Dong. It was to be about a twenty-mile move. The Bandits would have one night's respite!

With Lieutenant Cronin somewhere on temporary assignment, B Company now had four officers—Lt Palatas, Lt Morris, Lt Schryver, and Lt Nolan. At Sinny Yong I was debriefed then directed to move out the next morning on another patrol of the MSR leading to Uisong. I would leave one rifle platoon at the battalion command post, take the rest of the company, reinforced by two tanks and the necessary motor transport, and conduct a motorized security patrol about 20 miles northward, make contact with the 1st Marine Regiment there and return.

I requested an additional officer—Lieutenant Frank McDonald by name—and he was approved to join us. I assigned him to the 1st Rifle Platoon as relief for

T/Sgt Schmidt who served in that capacity in superior fashion. T/Sgt Schmidt would soon rotate.

Also, on February 13, 1951, we were warding off the fanatic guerrillas at Ha-Hoe-Dong. Over 20,000 Chinese forces made a counterattack in the Wonju area to our north and inflicted another heavy toll on U.S. Army units there. The EEI's (Essential Elements of Information) of these Chinese Army actions do not trickle down to our Battalion S-2 Section (Intelligence). Red Dog Keller's scouts had trouble even getting local intelligence. But the lack of intelligence didn't matter because of the army unit setbacks, we were abruptly pulled back 10 miles to our battalion's assembly area at Sinny Yong. We then were loaded on trucks and driven in convoy through the night through Taegu, then north over treacherous mountain roads (80 miles as the crow flies) to a staging area in the Chung-Ju–Wonju corridor.

*—M.V.P.—*

# The Road to Ha-Hoe-Dong

## Lieutenant Frank McDonald

In February 1951, I joined Baker Company as platoon leader of the 1st Platoon. I had been a platoon leader in Weapons Company, Machine Gun Platoon since Inchon. We had operated with air-cooled light machine guns (LMGs) from Inchon through the Chosin Reservoir battles, and had been equipped with water-cooled heavy machine guns (HMGs) at Masan. During the time we were equipped with the LMGs we operated as an independent platoon or in support of one or several of the rifle companies.

I had served with Lieutenants Hancock, Cronin and Palatas at Yudam-ni on Hill 1240 as part of the perimeter with two LMG Sections from Weapons Company. I was sorry to leave Weapons Company because of the fine men in my group, but I was pleased that Mike Palatas had asked for me to join Baker Company. I soon found out that fine men were not limited to Weapons Company alone, but were distributed in certainly equal measure in Baker Company as well. For a short time, until rotation, Dan Dyer was my Platoon Sergeant, and then came Frank Takeyama!

My first mission in early February with Baker Company was to be a motorized road patrol from Sinny Yong through a mountainous pass and north to either Ulsong or to Andong. This road patrol was part of the anti-guerrilla campaign of the 1st Marine Division. We were to seek out and destroy guerrilla elements of a NKPA division. The patrol had the responsibility to keep open the Yongchon–Andong road in the 5th Marine operating area.

The patrol was made up as:

- 1st Platoon w/Light Machine Gun Section (McDonald)
- 2nd Platoon w/Light Machine Gun Section (Nolan)
- 60mm Mortars—2 Sections
- 2 M-48 Tanks (Stewart)
- 6×6 trucks w/sandbagged beds
- Command Jeep w/commutation to battalion (Palatas)
- Lead Jeep w/radio
- Rear Jeep w/radio

I particularly liked having the tanks along, since I thought the patrol could use armor most effectively in beating down the surprise fire to be expected in a guerrilla-type ambush, for which we were vulnerable in vehicles on roads. Especially, I was, and am to this day, enthusiastic about the powerful support of the 90mm. tank cannon. The potential of this weapon and the tank, with a .50-caliber machine gun, was such that I thought we were a very powerful force indeed.

The patrol was organized so that we could respond to road block or ambush tactics from the front and rear at once.

The line-up was:

- Lead Jeep—me, radioman & driver
- 6×6's sandbagged—1st Platoon & driver
- M-48 tank
- 6×6's sandbagged—60mm Mortar Section & driver
- Command Jeep—Mike Palatas. Battalion Communications & Driver
- 6×6's sandbagged—60mm Mortar section & driver
- M-48 tank
- 6×6's sandbagged—2nd Platoon and driver
- Rear Jeep—Nolan, radioman & driver

The line-up provided good front-to-rear communications, easy dispersal for the rifle platoons and quick availability of the support weapons. Command was facilitated and we had, to repeat, the most welcome assurance of the 90mm cannons on the two tanks. Their firepower in the suppression of surprise fire from road block or ambush would be invaluable. The tanks were a great confidence building factor for the rifle platoons.

We left Sinny Yong at around 08:00 and went through Yongchon and then north into the mountains toward Uihung-Ulsong-Andong. We experienced no trouble at all through Yongchon and northward into the foothills of the mountains.

The mountains are part of the Taebaek chain which broadens out into a mountain and high valley province west of Pohang. The topography gave the guerrilla forces an excellent operations area with plenty of good hiding places in rugged terrain.

Shortly after entering the first part of the mountains

Truck convoy waiting for road clearing on the way to battle (Sydman)

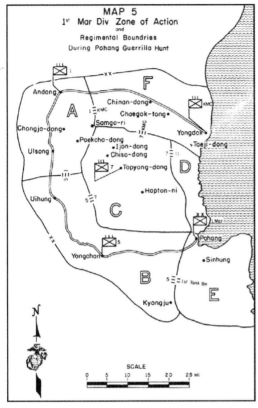

B Company was a motorized road patrol of the mountainous road to Andong (USMC Map)

along the north-bound road after leaving Yongchon, we came up on the rear of a stalled army convoy. This was an administrative convoy with various types of vehicles and no tactical organization. The head of this convoy had received fire from a guerrilla ambush. The convoy had halted to return the fire and to assess the situation. The convoy was blocking our patrol, so I went to the head of the column to offer assistance.

As I passed the rear vehicles on my way forward, I was surprised at the behavior of the men in the convoy. Those in the rear vehicles were just sitting in them and waiting for the men in front of the column to clear away the ambush. No one had gotten out, no one had established security and no one had moved toward the sound of the guns firing up front.

When I got to the head of the convoy, a few brave men, a captain and some NCOs, had driven off the ambush with carbine, M-1 and truck mounted LMG fire. I do not think that out of that large convoy more that 10–15 men were involved in the firefight to defeat the ambush.

I identified our patrol and asked if our Marines could help out? The army captain said "No" he thought they had beaten back the ambush and that they would now continue on. I asked if he would like for us to go ahead in front since we were a tactically organized combat patrol. Surprisingly, the captain said "No" again. They would start up and go ahead. He was a gutsy guy.

I started back to my Jeep to tell Mike Palatas that the army had cleared up its own ambush and that they wanted to go on forward ahead of our patrol. I had barely gotten back to my Jeep when here came the army captain shouting "Hey Marine!" He had thought the better of it, or his NCOs had, and he now wished us to go ahead of his convoy and clear the most difficult parts of the road passage over the mountainous terrain.

The manner of the road climbing and descending in the mountains was by switch-back or long straight or curving grades, and always with good elevation and observation provided from the flanking or frontal hillsides. While we had the tanks to immediately return and suppress hostile surprise fire, the men in the 6×6's especially at the head of the column were extremely vulnerable to surprise fire enfilading the column head on one of the switch-backs or long grades.

To reduce this vulnerability and to increase our ability to immediately use the tank and infantry fire, at critical switch-backs or grades, I had troops get out of the 6×6's in front of the lead tank and walk along the roadside. This way they were less vulnerable to enfilade fire, and they could return fire at once from cover in the ditch or along the hillside.

A Baker Bandit on road patrol though mountainous guerrilla territory (Palatas)

We went along in this manner, in and out of the trucks as the tactical situation demanded, and we passed through the passes, switch-backs and grades with no trouble at all. An occasional guerrilla could be spotted on a ridgeline moving away from us. We received no fire or ambush attempts. I feel to this day that we were not attacked because of the tanks and the dispersed infantry at critical moments. The presence of the tanks gave a feeling of great security.

I had seen the 90mm gun fired on the range at Quantico, and I knew what an excellent offensive potential existed in these guns.

The patrol came out of the mountains with no enemy contact. The road now went down a long straight grade to the village of Ha-Hoe-Dong, passing the near west side of the village, then across a dry wash and into a large, open valley towards Uihung, Ulsong and Andong.

At the top of the hill, looking down the grade to Ha-Hoe-Dong and the large open valley, I felt pretty safe. No more ambush sites were present. The long grade did not have close-by flanking hills, and I had been at Ha-Hoe-Dong twice before with Able Company when they had Weapons Company Heavy Machine Gun Sections attached. There had never been guerrilla activity at this village on either patrols, so I felt at ease.

I was just about to receive a rough lesson!

—Frank—

# The Ha-Hoe-Dong Ambush

## Lieutenant Frank McDonald

The village of Ha-Hoe-Dong sits just to the east of a north–south MSR type road from Yongchon to Wonju via Andon and Chechon. A high valley and dry wash extend eastward from the village up into the mountains.

Along this valley and wash, Able Company had been ambushed on our first patrol in the area, and on the second patrol with Able and Baker Companies, Lieutenant John Hancock had been killed near the village of Chorak. So, we knew that guerrilla units were at Chorak and along the upper part of the valley coming up from Ha-Hoe-Dong. At the culmination of the second patrol in the upper end of that valley, the area had been beaten by artillery fire. I did not anticipate guerrilla activity now at the western end of the valley.

Everybody got back in the trucks and we rolled down the long, straight grade into Ha-Hoe-Dong. As the lead Jeep and the front infantry trucks drew abreast of the village at its west side, things began to happen. I do not, to this day, remember hearing shots or seeing impacts or persons shooting at us, but I sensed that we were under fire. I probably did hear or see, but I can't come up with images. Somehow, I knew we were under fire. I yelled, "Stop, Stop" to the driver and bailed out of the Jeep into the ditch closest to the village. The driver and radio man bailed out across the road to the other side. The 1st platoon was leaping out of the 6×6's on both sides of the roadway and fire was being immediately returned into the village from where the initial surprise fire had originated. I think the leading tank had not yet gotten clear of blocking terrain to be able to open fire.

I remember looking back at the Jeep, and it was vibrating from the impact of hits on it. It had to be towed back to Sinny Yong as a wreck. (This is the Jeep that Mike Palatas says I owe the government!) I then looked at the village, and to my surprise, looked into the face of a guerrilla about 20 yards away. I remember that he had big ears and looked like he needed his adenoids taken out. I snapped a shot at him with my M-1 and went back down in the ditch.

All the fire we had received was from small arms; I do not recall any MG fire. It was now time to get a plan working. I called for Sam DiGiovanni's squad to come on down to me along the ditch, pass through to the north and set up at the wash to fire flanking fire into the village. I think they had a LMG Section with them because the amount of fire put out was a lot.

Sam, with a grin, brought his men down and set up a huge volume of fire. The fire was going into the village on a 7 o'clock–2 o'clock axis. It also sealed off the wash as an escape route. Meanwhile, the rest of the 1st Platoon was firing into the village proper and the lead tank was now in position to fire into the village, also. At this time in the firefight, the fire of the 1st Platoon had defeated and chased away hostile fire coming from the village. I got on the tank battle phone and was immediately asked by the tank commander if I wanted him to fire into the village? Since we were not receiving any more fire, and men were walking upright toward Ha-Hoe-Dong, I said that we did not then require fire into the village. (Some forty years later, Mike Palatas told me that the commander of that tank was Lieutenant Vaughn Stewart. I wish, to this day, that I had taken the opportunity to thank him and his tankers for being with us. The tanks were invaluable as support to the infantry, and the weapons on them awesome.

The 1st Platoon now entered Ha-Hoe-Dong where no dead guerrillas were found. I remember some civilians of the town came out of hiding to make overt gestures of friendship to the Marines. One of the images of that battle is standing with PFC Thomas Baggs, who had just had his baptism to combat, near where I shot at the guerrilla from 20 yards away. We found no blood or body, but I remember thinking to myself what a young tiger Baggs was. Marine training had done a good job on him. He was a good man all the time I was with Baker Company.

Sam DiGiovanni's group kept up fire up the wash to seal off that escape route, but had to cease fire across the village on the 7–2 o'clock axis. It was this fire, along with the frontal fire from the rest of the platoon that drove the guerrillas out of the village and onto the rocky and broken ridgeline to the south of the village. We would be in contact with this force again that night, but for now they were in hiding.

Sam DiGiovanni, a sea-going Marine (Dally)

A word about Sam DiGiovanni is due here. Sam had been a sea-going Marine before the Korean War, and had stayed in the reserves. Called up for Korea, Sam ran into the tender mercies of a reclassification section where the sergeant thought sea duty equaled infantry school, and so Sam showed up in Baker Company. A good-looking Marine, he seemed always to wear a quizzical smile and expression which seemed to say, "I'm sea-going, what am I doing here?"

Sam had that same expression on his face as he came down by me along the ditch, bullets flying all over us. When he got his group in position and opened up, it was irresistible fire superiority. That, and the frontal fire into the village, made it untenable to the NKPA. Maybe Sam put a picture of the reclassification sergeant out in front of his guns and then told his men to fire.

The ambush was now over, the village was ours and only sporadic fire from the hill mass south of the village was incoming. We had no casualties from the ambush. The army convoy now rolled by Ha-Hoe-Dong with all soldiers shouting "Yeah Marine" and so on. They all looked happy that they had let us go ahead.

Because of the surprise of the initial attack from the village right on the Andong-Woju MSR, and the knowledge that the valley did lead back into guerrilla infested country, Mike Palatas communicated with battalion and a new plan evolved. Palatas, and 2nd Platoon, the M-48 tanks and the mortar sections would remain and hold Ha-Hoe-Dong. The 3rd Platoon would come up from Sinn-Yong, and only the 1st Platoon would go ahead into the army military police at Andong and then return to the company at Ha-Hoe-Dong. On our return, Baker Company would be complete and would perimeter the area and secure the road.

No more guerrilla trouble was expected since travel to Andong was over open valley terrain, lacking in ambush sites and was heavily traveled. So Dan Dyer and I took the 1st Platoon in 6×6's up to Andong where we reported in to the Eighth Army Military Police unit responsible for that part of the road net. We reported to a 1st Lieutenant who was astonished that we had a firefight and still had come on through.

We then returned by truck to Ha-Hoe-Dong where the entire company was now assembled in a perimeter defense for the night.

—Frank—

# Night Fight at Ha-Hoe-Dong

## Lieutenant Frank McDonald

In the ambush at Ha-Hoe-Dong, we had suffered no casualties, nor did we receive any hostile fire on the open valley road up to Andong and our return. However, just before leaving the ambush site on our way to Andong, we noticed a Republic of Korea (ROK) truck on the bridge over the wash from which Sam DiGiovanni's squad had delivered the excellent flanking and cut-off fire. The truck was located about 50 yards to the rear of Sam's squad. Cries for help were coming from this truck. Some of us, including some of the army convoy men, went down to the truck to investigate.

A ROK driver who had been captured by the guerrillas was inside the truck and was being beaten and cut with a knife when our patrol came out of the mountains and started down the grade towards them. The guerrillas fled into the village before they could finish torturing and then killing this man. The Marines took him out of the truck and turned him over to Glenn Biddle, our corpsman. As I remember it, he had knife cuts, knife puncture wounds and he had been beaten very badly.

We came back to Ha-Hoe-Dong aster an uneventful patrol (Sydman)

When the army men attempted to move the truck off the bridge so their larger vehicles could continue, a booby trap went off by the left rear wheel. The NKPA guerrillas had time to set this charge before fleeing into the village. I remember hearing the explosion go off, and the next moment I remember is being in the wash below the bridge, scared, no; fast—yes!

We had wounded in that explosion, but thank God, nothing serious. Several Marines and army men had facial and hand wounds.

No fragments penetrated clothing. The blast had ample force, but produced few large sized fragments which could create serious wounding. Marines and army pushed the truck off the bridge, and the rest of the army convoy went on its way.

Dan Dyer and I went on up to Andong with the platoon and came back to Ha-Hoe-Dong in an uneventful patrol. As I mentioned earlier, I had Dan as Platoon Sergeant, actually he was there before I was and then I had Frank Takeyama as Platoon Sergeant. I think. If my memory holds, Dan left the 1st Platoon shortly after we jumped off at Wonju on "Operation *Killer*."

Dan was excellent, a perfect executive to do what had to be done on his own initiative. It was he, with the rest of the platoon, who developed the overwhelming fire superiority directed into the village. That fire permitted the maneuver to set up the flanking and cut-off fire. The fact that we had no casualties in that firefight clearly shows how quickly Dan got fire superiority established. A truly excellent Marine!

After rotation, I did not see Dan again until the Austin Reunion in '87, and then again at Camp Pendleton in '88. The day after the reunion at Pendleton, Dan retired from the Marine Corps Reserve as a Chief Warrant Officer, the best rank in the USMC with forty years of service. When he retired, Lieutenant General E.A. Craig took the salute at that parade and said goodbye to one of his best men.

Meanwhile, back at Ha-Hoe-Dong, the company had established a perimeter around the village. The terrain was difficult to defend. South of their village were two hills that dominated the village. Leading southward from each hill was a terrain saddle that led to a very high ridge with an east–west axis. This ridge provided good observation into parts of the village, the valley leading to high ground east of the village and the broad valley leading up to Andong. The two hills coming southward to this ridge masked any long-range fire that could be delivered to most of Ha-Hoe-Dong. For this reason, the Baker Company perimeter enclosed the village, which dominated attack efforts from the east down the wash, and included the two hills immediately to the south from which plunging fire could dominate the village and the entire perimeter. We expect that the NKPA guerrillas had taken refuge on the very high east–west ridge south of the two hills, and that, from that ridge they could only fire from long range into the two hills and into isolated parts of the village. That fire could be suppressed easily by airstrikes, and, in any case, would not be effective.

We did anticipate that after dark the NKPA might attack from the high ridge northward across the saddles connecting the high ridge to the two hills just south of the village. If they occupied either of the two hills, the plunging and enfilade aspects of their fire would be a disaster. We did not plan on that happening.

The 1st Platoon occupied the two hills south of the village as part of their assigned segment of the perimeter, including the draw between the two hills.

Once we had established the perimeter defense, facing south and looking across the saddles at the high east–west ridge, the night orders were given. These were:

1. No challenges were to be given to any activity or movement coming northward on the saddles.
2. If any activity or movement was detected, we were to open fire on it immediately. There was nothing south or east of us in that terrain compartment but NKPA guerrillas.
3. Alert condition was to be 50 percent, but actually was more because we expected attack.

Frank Takeyama had joined us by then, in anticipation of Dan Dyer's pending rotation. He was in charge of the Marines on the easternmost hill.

We settled in for the night with expectation that the NKPA would attack before morning. Frank had given instructions to all his men to fire alternately, so that two men close together would not have to reload at the same time.

Sometime after midnight, the east hill erupted in a vigorous firefight. The NKPA guerrillas had crossed the eastern saddle and were coming up our perimeter line. Frank Takeyama said you could hear them coming across the saddle. Apparently, they did not know the Marines were there. Someone forgot not to give, or in the tenseness of the moment involuntarily yelled a challenge. At very close range an intense firefight broke out. Frank's men very rapidly established a tremendous fire superiority, a nice habit within the platoon, and in the company also. That ended the attack. The NKPA were gone. Some sporadic firing continued through the night, all at long range. No more attempts were made to cross the saddles or capture the hills.

In the fight we had wounded, but no killed. One of the wounded men, Robert L. Knause, is certainly a very lucky fellow. He was shot seven times in the abdominal cavity, almost always a fatal circumstance. He was hit with fire from a "burp gun," and he was wearing his pile-lined parka. Although the bullets pierced the abdominal wall, they did not penetrate any vital organs or sever arteries or veins. We thought the small "burp gun" cartridge, with slow muzzle velocity and low entry was unable to give bullet penetration through the parka and abdominal wall and still have enough penetrating power to damage internal organs or blood conduits.

Glenn Biddle, our corpsman, worked on him in the darkness, and the young fellow survived to be evacuated the next day. I remember speaking to him at the ambulance in the morning, and hearing the corpsman say it was a miracle he had survived such wounds and that he was in good shape to make a complete recovery, Thank God, I thought!

The result of the guerrilla attack that night was that Frank Takeyama's men killed 13 NKPA. In the morning, Frank's group went forward on the saddle and found the bodies. Also abandoned in the rush to escape our fire superiority was a large-caliber machine-gun cart, a two-wheel trundle type. The guerrillas had intended to seize the eastern hill and to use the large-caliber weapon to fire into the village and perimeter. It cost them 13 men and their cart to find out they couldn't do that to Marines.

I want to say something about Glenn Biddle, our corpsman. There are no combat Marines who do not have great respect for the navy corpsmen who serve in combat with them, so it was with Glenn. He was a compassionate, brave, and loyal young man. He had personality that made it a joy to have him around us. He was at the platoon command post when Knause was hit so badly on the east hill. He crossed over to that hill in the dark, never an easy thing to do with infiltrators and tense, "no challenge" Marines on the alert. He treated that Marine in absolute darkness. Glenn was a brave and dedicated man in the best sense of those words.

In a letter from Hugh Bates, I learned that Glenn was Killed in Action on June 8, 1951, after I had gone home. Hugh has named his first son after Glenn. It was very sad to learn that Glenn was lost.

In the morning, after the firefight, we evacuated the wounded and then prepared to move back to base. We were relieved by a larger force of ROK army units who were to hold Ha-Hoe-Dong and patrol out of it. Baker Company returned to Sinny Yong.

In all our contacts with the enemy, the ambush and the night fight, we were always able to dominate the situation because of our ability to immediately develop overwhelming fire superiority. This ability was a characteristic of Baker Company. The legend of the "Bandits" had in it a quality of aggressiveness that was of very great worth in battle, and no doubt saved many of our own lives. Of course, Marine training in tactics and weapons utilization and "Esprit de Corps" had a lot to do with it as well.

*—Frank—*

# Sinny Yong

## Lieutenant Mike Palatas

It is February 17, 32 degrees, overcast, with light snow cover. B Company is ordered back from Ha-Hoe-Dong to Sinny Yong where Lieutenant Colonel Stephens, the Commanding Officer of the 1st Battalion, 5th Marine Regiment, has established an assembly area. This is done on warning order from higher authority in preparation for a forthcoming major move of the entire 1st Marine Division into central Korea.

The move of B Company from its remote forward defense position at Ha-Hoe-Dong is made by motor convoy. The convoy of 16 2½-ton 6×6 trucks from the 1st Division's Motor Transportation Battalion. Transport Sergeant "Rocky" Williams, the 5th Regiment's Motor Transport Chief oversees the administrative details of the convoy. The distance we are to move is about 15 miles southward and the trip is uneventful. The guerrillas in their mountain enclaves east of Ha-Hoe-Dong have to be overjoyed at our departure.

It was only a month ago when we embarked at the fish-smelling seaport village near Masan (Chinhae). The embarkation was not without incident—though minor. A couple of Bandits from Lt McDonald's 1st Platoon somehow managed to get some "torpedo juice" from an enterprising swabbie and "bombed" out not realizing the power of the concoction on the physiology of the combat-conditioned Marine rifleman.

Aboard the landing ship tank (LST) 679 we enjoyed the amenities the vessel had to offer (the break in routine, hot chow and even eggs to order, and best of all, long hot showers of the salt water kind). This was the beginning of the "Guerrilla Hunt."

The B Company Unit Diary showed our strength at five officers and 155 enlisted men including our attached corpsmen. Our T/O calls for a rifle company strength for war time at 250. Thus we begin this phase of the war at not much more than 60 percent of operational strength.

Now, here at Sinny Yong we close the operation. The relatively few surviving members from the days of Brigadere General Craig's 1st Mar Brigade in the Pusan

Perimeter, have earned their fourth battle star to affix on their Korean Campaign ribbon. A majority too, will wear a Purple Heart. A separate Unit Diary entry shows Staff Sergeant Walter L. Wolfe USMC awarded a Gold Star in lieu of a third Purple Heart Medal.

Sinny Yong is a small village and of no major significance. The main thoroughfare through it is composed of gravel and is narrow—two-lane with the few buildings on main street crowding the road's edge. The "yong" means mountain pass in the map's glossary. Our stay here will be but a brief respite. What one might remember about it was the huge stack of rice-filled bags piled to look like big buildings. These were on the northern edge of our encampment. Official-looking Korean men doled out these rice supplies to other Koreans in the distribution chain and the piles were guarded around the clock to prevent the stores from getting onto hands of irregulars in the mountains.

The business at hand for B Company will occupy all of our key NCOs down to the fire team leader. The busiest will be our 1st Sergeant, Gunnery Sergeant Wright, and our property NCO, Supply Sergeant Willie G. Shoemaker.

Gunnery Sergeant Wright oversees the line-up of B Company in alphabetical order for signing of the payroll. There is the usual grab-ass and skylarking. PFC Corso can be counted on as a ringleader of such mischief. Inside the pyramidal command post tent, the Top is seated on a small folding stool behind his small folding table wearing his bunny-fur hat. He has the pay roster on the table and each man is to sign and designate the amount he wishes to draw or indicate "none." (The actual "pay call" will be held in a couple of weeks time). The pay roster shows what's on the "books" for each officer and enlisted man. A private might wonder at his paltry sum for the risk and deprivation he goes through. Even the sergeants' pay shows less than $70.00 for one month. Most men will let the money "ride" on the "books" since there is no place to spend it in our operational status. Others will draw some monies to engage in a card game or craps if the opportunity presents itself. (SSgt Wolfe always carried a deck of cards for a chance game of pinochle). There was always that private or corporal who carried a poker deck and/or a pair of dice!

We got hot chow here also from the battalion galley set up in the battalion command post area. We also get a rare treat of fresh baked bread from the 1st Marine Division bakery—way back in the "rear." Even though the loaves have been compacted a bit in transit, the bread is a treat with or without the canned butter spread and jam, it's hog heaven.

We haven't showered in a month—since leaving the LST and Pohang we won't get one for another week or so, until the time to complete our move into Central Korea. So, we still bathe with washcloth and steel helmet full of water which isn't always heated.

Working parties are provided to the Battalion Supply Officer. Lieutenant Daly. These are mostly for handling C-rations, ammo replenishment, survey of 782 gear and items of clothing and footwear.

Planners on all levels from Battalion to Division are wrestling with the logistics of our next move, the entire 1st Marine Division (over 20,000 officers and men) into Central Korea.

First Lieutenant Timothy J. Cronin rejoins us from his stint to division as a ROK liaison officer and Lt Palatas is reassigned as executive officer and Cronin is assigned as commanding officer. On the upper levels of leadership and command, changes are also in the mill. Colonel Hayward takes over as commanding officer of the 5th Marines from Colonel Raymond Murray who rotates to U.S.

*JOB WELL DONE, SIR!*

—*M.V.P.*—

# Truck Accident

February 21, 1951 USMC Historical
Diary SECRET Declassified

**Feb. 21.** The first serial was scheduled to depart Chunju at 2230, 20 February, but as the trucks were late, the first serial departure time was 0120, 21FEB and the fourth serial departed at 0215.

The first serial arrived at the assembly area at the city of WONJU at 0620. The last serial, B Company, arrived at about 0720, less one (1) overturned truck and seven (7) other trucks delayed by the accident. Two (2) men were killed and eleven (11) injured in the overturned truck. The 5th Marines in their operation order 5-51 ordered the 1st Battalion to move out from WONJOU, pass through elements of the 187th Airborne Regiment, cross the line of departure at 1000 to seize that portion of Division Objective One in the 5th Marines zone. In spite of the all night truck movement from CHUNGJU, lack of sleep by the men and the fact that elements of B Company had not arrived, the battalion executed orders as scheduled. A and C Companies departed from WONJU in route column at 0835 followed by Weapons Company, Engineer Platoon, H&S Company and B Company to march the distance of three (3) miles from the assembly point to L.D.

# Death on the Road to Wonju

## Lieutenant Mike Palatas

While we were at Chungju, B Company joined Lieutenants Ables and Cowart, plus numerous good men, who are yet to receive their "baptism by fire." Our own Lieutenant Colonel Stephens will be relieved by a newly promoted Lieutenant Colonel Hopkins out of the 3rd Battalion. We get to see the replacements for "Ole Top" Dierickx and Gunnery Sergeant Wright. These are a non-smiling and serious-looking Master Sergeant Heacock who wears an unkept black menacing-looking mustache and an amicable and eager-appearing Gunnery Sergeant Long. Both are tried veterans of World War II. Our own heroes like Lischeski, Schmidt, Lyles, Palmer (our field music), and a dozen more will leave us here to rotate to Conus. The Jeep that brought a smiling Lieutenant Cronin to our command post was driven by Transportation Sergeant "Rocky" Williams.

We were caravaning and then dust in the air and a jeep and a 6x6 roll-over (Sydman)

"Rocky," nursing his cigar butt, sought me out to inform me that we should break our company down into 13-man truck loads and that our move, a night move at that, was to go through the mountains a long distance to a town of Wong-ju and the move was imminent.

On February 20, 1951, the battalion commenced preparation at 0800 for the overnight trip to Wonju. It was one of those grey winter days. The afternoon air was filled with monoxide fumes. The division NCO designated as "Roadmaster" went down our line of trucks and designated which drivers would have their lights on. It was every fifth vehicle, a tactic to deceive or confuse any enemy intelligence gatherers when the long convoy wended its way across the mountains northward. The rest of the vehicles used their blackout lights.

Our move was not made without incident and casualties! I rode in the passenger seat. My truck's engine sounded like it wouldn't get very far. It idles so rough! Sometime during the night of February 21, 1951 and in between dozes, we came to a crawl, moving very slowly. Just ahead, but not yet seen was a sharp curve in the road (these roads were all gravel or sometimes just dirt and mud). When we reached the curve, a pallor of dust hung in the air. A Jeep had its lights facing the darkness downhill and not far down a 6×6 rested on its top. Marines were scrambling downhill to render assistance. I knew men were hurt and/or killed in this unfortunate accident. The truck driver negotiated the turn too sharply and the left-side wheels dropped over the embankment causing the truck to roll.

Sometime the next morning we arrived at our destination, but we really had no idea of where we were or how we got here.

—*M.V.P.*—

*A Note from Ole Emmett: We all remember riding in a 6×6 on roads meant for an oxcart. The truck just barely fit and the roadway dropped away on one side or the other. I have had several men tell me of that fateful night when the truck ran off the road and overturned. A piercing plea came through the darkness as one of the men pinned under the truck begged to be put out of his misery. I understand that he later died. This made a real impression on the minds of lots of young Marines.*

# A Mine Caused the Truck Accident

## Private Bill Dove

The article about our Commanding Officer Lieutenant John Hancock brought back a lot of memories that I try to forget. I guarded his body that night as he lay lifeless on the Jeep.

As I read the story, I could see the tank that arrived to give supporting fire to the ones on the high ground.

In reference to Lieutenant Mike Palatas' story on the truck accident, I would like to give another version and what happened to the injured.

As you know, most of us were asleep as we made the journey that terrible night of February 21, 1951. As usual, the sounds of artillery could be heard all through the night.

I don't know what hit me in my sleep but, when I regained consciousness, I was on a stretcher on the road, there were two live Marines, and two dead Marines, on stretchers next to me. I asked the two live Marines beside me what happened? Both remarked, they heard a small explosion that sounded like a land mine or a blown tire. I have accepted this story all of my life. I can remember and see the curve, as though it was yesterday.

As told to me recently by a Baker Bandit by way of e-mail, he had yet another story. I don't guess we'll ever know what really happened, but I'd have to go with the two Marines that were there. We hit a small mine on the side of the road.

Reason being, it was a nice curve, but it had plenty of room. The driver had no need to drive off the road. I do think he got too close to the shoulder. We hit a small mine, the ground gave way and the truck rolled over. The only reason I settle on this version is for the driver's peace of mind!

Unknown to us at this time, we were about to begin a long journey of which we can tell our grandchildren. They loaded us into an ambulance and proceeded to an army medical station behind the lines. While en route, the driver took a wrong turn and we met with small-arms fire from the enemy. One driver returned the fire while the other was frantically trying to turn the vehicle around. All this time, we lay helpless on the stretchers in the back of the ambulance. The Lord must have been on our side, because we made it to the medical aid station.

When we arrived, I was placed in a tent full of Chinese prisoners. From what I could see, most were suffering from frostbite. I lay there for about three or four hours waiting to be killed by the enemy before being seen by an army doctor. He decided that I should be moved by train to Pusan, where two hospital ships were docked, the USS *Constellation* and the USS *Repose*.

Both of my legs were placed in temporary casts which stuck out about six inches from the ends of my feet, making it impossible to stand or walk in case of an emergency. I was placed on the train, and as the train began to move, I felt renewed and safe for the first time in quite awhile.

Several hours later, as we rounded a curve, I could see a flat bed truck with ROK soldiers, sandbag fortifications and a machine gun sitting beside the tracks.

As we moved peacefully southward, it dawned on me—my insulated boots were gone! The military was taught a lesson during the winter of '50 when we only had those rubber shoepacs. They began issuing Thermo Boots at Pusan to prevent frostbite. The army had relieved me of mine at the Med Station.

Suddenly, out of the quietness came a loud explosion… the shattering of glass and I felt the train car leave the tracks and gently roll over on its side. I'm not sure how, but I found myself out of the car and on the ground. I'm do not remember anyone able to help me out and I could not walk… but I was out. I had survived yet another ordeal. The Lord surely must have had something in store for me!

I was then loaded into another truck and transported to the Hospital Ship *Constellation*. To get me aboard they lowered four ropes, which looked a mile long to me, with concrete below. These ropes were attached to my stretcher and I was pulled up to the deck. I've been scared of heights ever since!

*Editor's note: Bill doesn't say what happened next, but I know that after he recovered from his injuries, he went back to B Company in Korea. One young Marine PFC John A. Evans, Jr, survived with injuries, but the other another, PFC Wilbur B. Gray, died in that 6×6 overturn of February 21, 1951. May He Rest In Peace.*

# B-1-5 Casualties and Medals— February 1951

## Killed in Action

*Confirmed through Korean War Project*

1LT John Hancock, from Craig, Nebraska          KIA    7FEB51 Silver Star
CPL Henry C. Eggenberger, E. White Plains, NY   KIA    24FEB51

## Wounded in Action

*Confirmed through USMC Unit Diaries*

CPL Carl L. Cash                WIA    7FEB51
PFC Daniel Garza               WIA    7FEB51
CPL William D. Nesmith         WIA    7FEB51
SGT Francis P. Hogan           WIA    7FEB51
CPL Cecil K. Lambright Jr.     WIA    7FEB51
CPL Tommie S. Ray              WIA    7FEB51
CPL Hugh M. Bates              WIA    7FEB51
PFC Charles J. Murphy          WIA    23FEB51
PFC John A. Evans, Jr.         WIA    21FEB51
                                      (truck accident)

## Killed Accidentally

PFC Wilbur B. Gray, from Austin, Texas    KIA    23FEB51
                                                 (truck accident)

# Silver Star

First Lieutenant John Hancock (Posthumously)

The President of the United States of America takes pride in presenting the Silver Star (Posthumously) to First Lieutenant John Richard Hancock, United States Marine Corps, for conspicuous gallantry and intrepidity as Commanding Officer of Company B, 1st Battalion, 5th Marines, 1st Marine Division (Reinforced), in action against enemy aggressor forces in Korea from November 28 to December 11, 1950. On November 28, when his company was ordered to occupy and defend a ridge overlooking Yudam-ni, First Lieutenant Hancock personally reconnoitered the ridge, returned to lead his men up its slope, and succeeded in relieving elements of a friendly unit under heavy fire. Successfully directing the attack of two of his platoons, he aided his company in attaining defensible ground and in preventing the enemy from firing into the regimental area. For three nights and two days he directed the fighting of his company against a numerically superior hostile force which occupied well-concealed positions on commanding ground. Foregoing rest, and despite badly frostbitten feet, he courageously exposed himself to heavy enemy fire, guiding and controlling the defense of his positions and supervising the evacuation of casualties. On December 1, after having covered the movement of other regimental units, he was ordered to withdraw his company, the last unit to leave the original regimental defense perimeter. Despite a lack of artillery and air support, and although the enemy was in immediate pursuit and rapidly gaining advantageous firing positions, he successfully covered the movement by the skillful use of machine-gun fire. On December 7, when a strong hostile force penetrated the regimental defense perimeter and he was ordered to reinforce the unit under attack, he personally led his platoons into the penetrated areas during sub-zero temperatures and darkness, reformed the defense line and guided his sector in the repulse of the hostile assault. His daring initiative, outstanding leadership and superb courage in the face of enemy fire reflect the highest credit upon First Lieutenant Hancock and the United States Naval Service.

# Operation *Killer* Begins—March 1951

## Lieutenant Frank McDonald

While in Wonju, the 1st Marine Division left the 10th Corps and became part of the 9th Corps and part of the Eighth Army under General M.B. Ridgeway.

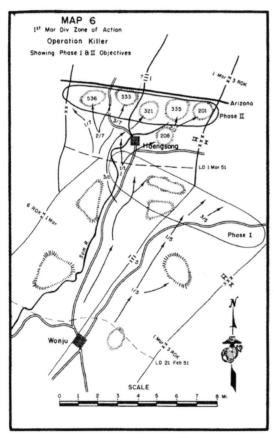

We were to go on the offensive in an attack named "Operation *Killer.*" The attack concept was the limited offensive, combining our superior fire power, air support power and ability to maneuver to offset the Chinese advantage in numbers. The operation was to be a great success, and the 1st Marine Division was a major participant.

We jumped off from Wonju in late February–early March. As we left Wonju, the Marines in Baker Company turned in their winter parkas. We had made it through the Korean winter. It would still be cold, but with sweaters, field jackets and gloves, we would be warm. Spring was just ahead and so was some magnificent campaigning.

—*Frank*—

We turned in our parkas and jumped off on Operation *Killer*
(USMC MAP)

# Close Call in Operation *Killer*

## Corporal H. J. "Syd" Sydnam

After we returned to company-sized patrol advances, probably in early March 1951, I had a close call. We caught up to a main body of the enemy and encountered fierce resistance from our front. There happened to be a Marine Corps Photographer with my squad at that time and his presence served to heighten the squad's chatter and activities. Hidy and Nail were hunkering down behind a couple of large boulders. Hidy popped up now and then to do some shooting while Nail was busy shooting rifle grenades over to where very hot small-arms fire was coming at us.

It was a very hot zone and we were all telling the photographer how we planned to "charge over the top" and take the enemy when Nolan yelled down for Hidy to come up to him. The slope Hidy had to climb was quite exposed to enemy fire. He took off running full-speed up the open slope with the photographer snapping pictures and suddenly Hidy stopped, turned around and ran back to us, saying "I forgot my rifle!" Then he took off again up the slope. When he returned, the firing had died down a bit. He said, "Syd, you are to take your squad out front along that ridge and see how far you can go. There is an airstrike called in for later so be sure that you have air-panels." Now, his delivery was incredulous and so was our reception! None of us, especially the photographer, could believe anyone could cross to the forward slope and live! However, we set out and drew very little fire. We progressed quite a long way out ahead of the company, perhaps

Hidy and Nail were hunkering down behind some boulders (Sydman)

a mile or more and the lack of resistance was unbelievable after how hot it had been such a short time before.

I was quite far ahead of the rest of the squad and Hidy, who had come along with us, was the next man behind me. As I negotiated a dip in the ridge, where a path crossed it, I received "incoming" from my lower right front. I spotted an enemy armed with a burp gun in a paddy drainage ditch perhaps 100 yards from me. I fired my rifle at him and could see a splash of mud from where I missed him. Thinking that if I walked my rounds into him, I could keep him pinned until I could take him out, I kept a rather steady fire going, as my splashes grew closer. Suddenly, he popped up and let loose a burst from his machine gun and I heard a great, metallic, "clang!" from my helmet as I pitched backwards onto the reverse slope. I sat there a moment thinking I had been hit in the head and feeling for holes and flowing blood. My ears rang far louder than usual and I very gingerly removed my helmet and felt my skull. When I could find no wounds, holes or blood I checked a lot closer and saw that I had a bullet hole in my helmet strap which had been just forward of my left ear!

About this time, Hidy was coming up on the dip in the ridge and I yelled to him to "Watch it, it's hot there!" just as a burst of fire went past him. I really didn't want to stick my head up over the ridge again so I told him that I would pitch a grenade down there to flush the enemy out if he would shoot him. That worked. After we had gone a bit further, we decided that we had exceeded our instructions and we returned to the company's area. There, I found that both ends of my shelter half, which was rolled on top of my pack, and both sides of my parka hood had been shot through! The bullets had passed me just above shoulder-level lacing my gear on both sides of my head. It could not have been closer without killing me! When we left "the beach" months later to return home, I cut those straps off of my helmet. I still have them, with a burp-gun cartridge thrust through the hole, as souvenirs of one of my closest calls.

*—Syd—*

# B-1-5 Casualties and Medals— March 1951

## Killed in Action

*Confirmed through Korean War Project*

PFC Hugh McKenna, from College Point, NY   KIA    29MAR51

2LT Carey S. Cowart, Jr., from Tulsa, Okla.    DOW  22MAR51 Silver Star

## Silver Star

Second Lieutenant Carey Shaw Cowart, Jr.

The President of the United States of America takes pleasure in presenting the Silver Star to Second Lieutenant Carey Shaw Cowart, Jr., United States Marine Corps, for conspicuous gallantry and intrepidity as Leader of a 60mm Mortar Section of Company B, 1st Battalion, 5th Marines, 1st Marine Division (Reinforced), in action against enemy aggressor forces in Korea on March 20, 1951. Participating in a company attack against a series of strongly defended hostile positions in difficult terrain when automatic weapons and small-arms fire temporarily halted the advance, Second Lieutenant Cowart immediately placed his section in tactical positions to deliver supporting fire and boldly moved forward to direct the firing. With visibility limited by several small forest fires which were burning in the area, he advanced to the forward slope of a fire-swept ridge from which he could observe more effectively. Courageously refusing to seek cover, he remained in his exposed position and continued adjusting accurate fire until he fell mortally wounded. His cool leadership, tactical skill and indomitable courage were contributing factors in permitting the company to maneuver successfully and seize the hostile emplacements, thereby reflecting great credit upon Second Lieutenant Coward and the United States Naval Service. He gallantly gave his life for his country.

# Massacre Valley—January–May 1951

## Corporal Emmett Shelton, Jr.

I've heard Bandits tell of recovery work in a place called "Massacre Valley," also another called, "Slaughter Valley." These two places involved army troops. One of them was troops on line, and a battalion in rear echelon in warm weather. The other was a convoy in cold weather. After each incident, the army sent some officers and had Marines sign forms that said we would not divulge anything of what happened. Does anyone remember? It was a great tragedy.

*—Emmett—*

### Private Bill Dove

In January or February of '51, as we made our way north, we came upon an army camp that had been overrun by the enemy. I think about what we saw that

Men of B-1-5 inspect a downed helicopter (Sydman)

day and wonder what outfit it was, and if there were any survivors, what story would they have to tell.

As we entered the command post area, it was as quiet as death. The command tents stood empty and silent as the entrance flaps waved slowly in the breeze. On the ground over a wide area, lay hundreds of pictures of loved ones. It was a though the enemy assembled here to celebrate their victory and decide what pictures to keep and what to throw on the cold ground, never to be viewed again by the owners.

As we made our way to the Main Line of Defense on the high ground, bodies lay motionless, everywhere, stripped of their weapons, gear, and clothing.

As we made our way to the low ground, we were met by a downed helicopter, stripped of its radio and the pilot who had flown his last mission.

We entered two huts, both of which contained two bodies each, all in the sitting position. It looked as though the few had escaped to the safe haven of these huts only to be shot or die of their wounds. GOD BLESS & SEMPER FI,

*—Bill—*

## Private Don Roush

Massacre Valley is something I can never forget. This is where the U.S. Army 38th Regiment, 2nd Division was overrun and lost 1,000 men. Our Battalion went through this area May 23–24, 1951.

Our Battalion was in reserve near Hongchon. We left May 22 to move up and reinforce the line. We traveled part of the way by truck. Soon after we got off the trucks, we came to a creek and filled our canteens. We hadn't gone far when the word was passed "Bad Water" and to empty our canteens. Up ahead the creek was littered with dead Chinese.

We saw many enemy and G.I. dead and also a helicopter that had crashed. Bobby Hickey, a Jeep driver, told us that he and another fellow rescued an army major who was wounded in the leg. They found him in a house with a South Korean family. They carried him out using their arms as a stretcher.

As we went through this area, we came to a small hut. Inside was a G.I. that they had hung up by one knee and bayoneted him in the throat. Someone cut him down. I can never forget.

*—Don—*

## Corporal Vinton H. Sholl

Mention of "Massacre Valley" has brought back memories from the dim past and I thought I'd pass them on.

I was 1st Squad Leader, Second Section, Heavy Machine Guns, Weapons Company, 1st Battalion, 5th Division, in May of 1951.

We entered this river valley with elements of the battalion, one afternoon. I was told to dig in the gun and afterward I could give the squad permission to go swimming. We did that, but orders came down to pick up and move out. There was the customary bitching and complaining as only half the squad had been able to swim after digging our foxholes and a "horse-shoe" gun position.

Some miles down the road, we came across a burned-out Jeep heading our way with three dead army soldiers in it. Farther in the main regiment area, there was complete havoc, burned squad tents, wrecked equipment, and bodies.

Memories fade over the years, but I think we were all in a state of shock over the devastation to a unit of this size. Of course, all sorts of stories came drifting by.

There were high ridgelines on each side of this valley and of course we had to struggle up to the top to set up defenses, although by this time it was nearly dark. During the climb, we passed a foxhole with three army boys, still there. Their throats had been cut without question. I remember wondering what kind of leadership would permit a position only halfway up the slope? I had no trouble getting my guys to the crest after seeing that!

The next few days, we kept moving along the ridgelines and finding bodies. I remember being told that one of the companies found several dead army guys, hands tied behind them.

I believe, later we caught up to the enemy one afternoon digging in on a cross ridge quite a way in front. The 11th Marines (Artillery) F.O. called in a proximity fuse barrage fire, for effect. It caught them completely by surprise and it was devastating to them. It's hard to remember details after forty-some years, but the shock of the scenes; the number of dead, the devastation will never fade.

I had a very deep appreciation of being a <u>Marine</u> after that because, I knew our officers would have never permitted such weak defensive positions in the first place. God bless all who died.

—*Vinton*—

## Lieutenant Angus Deming

You might be interested in yet another version. In May 1951, various units of the 5th Marines made a grim discovery in Korea one day—the remnants of a U.S. Army battalion that had been overrun by the Chinese and virtually wiped out. This was once the 2nd Battalion of the 2nd Infantry Division, 38th Infantry Regiment. The massacre—for that was what it was—took place during the Second Chinese Spring Offensive of 1951. I have heard various accounts of this story from Marines who were in all three companies of the Marines 1/5 (Able, Baker and Charlie). I served in 2/5 as a rifle platoon leader in Easy Company. I would like to add my own account of what many of us saw, as I believe my platoon, 2nd Platoon, may have been the first to arrive on the scene.

Easy Company had been tasked to lead 2-5's advance that day and my platoon had the Point. The morning was sunny and mild. A couple of tanks from the Tank Battalion provided support. We trudged up a seemingly peaceful valley, along a narrow dirt road bordering a wide and swift flowing stream. No one had given us a clue as to what to expect up ahead. We were prepared for anything, or so we thought.

As we approached, I began to notice things scattered on the ground. First, I saw some "Indian head" shoulder patches, the insignia of the Army's 2nd Infantry Division. We were familiar with that outfit, as we had often served in the same sector with it on the East Central Front. Then, I saw some U.S. Army field manuals littered on the ground and a helmet liner. Why were these shoulder patches lying in the dirt, I wondered, and why here, in this no-man's land? There was something creepy about it, and it made me distinctly uneasy.

As we proceeded up the road—very cautiously, now—we suddenly heard someone, who sounded like an American. Then, we saw him: an American soldier, in olive drab trousers and dirty white shirt, waving weakly to us from the opposite bank of the stream. He seemed to be lying in a sort of improvised cave or shelter in the river bank. Then, about 50 feet upstream, we saw another soldier waving to us. Both of them had somehow survived the Chinese assault that had overwhelmed their battalion several days earlier, on May 17. They had hidden beside the stream, hoping against hope that other U.N. troops might eventually rescue them. You can imagine how they must have felt, seeing a platoon of Marines arrives just in the nick of time.

The two men were in pretty bad shape. They had survived on scraps of food. They were undernourished, exhausted and had lain exposed to the elements for days and nights on end. Too weak and disoriented to find their way to army or Marine positions—and not knowing where friendly lines were, anyway—they had remained near their devastated battalion command post. Both men were traumatized by the surprise attack that had all but wiped out their battalion, and by the ordeal of trying to survive. They shook and trembled uncontrollably as we gently placed them on stretchers and prepared them to be evacuated to a MASH unit. Their war was over, but they would probably never forget the terror of being overrun in their last battle.

Up around a bend in the river, we came upon another scene: the remnants of the battalion command post. Bodies littered the ground—dead American soldiers (no Chinese), quite a sight.

While I was on the radio reporting the gruesome scene to our battalion S-3 (the legendary Major Gerald P. Averill), some of the men in my platoon fanned out and reconnoitered the area. Just around another little bend they found the battalion command tent. The body of the battalion commander, a lieutenant colonel, was still in it. Some said the Chinese had propped him up with a bottle of whiskey in front of him, to make it look as though they'd caught him drinking when they launched their attack.

My platoon and I were not able to linger for long on the scene. After I radioed in my report and had seen to it that any survivors were evacuated and cared for, we were ordered to move on to the next objective. I never had time to question the two traumatized soldiers at any length, though I'm not sure they'd have had the strength or will to answer very many questions at that point.

I know that others in the 5th Marines discovered bodies of American soldiers in foxholes in the hills above the battalion command post, along with abandoned equipment. ("Mess Kit Hill" is how Marines from Charlie Company, I believe, dubbed one gear-strewn scene. Others called it "Quartermaster Hill,") but to this day, I still don't know how many men in the battalion were killed, how many were wounded, how many survived or were able to make it to safety? Nor do I really know how the Chinese managed to make such quick work of an entire battalion. I have looked in histories of the Korean War—including the unit history of the 2nd Infantry Division—but have found no mention in any of them of the disaster that befell the 2nd Battalion, 38th Infantry Regiment, back in May 1951. I think there should be a record. Bless them.

*—Angus—*

# Hwachon—Hill 313, April 1951

My thanks for what you did for our country and corps. The chips were down and you proved your worth.

Baker Company sets an example for all other great Marine rifle companies. You fought in many bitter battles from the Pusan Perimeter and on to Inchon, Seoul, Wonsan and the Chosin. Most of you here today made the whole circuit.

**I am so proud of your service.**

You were front line troops. The outcome of every battle depended on you. You endured great hardships and danger. Many of you here today carry the scars of war that you can never forget. You are the survivors of a company that despite very heavy casualties, always took its objective. Many paid the supreme sacrifice and today you honor those heroes and keep their memory bright.

Baker Company lives on, because it made history for our nation in its time of need, and because you are here today to remember. God Bless you All.

Semper Fidelis,
*—Edward Craig—*
*Lieutenant General Edward A. Craig,*
*USMC Retired, March 1987*

# Hill 313—Hwachon

## USMC Historical Diary for the Month of April 1951 ~~SECRET~~ Declassified

**April 22** After an active day securing multiple objectives, Company A, B and C had made considerable progress. However, at 1940, Regimental S-2 received a statement by a wounded Chinese POW that 3 enemy regiments were planning to attack tonight in the zone of the KMC from the northeast. All of B Company was on the high ground of Hill 313 and advised of the pending attack.

**April 23** At 0230, Regimental reported 300 enemy had penetrated the KMC lines moving towards Hill 313. This hill constituted the commanding ground overlooking the city of Hwachon. The hill was very steep with narrow pathways and cover was non-existent. Possession of Hill 313 by enemy forces would have constituted a very real threat to the 1st Battalion, B Company tanks and to the 2nd Battalion, 11th Marines who were below the city. On approaching Hill 313, B Company was engaged by 200 enemy troops that had occupied the hill. Tanks were in position. A platoon clambered up the steep slope and, about 30 yards from the summit, heavy fire opened up with a deadly shower of grenades. The platoon moved down the slope and reorganized. The platoon made another assault also in the dark with bayonets fixed. Again the platoon was thrown back with heavy casualties. Supporting fire from B Company tanks, mortar and heavy machine-gun fire was brought down on the enemy. At dawn, the platoon, which now numbered only 15 men, once more stormed up the hill and drove the enemy from Hill 313. At 0645 Hill 313 was secured with 7 KIA and 23 WIA suffered by B Company. The more seriously wounded were evacuated by 2 helicopters.

**April 24** In the early morning, Chinese crept up and launched a grenade volley—then attacked with small-arms fire. Hand to hand fighting ensued. By 0100, A Company suffered an additional 3 KIA and 17 WIA.

NOTE: By the end of March 1951, although the Marine Corps had meanwhile almost tripled its active duty strength of 30 June 1950, reservists comprised 45 percent of the Marine Corps total active duty strength. By the end of April 1951, the reserve had hit its peak strength during the Korean conflict—859,538 reserves on active duty.

# My Last Battle in Korea Was on Hill 313

## Private Harlan Pope

*Hill 313 was where my tenure in Korea and my Marine Corps career came to a sudden halt. In the early morning of April 23, 1951, I left the rear base of this hill in a wire basket on the starboard side of a south-bound chopper. There was another Marine (I never knew who he was) in a basket on the port side.*

The day before was Sunday April 22 and we moved through a small valley. The day was cool, but dry and field jackets were comfortable. Late Sunday afternoon we were on the Main Line of Resistance (MLR). Sometime before dark, we halted, a short time later the Second Platoon started to the rear to be in reserve. Second Platoon supporting weapons went with them, which was standard operating procedure. We did not travel a great distance when we stopped on flat ground, but we <u>did not</u> dig in! Around midnight we were roused from sleeping bags and advised that we were moving out to higher ground. We also were told to leave everything but our sleeping bags and weapons. I don't recall any <u>racing</u>. We moved

Men of B-1-5 check the map (Palatas)

out in column with no loose gear rattling. I can't recall the distance, but do not believe it was more than maybe an hour's walk.

There were positions on Hill 313 from all the push and shove of the previous summer. We were doing our best to get to these positions before the Chinese, however, they beat us there and really sucked us in. We were moving up a trail in a column, my machine-gun squad was somewhat to the rear. A number of riflemen were ahead of us and there was a great deal of firing, but well away from us, it was still dark and it just happened that I was carrying the machine gun when all of a sudden, I saw the muzzle blast of an automatic weapon and he wasn't more than eight or 10 feet away! We scattered like a covey of quail. I lay down on my back and drew my .45 pistol with my machine gun lying across my mid-section. If any of the bastards had stood up I would have them outlined against the sky, but they elected not to come out after us.

Some time later, Lieutenant Nolan got things organized and sent a squad around each side of the crest and another squad straight up the middle. Pfc Dell Green was a forward scout. He was hit and spent most of the remainder of the night hanging onto a stump and kicking those damn potato masher grenades away from him. My section leader had me set up my gun for covering fire. Mainly in an attempt to keep the Chinese heads down. I fired several boxes of ammo and word was passed down to cease fire, as machine-gun rounds were ricocheting off the hill and back into our own people. Hell, the boulders up there were as big as a six-room house. Prior to this time, Weapons Company had sent up some heavy water-cooled .30s, so we must have had eight or 10 guns going by then.

Lt Pat McGahn and men of B-1-5 (Palatas)

There were steel transmission towers going across country carrying electrical power lines coming across Hill 313. I shifted my fire to the left connecting ridge to estimated (it was still prior to daybreak) ground level. I figured that if our people could push them off, hell, they would have to come through my fire. Come daybreak though, we had the hill. After a tough day at battle on Hill 313, Commanding Officer Lt Charlie Cooper was briefing

B Company on the day's actions, Lt McGahn stood up and said, "Sir, if we make it out alive, I'm going to invite everyone to one hell of a party in Atlantic City." The B Company men were dog tired but most chuckled at the idea of a party. Pat was seriously wounded in an intense battle the next day. His heroism earned him a Navy Cross.

After full light, my squad was preparing to move out and stopped by the platoon command post. There were three or four Marine bodies covered by ponchos. One was raised and it was a friend, Corpsman Sutton, who was from Shawnee, Oklahoma. This was a blow to me. He was being held COG (Convenience of the Government) because his enlistment had expired. He had died attempting to save two Marines. The result being he, and the two Marines, all died.

About 10 minutes later, while moving out, I was hit hard by one of our tanks at the base of the hill. I have been told it was due to an order from a certain Lieutenant Colonel. I will not elaborate because it would be hearsay on my part. I would like to remember this Marine Officer as a man who tried to look after his men. I know he must have been a fine officer or he wouldn't have held the command that he had, maybe I'm wrong.

One more note: When I was hit, I came to my senses with two corpsmen working on me. I was worrying hell out of both of them because I had lost my damn machine gun! I could just hear Ole Waldo, "The only asshole I ever had who could lose a goddamn machine gun!" (Waldo had rotated back stateside, but he still held me in fear of his wrath.) I was told later that my gun was found sticking muzzle into the ground and was put back in action immediately, with no damage. I never saw it again. I never saw my friends again until our reunion in Austin, Texas, 36 years later.

I do not know if Corpsman Sutton's family received any award in his name, but I feel he should have at least been awarded the "Silver Star." Maybe even a higher award was in order.

Sutton saved Dell Green's life too, and others that night. I will not single out Sutton, as all of our corpsmen were damn fine and dedicated men, but on this dark morning, he went a little above and beyond in this Marine's eyes.

Hill 313, seven dead, 17 wounded. All good men, all Marine buddies!

—Harlan—

# FMF Corpsman

## Chuck Hall, 1990

The navy calls them corpsmen,
Though they seldom saw a ship
Their major tools of battle,
They carried on their hip

Trained to go with field Marines,
In every clime and place
They risked their lives most every day,
With compassion, skill and grace

Where they found these people,
I'll never understand
A breed apart from other men,
Serving in this foreign land

To hear the cry of "Corpsman,"
Would chill you to the bone
As these brave men came running up,
Unarmed and all alone

They saved the many wounded,
And stood along their side
Without these valorous corpsmen,
A lot more would have died

We dearly love our corpsmen,
And defend them to this day
As much Marine as navy,
They served a special way

When they get to Heaven,
And streets filled with Marines
We'll call out for our corpsmen,
And show them all our scenes

# Wishes Do Come True—Sometimes

## Private Jim "Poodles" Redding

Many of us from the 1951 "Bandits" remember a Marine we called "Big Smith" (Private Gerald Schmitz). Ole "Big Smith" was really getting tired of climbing those awful Korean hills in the face of enemy fire.

One day, as we were about to jump off on yet another assault up another hill and the enemy was not going to let us just walk up and take it (as it turned out, this was Hill 313), "Big Smith" said, "I'd give one of my legs to get out of this hell hole!"

With that, we jumped off. Later that morning, here came "Big Smith" back down that hill on a stretcher with one leg all shot to hell. He had a million-dollar wound.

When I was rotated back, I saw "Big Smith" while on liberty in Osaka, Japan, AND HE HAD BOTH LEGS!

**Thank a corpsman!**

*—Poodles—*

# Thanks to Lieutenant Pat McGahn

## Private Gene Keyton

Dear Lt Pat McGahn,

I was recovering from a heart attack at the Wala Wala, Washington VA Hospital when I was looking through some Readers Digests and with the first paragraph on you, I set off the monitor.

I am Gene M. Keyton, on that morning, April the 23rd I was a private, 5th ammo carrier, under your machine-gun squad leader Corporal Raymond F. Hill. We were following you up Hill 313 to see what happened to the Korean 6th Division which had vanished. Two men were out forward on each side and you were leading the main body when we were hit with heavy automatic fire.

I thank you for saving my life, because I was ready to run and I'll bet others were too. But you dived for a depression and we all followed you, and the fire went mostly over us, but heavier than any movie firefight that I have ever seen. I saw the grenade come in that hit you. I'm sure it was a concussion-type. Blood came out of your eyes like a horny toad. I thought you were blinded.

When the incoming fire died down, the Marine on the right side out front was groaning. I was too scared to talk, but I was the only one big enough to get him, so I left my carbine and went out to get him and I got shot in the ankle.

Corporal Hill and I both went and got the Marine on the left side, but he didn't have a chance. Later that morning, Cpl Hill was shot and killed. He was very nice to me.

You and Sergeant Donald J. Garrett performed a miracle in getting us over the top of that hill and in position to, as one Marine said, "Have a Turkey Shoot." Considering enemy fire coming at you from one side, and friendly tank fire coming from the other side, I guess your commanding officer just didn't believe you could take that hill.

I want to thank you for being a part of American and Marine Corps history.

*—Gene—*

# Marine Taken Prisoner of War

From Vol. 1, No. 10 of the *Haven Herald*. Published aboard the USS *Haven*, May 27, 1951

One of the most interesting stories that we have come across is that of PFC Bernard W. Insco, USMC, who hails from the Buckeye state of Ohio.

Bernie, as he was called aboard ship, was born in Cincinnati, Ohio on May 27, 1932. He grew up there and attended Roosevelt High School in Dayton, Ohio, incidentally, it seems fitting that we should tell his story on his birthday.

He entered the Marine Corps on September 1, 1949, and on August 18, 1950, he embarked for Korea.

Insco first heard the noise of battle during the landing at Inchon. From here on in, his was the path of the traditional Marine, getting hit, but more usually hitting first. His team was put into operation at Majoni where it became isolated and necessitated the airlifting of supplies. The army fought their way to them and relieved them on November 19. The Chosin Reservoir marks the spot where they met their first real Red Chinese resistance. He was in the famous march down to Hamhung. He rested at Masan from December 15 until January 5, 1951. At this time his outfit shoved off for Pohang and a little later to Wonju. It was at this time that he was given the job of forward observer in the 3rd Battalion for the 1st Regiment for Operations *Killer* and *Ripper*. These being brought to a successful completion, he, along with other men with the 2nd Battalion of the 11th Regiment in Hwachon, was attached to the Korean Marine Corps as forward observers.

On the evening of April 22, 1951 at about 2000 hours, the blare of bugles broke the silence. The rattle of automatic weapons fire punctuated the bugle calls, Private Insco and his six companions jumped into a dugout. The battle was on and it continued into the night. At about 0400 hours it slackened and the men decided to make a run for their own lines.

It now being dark, the men stumbled over everything. Insco hit a tree, was knocked down, but recovered and started running again, only to discover that he had lost his weapons! At that moment, he noticed two figures coming over the hill. Thinking they were friendly, he yelled, "11th Company KMC!" A burst of fire from a "burp gun" gave him his answer and he circled the hill, presently coming onto a dugout. By this time it was relatively light, so he decided to wait in this dugout, thinking the Chinese would stop their offensive at break of dawn; but, unknown to him, his company had been overrun and the offensive continued. An enemy machine gun had been set up 29 feet from his dugout and he was caught between this fire and fire coming from his own lines. In the meantime, the Chinese had moved up and what seemed to be a command post (everyone was saluting) was set up.

At about 0930 hours on April 23, 1951, things eased up a bit. Consequently, the Chinese started investigating the dugouts, caves, holes, etc. located on the hill. Four of them looked in the dugout Insco was in, and as they looked in, he walked out. They were very excited and motioned for him to raise his hands. As one of them reached for a "burp gun" Insco thought it would be a good idea to obey.

They searched him for weapons and then took him to the command post. Later, he was taken to a house a mile north which served as intelligence headquarters. Before his interrogation, however, they let him wash up, and then fed him.

At this point, he mentioned the fact that all that they had to eat was barley and millet. This is the field ration of the Chinese Army. He also said that some of the prisoners, whom they had held for about six weeks, told him that for 30 days they had been fed a ration of corn. Rice and millet was prepared in several ways such as; rolled in balls, mush, baked much like our pancakes, and eaten with hot pepper sauce, rolled around a few beans, etc. They had plain beans once during the time he was held prisoner. Water was the only beverage. Meals were served twice daily, morning and evening.

PFC Insco's next experience was an interrogation by a Chinese officer, who spoke through an interpreter. The questions at first were related to the armed forces such as: his outfit, the size of our forces in Korea, where the various divisions were deployed, etc.? Later on they showed him a map which had more information on troops than he had ever seen. Bernie's next quizzing took place 4 miles further north where they had asked him questions of a personal nature—about his sweetheart (he had none), his home, family, father's income and job (he's a foreman in a factory), school and education, why he had joined the Marines, etc. He later found out that the fact his father was a working man had much to do with his release. That fact, among countless others, made him a favored candidate for Communist "Indoctrination School." He then was taken a mile south to a building where 13 GIs and another Marine were being held for the same school. On April 25, 1951, they started classes. The 15 men were divided into two groups of eight and seven, given books and sent off to school in a cave! They were told that the harder they studied, the sooner they would be released.

The literature reiterated the typical Communist line of propaganda. The "rotten" Capitalist and Imperialist Americans were favorite targets. They also tried to point out that we shouldn't be over here fighting at all, but should let the Koreans fight it out by themselves. They compared the Korean War to the Civil War in the United States.

After two weeks of classes, they were given haircuts, shaves, and eyebrow trims. With that, a one-star general gave them a speech on how to obtain peace in the world today, and sent them on their way on the evening of May 9, 1951, under guard. They walked nights and slept during the day. One memorable incident happened during the wee hours of the morning of May 11, 1951. As they were walking along the troop-filled road, an American light bomber started bombing the troops, trucks, and supplies. That was barely the end of Insco's adventure. That evening, the guards and interpreters left the group, giving them directions to stay on that road and they would meet friendly troops on the other side of a mile-distant bridge. The enemy was proved badly mistaken, however. "We had to walk nearly 45 miles," commented Bernie.

The men reached friendly lines on the morning of May 12, 1951 and from then on everything was a maze of questions and CIC men.

Private Insco was sent to the USS *Haven* for a brief recuperation period, and during the past week he left to rejoin his outfit.

# My Life Changed on Hill 313

## Private Milton L. "Dell" Green

I signed up for one of those three-year stints in the Marines in 1947, with an additional amount of time to be spent in the Reserves. I got off active duty in 1950 and joined the USMCR in Austin, Texas just in time to be called back on active duty for the Korean War.

I went to Korea and joined Baker Company-1-5 in March 1951 and was doing pretty good until a place called Hill 313 on April 23. The Second Platoon was ordered to run the Chinese army off Hill 313. This particular hill seemed steeper than most of the others we had encountered so it was a real tussle just to climb to the top, let alone dodging enemy fire.

As usual, the Chinese let us get way up to the top before they opened up with everything they had. They were shooting down all the trees as well as the Marines and things were really up in the air.

I had gotten up a particularly steep area and was positioned right under the enemy positions, hanging onto a tree. They knew I was there, but they could not get a shot at me without exposing themselves so they were throwing grenades down the hill at me, and all the other Marines.

Here I was, hanging on to this tree for dear life with grenades rolling all over me. I kicked them away as best I could, but a couple went off and they pretty well messed up my legs in doing so.

We prevailed and I was taken down this hill along with Lieutenant Pat McGahn, Harlan Pope, and many other wounded Marines.

I spent the next five years in hospitals all over. Semper Fi.

—*Dell*—

Dell Green (Schryver)

*Editor's note: Dell was permanently disabled due to his injuries from the Battle of Hill 313.*

# Caruso on Hill 313

## Frank Caruso

I remember the company clerk running up with an air panel to try to get the tank to stop firing on our men. The tank on the left, with a clear shot at the Chinese, was only using his .50 cal. machine gun, while the other one was firing his 90mm.

I remember being one of the first up Hill 313 in the morning and coming on a wounded Chinese. The commanding officer asked me to take him prisoner, but my 3rd Platoon Leader, Lieutenant James Ables radioed back that he might have a grenade under him. We checked, but he didn't. We headed south after that to re-group and straighten out the line. We took trucks for awhile, and then switched to riding tanks.

We saw tanks facing north covering us—then a little further down the road they were facing east—a little later we knew we were in trouble when we came up on a group of tanks in a circle covering every direction. The tank I was on had a cooling problem and the tank commander pulled over and opened the grate over the engine to cool it off. One of the guys dropped a cartridge belt into the engine and knocked it out. We had to be towed by a tank retriever and were separated from the rest of the outfit. When we finally caught up, we learned that Lieutenant Ables had been Killed in Action by an accidental discharge of an M-1 while riding on one of the other tanks. Semper Fi.

*—Frank—*

# Jack McCain on Hill 313

## Jack McCain

Fire Officer W.C. Clark, along with me and our radioman, Corporal Harris from Seattle, Washington were ordered to go along with the 2nd Platoon in case they needed mortar support. As we moved up Hill 313, we were pinned down by heavy fire from a bunker at the crest of the hill and from the ridge on the right. My map also showed a ridge running down the back side. Our guns were right below us in the valley, so we called in a firing order.

We were limited as to the amount of rounds we could fire in a day so we called for six rounds of H.E. heavy 10 seconds delay, three from each gun to try and knock out what we assumed was a bunker. We also called for 12 rounds of H.E. light and tried to walk them down the ridge. We were using World War II ammo and 50 percent of the time, they were either duds or short rounds, as the charges wouldn't burn even, or not at all. We were in real close and I believe some of the rounds hit among us. I do know, we hollered that there were going to be incoming mortars, but who could hear? I have no idea what the results were from our mortars as my nose was three inches in the dirt at the time, but I'd like to think I helped the enemy make up their mind about pulling off the hill.

Jack McCain, Mortars F.O. (Palatas)

I later moved up the right side of the ridge along with a fellow who said he was with machine guns.

As we hit the top, he got hit high in the chest, right side. I didn't know his name, but the corpsman said he wasn't hit too bad. He later died of shock, I believe.

I was about 100 feet to the right of the bunker, when the tank opened up on us. It looked like he was shooting at the bunker. I later heard they thought we were Chinese forces. I could see a radioman and another man in the foxhole from where I was. I do know a Sergeant Clark was Killed in Action. At first I thought it was the other F.O., as we had gotten separated during all the confusion, but it turned out to be another Clark.

About Lieutenant Ables' death, some time later, Baker Company was moving up. We had to cross a river. The engineers had set up a bridge for us. It was dark and raining. Trying not to make any noise, I slipped and broke my right wrist. The company corpsman wrapped it up and I went back to Weapons Company for some penicillin shots and what have you.

A few days later, was when Baker Company hitched the rides on the tanks, F.O. Sergeant Clark radioed ahead that a Marine had accidentally killed Lieutenant Ables with his own rifle. I later checked with the Marine. He was giving the Lieutenant his rifle when the tank moved and the butt of the rifle hit the track of the tank, the safety was not on and Lt Ables was shot in the chest.

I rejoined Baker Company as we went back into the attack. We had just taken a ridge and started getting incoming mortars. At that time, Sergeant Howard Clark, the other F.O. was Killed in Action along with, I believe, a Lieutenant Fisher, an interpreter, and others. Several were wounded. A few days later, after unsuccessfully trying to take another hill, Baker Company was relieved and went into reserve for awhile. I stayed with the company until I was relieved sometime in September.

*—Jack—*

*Editor's Note: Jack allowed me to omit the name of the Marine who accidentally killed Lieutenant James Ables. I am sure he has relived that accident over and over, every day of his life, so let's let him put it behind him now.*

# Why Our Tanks Fired on Us

## Corporal Emmett Shelton, Jr.

I have had three Marines from Baker Company who were at the foot of Hill 313 when the decision was made for the tank to fire on B Company. Two were ammo carriers from our machine guns, down there to get ammo, and one was down there for other reasons. Here is what they all agree on:

A certain Lieutenant Colonel ordered one of the tanks to fire his 90mm on the troops at the top of the hill. The tank commander said, "But those are our Marines!" The Colonel replied, "I order you to fire!" And it was done!

Second Platoon, Baker Company received about four rounds of 90mm injuring and killing several Marines.

*—Emmett—*

*Editor's Note: We have chosen to omit the name of the Lieutenant Colonel as did Harlan Pope's story.*

# Memories of Late May 1951

## Bill "Horny" Horton, A-1-5

*The Guidon* story about the army 8-inch gun outfit brought back memories of late May, 1951. B-1-5 was in position around the road that comes down from the Punch Bowl eastward and goes across the river.

We were on a hill above the river and were told that we were the plug if the Chinese broke through, so everybody else could get out. Anyway, we could look down and across the river where there was a battalion of army 105s in place and firing from time to time. All of a sudden the Chinese artillery started firing and they must have had a FO behind us, because the first rounds started with the northernmost army gun pit and worked their way south. The enemy must have been afraid of planes or counter battery fire as they did not fire again. We could hear the calls of "MEDIC" and there were quite a few people lying on the ground in gun pits.

It was in the same place that one night around midnight, way back up on the hill towards the Punch Bowl, there was a hell of a rumbling, booming and white lights flickering on the horizon. This went on for a half an hour or more. We thought the enemy artillery was laying it to 2-5 and 3-5 who were up there. Next morning, Alvin Pope and I went down the road coming from the hill and asked a weapons carrier driver what the hell happened? We mentioned artillery and he said no, it was a mine-field that went up.

Another interesting thing happened one morning just after sunrise. We were on line about 200 yards east of Baker Company who were on the Rock Pile. It was Hill 8-something. I had gone to the reverse slope to visit the "facilities" with entrenching tool in hand. I looked back down the valley to the south and could see a weapons carrier parked pointing to the south and four guys with a field rocket launcher pointed north. They started firing as fast as they could twist the firing switch. Before I could go back to the other side of the ridge to see the impact, the Chinese artillery started searching for the rocket unit. They had immediately, after firing everything, hitched up the launcher to the weapons carrier, jumped in and took off like a scalded ape. As they went down the road, the artillery rounds followed them and all of a sudden the road took a sharp left behind a ridge and I hope they got away. At least the artillery stopped. Semper Fidelis,

—*Horny*—

# B-1-5 Casualties and Medals— April–May 1951

## Killed in Action

*Confirmed through Korean War Project*

| | | |
|---|---|---|
| SGT Anthony M. Cappucci, from Bristol, RI. | KIA | 23APR51 |
| SGT Howard F. Clark, from Los Angeles, Calif. | KIA | 23APR51 |
| PFC Louie O. Gerue, from Kalamath Falls, Oregon | KIA | 23APR51 |
| CPL Raymond F. Hill, from St. Louis, Missouri | KIA | 23APR51 |
| PFC Norman I. Podos, from Los Angeles, Calif. | KIA | 23APR51 |
| PFC Theodore M. Skeals, Jr. Baltimore, Maryland | KIA | 23APR51 |
| HN Merle E. Sutton | KIA | 23APR51 |

## Wounded in Action

*Confirmed through USMC Unit Diaries*

CPL Russell J. Bittinger
CPL Michael A. Daskalakis
PFC Charles E. Doyle
PFC Charles H. Elmer
PFC Harold E. Evans
PFC Donald R. Fay
PFC Cornelious E. Fineran
PFC David R. Gelb
PFC William L. Giguere
PFC Robert E. Gill
PFC Milton L. "Dell" Green
SGT Billy R. Hidy

PFC Gene M. Keyton
PFC Clarence Marchington
PFC Savino G. Mahin
2LT Patrick T. McGahn, Jr.
PFC Thomas R. Mortimer
PFC Daniel Pena
PFC Francis L. Pieri, Jr.
PFC Harlan B. Pope
PFC Billy C. Prescott
PFC Gerald Schmitz (Big Smith)
CPL Arthur H. Talken

*These were the MIA–KIA listed on pages 103 & 104 of the B-1-5 Company Record Book for April 1951. I am sure other wounds occurred, but were not reported or not put in the book at that time. Sutton is listed on page 1037 of the H&S-1-5 Company Record Book.*

# Navy Cross

Lieutenant Patrick T. McGahn

"As a Platoon Leader of Company B, 1st Battalion, 5th Marines, 1st Marine Division (Reinforced), in action against enemy aggressor forces in the Republic of Korea on the night of April 22–23, 1951. When the enemy launched a strong offensive and seized a key terrain feature which dominated the approaches to his company's position and provided the enemy with a direct observation of friendly units and routes, Second Lieutenant McGahn gallantly led his platoon through heavy enemy fire in a counterattack. Although seriously wounded, he spearheaded a daring bayonet charge up the rocky terrain and succeeded in capturing one strategic position, personally killing several of the enemy. Despite the intense pain of his wounds, he courageously assisted in leading a successful attack on a second objective and steadfastly refused medical aid or evacuation until assured that all other casualties had been given medical treatment. By his indomitable fighting spirit, exceptional fortitude and resolute determination in the face of overwhelming odds, Second Lieutenant McGahn served to inspire all who observed him and contributed in large measure to the successful accomplishment of the regiment's mission. His great personal valor reflects the highest credit upon himself and enhances the finest traditions of the United States Naval Service."

# Navy Cross

Lieutenant Harvey Nolan

"As a Platoon Leader in Company B, 1st Battalion, 5th Marines, 1st Marine Division (Reinforced), in action against enemy aggressor forces in the Republic of Korea on April 23, 1951. When numerically superior hostile forces penetrated an adjacent unit and threatened the security of the Battalion, Second Lieutenant Nolan boldly led his platoon up a steep slope during the hours of darkness in an attempt to dislodge the enemy from their well-entrenched hill positions dominating the city of Hwachon. Although painfully wounded when the unit was subjected to a sudden hail of hostile automatic weapons and grenade fire near the summit of the slope, he bravely refused to be evacuated, seized an automatic rifle from one of the casualties, put it into action and, at the same time, directed his leading elements in delivering effective fire on the enemy, thereby gaining the initiative. After successfully evacuating the dead and wounded, he skillfully reorganized the remainder of his unit and led a vigorous fixed-bayonet assault on the objective in the face of intense hostile fire. Unable to dislodge the enemy, he led his platoon to an adjacent hill and, throughout the night, moved among his unit, encouraging his men and directing heavy automatic weapons and mortar fire on the hostile positions in an effort to deny the enemy the use of the vital ground. At dawn, he gallantly spearheaded the remaining fifteen men of his platoon in a second determined attack, completely routing the enemy and driving them from the hill. By his brilliant leadership and sound tactical ability, he served to inspire all who observed him and contributed materially to the security of friendly forces within the area. His outstanding courage, aggressive fighting spirit and unswerving devotion to duty reflect the highest credit upon Second Lieutenant Nolan and the United States Naval Service."

# Hill 907: June 1951

After the Battles of Hil 907, General Almond lent special meaning to the sacrifices of so many when he sent the following message:

Please express my appreciation and high commendation to the officers and men of the 5th Regiment, U.S. Marines, and its supporting units, for their valor, persistence, and combat effectiveness in the fighting of the past 10 days. Today, I made an aerial reconnaissance of the near impossible mountain peaks east of Taem-san captured by the 5th Regiment. I have nothing but admiration for the dauntless men who scaled those peaks and now remain on their assigned objectives.
*—General Edward Almond,*
*Commanding Officer U.S. X Corps*

# Hill 907

## Lieutenant Charles Cooper

It was June 1951, we never knew when Operation *Mousetrap* ended and another counter-offensive, Operation *Killer*, began. Not that it mattered to us. The real issue was how much longer we could go on doing the things that had to be done.

The Chinese continued to attack, but in smaller units, and they continued to surrender, but in larger numbers. The North Koreans remained, unchanged. They fought until they died.

We received new battle maps imprinted with a symbol of hope called the "Kansas Line." The line followed commanding terrain features across our front from southeast to northwest. The dominant mountain peak in our area, named for its height in meters, was Hill 907. Nearly 3,000 feet high, it looked to us like a smaller version of Mount Fuji.

In early June of 1951, most of the enemy long-range antitank and mortar fire came from Hill 907. Our forces believed that Hill 907 housed the command post of the 10th North Korean division serving as the rear guard of the Chinese Corps.

Lieutenant Kerrigan let us in on the general campaign plan. We would continue to attack until we reached the Kansas Line, then we would stop. Hill 907 dominated the surrounding area and would be the 5th Marines' regimental objective.

Our battalion commander, Lieutenant Colonel Hopkins, was anxious to reach the

Our new C.O. Charlie Cooper, fresh from Annapolis (Cooper)

Kansas Line. He was scheduled to be relieved of command, but wanted to conduct the attack on Hill 907 before he left. He was running out of time. To make matters worse, he had lost his operations officer, Captain Jack Jones, who had suffered severe wounds from a booby trap. Jones was no longer available to control our operations or to give calm, professional advice to the battalion commander.

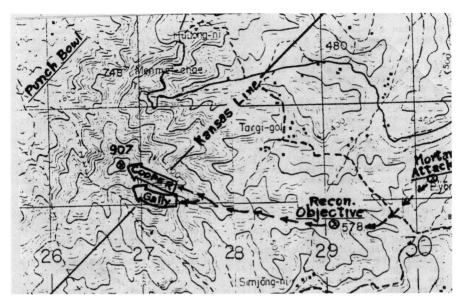

Lt Cooper's map (Cooper)

Several days before the actual attack on Hill 907, we heard that the 5th Marines would be launching a coordinated two-battalion assault when the time came. A coordinated assault by several companies seemed essential because the hill had at least half a dozen large finger ridges leading to its summit and because a determined enemy, who knew how to use terrain, was there in strength.

We expected the 3rd Battalion, because of its location, to conduct a flanking attack down the ridgeline from west to east. Either we, or the 2nd Battalion, would have to carry out a frontal assault, because we couldn't get to a flanking position from where we were. Except for the six or so fingers leading down from the summit, the sides of the hill descended almost vertically into the valley.

The soldiers of the American Civil War called battle casualty lists "the Butcher's Bill," and that's as good a term as any. Everyone from the newest rifleman on up knew that the Butcher's Bill to be paid for taking Hill 907 was going to be big. The only real question was which names would be on it.

Early in June of 1951, the 5th Regiment was attacking northward just west of the Soyang-gang River. The 3rd Battalion was on the regiment's left, and our 2nd Battalion was on the right, with its right flank stretched out to the river bank. The 2nd Battalion, following in the tracks of the other two, was in regimental reserve. B Company was more than busy. Before he was wounded, Captain Jones had identified 14 intermediate objectives leading to Hill 907, the regimental objective. Of the 14, 10 had been assigned to our Baker Bandits.

The B company had been attacking cross-compartment—from one ridgeline straight across to the next. Just the climbing itself would have been exhausting, but that paled by comparison with the fighting. Each of the objectives was stoutly defended. The Baker Bandits had 10 heated firefights and conducted 10 casualty-producing assaults before reaching the base of Hill 907. As we had done for weeks, we attacked during daylight hours and defended ourselves at night against the waves of Chinese soldiers sent to destroy us. Baker Company was wearing out.

On June 6, we received two lieutenants and several enlisted Marines, as replacements. This infusion of new blood helped. The 1st Lieutenant Dave Gally, was assigned to lead the 1st Platoon, and 2nd Lieutenant Ray Fagan was assigned the Second Platoon. Typical of the company's trials was the June 16 death of Lieutenant Ed Fisher, the mortar section leader. Ed and several others were killed by mortar fire just as we reached the base of Hill 907.

Our arrival at the foot of the Hill 907 fortress was to have ended the daily routine of attacking into the teeth of well-prepared enemy positions. We expected A Company to relieve us and allow us to get at least a brief rest. As planned, A Company joined us on June 16 and took over our defensive positions of the previous night. We moved to a nearby place and established new positions. That night, A Company took a heavy attack and had one of its platoons overrun. It was a close thing, but they held on, and finally ejected the enemy force. In the process, the company took many casualties and lost a light machine gun. B Company was not called on to assist, but after it was over, the air around the company was heavy with foreboding. We could all feel it. The A Company had been hit hard. It had fought most of the night and in the process had lost something. We were no longer certain that A Company was going to replace the Bandits and take over our assault duties. Hill 907 loomed even larger in the foreground, both geographically and psychologically.

Art Conley, "I was there and ready" (Conley)

Sometime during mid-morning of June 17, battalion ordered Lieutenant Kerrigan to conduct a company-level patrol to Hill 578. This hill, a prominent knob, was the gateway to the maze of climbing ridgelines that culminated in Hill 907.

Hoping to lighten our load, or perhaps trying to get a better feel for our future, the Skipper sought battalion's permission to leave our packs behind. We would be returning once we were relieved by A Company. The response came quickly—an ominous "negative" that was a strong clue to future possibilities. With Dave Gally and the 1st Platoon in the lead, B Company moved to Hill 578 and climbed it without incident. Reporting no enemy in sight, we took up tactical positions and waited for A Company to appear and relieve us.

The wait gave us an opportunity to look over Hill 907, above. A wide, well-used path led up the nearest finger. Large trees along the path formed a canopy that filtered or screened out entirely a bright sun that beat down with increasing intensity as it climbed the mid-day sky. The enemy had cut most of the underbrush away, a sign that it had cleared fields of fire for defensive positions somewhere on the slope. Using binoculars, I finally picked out at least 10 of them—well-camouflaged bunkers, some two hundred yards up the hill. It looked like a Gibraltar!

Unlike the previous several days, this day was quiet, almost peaceful—so much so that the troops relaxed and began to doze in the hot sun. Fighting the temptation to do the same, the officers studied what they could. They silently examined the terrain and defenses in front of us. Shortly after noon, a stirring around the company command post showed that the battalion radio was demanding attention. It was the battalion commander and he wanted to speak to Lieutenant Kerrigan. The conversation was brief, its message unwelcome but in some ways, not unexpected. Lieutenant Colonel Hopkins told the Skipper that the 5th Marines had given the 1st Battalion permission to seize Hill 907. He ordered B Company, alone, to go and do it. All thought of a coordinated, carefully planned, and heavily supported two-battalion, multi-company attack floated away into space—to the never-never land of tactical plans that should have been executed, not discarded. None of us ever learned why.

It was late in the day to start an attack of this magnitude without either planning or advance preparation, but that is exactly what the battalion commander was demanding. To make matters worse, he pre-empted the company commander by specifying that "Charlie Cooper's 3rd Platoon will lead the attack."

The terrain was an enemy-dominated area, and there was no doubt that, having observed our climb to Hill 578, the enemy knew our strength and the nature of our weapons. Soon, they would know our intentions, as well. We, on the other hand, would be moving directly into the enemy's main battle position with no more information than what we had gleaned from our limited view up the hill. The 3rd Platoon, followed by the rest of the Bandits, would have to attack on a narrow front with no planned fire support, with both flanks exposed, and with no reinforcements: Just Move Out and Attack. The concept was almost overwhelming, but there was no alternative. It was time to remember that for a Marine officer, the one thing worse than dying—is failing his troops in battle.

When confronted with an operational problem in combat, an officer must suppress personal fears and concentrate on the professional things that can, and should, be done. The problem was simple enough to describe: in many respects, our situation and mission bordered on the suicidal. What we had to remember was that there were strengths, as well. First and foremost, we were Marines, a point that may seem trite or even juvenile to the outsider, but one that meant much to us—and of at least equal importance, it also meant much to the enemy. The Marines of this platoon had been through a great deal, together. They were experienced, they knew what they were doing, and they were like Brothers. They had never failed me or the company, and they understood the meaning of "orders" just as well as I did.

If those factors were not enough, we also had a potential hole card. Marines have a penchant for taking combat souvenirs: We had our own stock of captured enemy ammunition and weapons. We had brand new, mint-condition burp guns, not especially accurate at a distance, as the enemy had so often proved, but handy for close-in fighting. The troops had been intrigued by these sparkling new weapons ever since we had captured them, and although we had turned in most of them (too much to carry), we had managed to hang onto a dozen, along with sizable amounts of ammunition. It was time to do something different. We might confuse the enemy by using his own weapons against him. If we did, we would be saving our own limited ammunition. More important, our using his weapons against him would give our platoon a psychological boost.

Agreeing with that rationale, Lieutenant Bill Kerrigan approved the idea of arming the two lead squads with burp guns. He also said that battalion had just confirmed that Hill 907's defenders were North Koreans, and probably our old enemy, the Tenth Division. We knew what to expect. There would be no surrendering, and there would be a lot of dying—all of the North Koreans and maybe most of us.

There was little time to make a reconnaissance. Staff Sergeant Reiman, the platoon guide, the machine-gun section leader, three squad leaders, and I moved forward to a large boulder to learn what we could. It wasn't much, but it helped. The cut undergrowth had left the area open, but there were boulders and folds in the ground that we could use to mask our movements. We developed the plan, and then explained it to our men. Hiding behind the terrain folds and boulders, the two lead squads would work their way around the bunkers and take them from the rear. In a procedure unlike that used in most other attacks, the machine guns would move with the assaulting squads, constantly changing position and always furnishing support. The plan may not have been the best way to deal with what appeared to be mutually supporting bunkers, but it was the best we could come up with.

In my final conversation with Lt Bill Kerrigan, I expressed confidence that we would be able to penetrate a number of the bunkers. The problem was that each penetration would leave us more vulnerable to enemy fire from both flanks. It was clear that our frontage and maneuver room would narrow as we moved upward. If the assault went as planned, we were going to need impressive quantities of accurate fire support on both flanks.

We finished making preparations. We had issued the orders, and everyone understood them, down to the newest rifleman. Glancing up the hill as they listened to squad or fire team leaders explaining how we would operate, the troops steeled themselves for what they knew would be, at best, a long afternoon. At worst, it could be the last afternoon. We issued burp guns and ammo to the two lead squads, an action that had helped divert their attention from the coming ordeal. To lighten the load, the men had removed their packs and put them in squad stacks for retrieval after the attack. We carried canteens and ammunition. It was time to go.

Once I informed Lt Bill Kerrigan that we were moving out, the lead troops started forward in a series of fire team rushes that produced early successes. In the first half hour we took four bunkers from the rear and destroyed them without meeting any enemy resistance. Then the North Koreans began reacting. They had us pinpointed. Scattered rifle fire gave way to persistent and accurate firing. Suddenly, when we were halfway up the hill and fully deployed, a murderous fire erupted on three sides: from directly ahead and the two flanks. We were in real trouble. Only the rear was secure. We called in airstrikes and artillery fire without letup. We used everything that was available, and there was plenty. No one else was fighting that day, so we had it all.

In spite of the continuous curtain of supporting fire to our front and on the flanks, we were taking casualties. The North Korean machine guns were relentless. My platoon radio operator took a round through the neck, and appeared to have died instantly. A Marine sprang forward, removed the radio from its dead operator, started moving toward me, and was killed before he could get to cover.

Inexplicably, Lieutenant Colonel Hopkins's voice suddenly came over the company radio net, screaming obscenities at the enemy. He knew they were listening. Maybe he was trying to rattle them. Whatever his intent, he was clearly getting out of control and his tirade was having no visible effect. The well-concealed North Korean machine guns chattered the language of death, and Marines were dropping in increasing numbers when Hopkins decided that he wanted to talk to me. It was a short conversation. We had to have him call in additional air support on the crest and more heavy artillery fire on the flanks if we were to continue to move. I hastily gave the proper map coordinates for both.

The ground shook under our feet and red hot machine-gun shell casings dropped on and around us as strafing aircraft swooped in overhead, hosing down the area to our front. But each of the platoon's successes in the tortured progress upward brought more difficulties. As we moved deeper into the North Korean defenses, our location and tactics became more obvious, and our maneuver room shrank to almost nothing.

We had used confusion, maneuver, envelopment from the rear of their bunkers, and the shock effect of massive supporting arms. I remained with the two assaulting squads and kept the two machine guns close, because a counterattack could come at any time. With all we had done, the volume of enemy fire did not reach its maximum until the ground began to level. We were nearing the top, but could move no farther—and Marines were dying. The noise, smoke, confusion, killing, and increasingly fanatical enemy resistance were almost overpowering. The issue was in doubt.

During our move up the hill, the Skipper had sent Lieutenant Dave Gally's 1st Platoon up an adjacent finger on our left flank with orders to suppress enemy flanking fires that were hurting us badly. About the time we assaulted, the 1st Platoon uncovered and destroyed an enemy outpost that was causing our problems. In turn, they began receiving fire from slightly ahead on flanks, losing one killed and three seriously wounded in the initial exchange. They returned fire, and received orders to hold their ground. Sooner rather than later, they and their casualties would have to be removed from that exposed position.

While this was going on, Lieutenant Ray Fagan's Second Platoon had been sent forward to assist in moving our dead and wounded. Ray became one of the assisted when he went down with a hit from a machine-gun burst that eventually resulted in the loss of a leg.

About 16:30 we seemed to be on the military crest, just short of a final assault position. There weren't many troops left, but we still had the machine guns and we couldn't stay where we were. If we stopped, the North Koreans would pick us all off in short order. There was no turning back. It was move forward or die. I asked for one more airstrike. Hopkins radioed that two Air Force F-80s armed with napalm tanks were orbiting overhead. Eavesdropping on our tactical air support radio net, they had checked in to offer help. We agreed that I would mark the target area with my last white phosphorous grenade. The cloud of white smoke would rise through the trees, the pilots would see it easily, and all they had to do was drop on the smoke. The pilots "Rogered" the instructions and reported themselves ready to turn for the "hot" run to the target. I signaled what was left of the platoon—12 to 15 Marines—to move forward with me, then pulled the pin on the grenade. We were moving forward, screaming madly: "Gung Ho, you bastards, we're Marines!" The volume of fire swelled when I heaved the grenade as far as I could.

The grenade had flown some 30 yards between the trees when a massive blow on my left side flattened me. It was like being hit with an ax—a large ax. It spun me completely around. The senior corpsman, Doc Roderick, moved like a flash, trying to plug the hole in my left side. I looked up to see enemy troops forming a line beyond where the grenade had exploded and apparently confused them. They seemed to be milling around in the grenade's smoke. Considering the F-80s on their inbound run with the napalm, from our viewpoint there was no better place for North Korean confusion. My platoon, or what was left of it, was on the ground, firing at the line of North Koreans. The machine-gun section added its weight and I was able to continue firing my carbine. The North Koreans were feeling the punishment.

As the smoke rose, the shadowy figures of the enemy became more visible. It was a long line of North Korean soldiers, dressed in camouflaged uniforms, each with leaves and twigs added for additional effect. They looked much like clumps of bushes. Armed with burp guns, they were firing from the hip: had they been more accurate, they would have killed us all. We took them under fire with everything we could muster and couldn't miss at that range, particularly with machine guns. It was the North Koreans' turn to fall like bowling pins. But they kept on coming. The yells, the screams, and the noise of chattering automatic weapons, all hemmed in by the trees, shut off outside sounds.

We couldn't kill them fast enough and, heavily outnumbered, were about to take on the North Korean counterattack in hand-to-hand combat. As they started moving, my carbine was hit on the stock and literally blown out of my hands. Conscious but unable to move my legs, I drew my fighting knife. It would be the last resort. There was nothing else left.

We never heard it coming. Hell exploded through the trees. The napalm bombs burst in the branches directly over the North Korean troops, not 30 yards away. Fire and flames were everywhere. The heat was unbelievable. We had burns and almost suffocated, but the North Korean counterattack had been incinerated, en masse. It was no more. Hanging by our fingernails some 100 yards from the peak of Hill 907, we were no longer an effective fighting force. Our courageous machine gunners and that lucky, perfectly timed napalm drop had saved what was left of the 3rd Platoon. We could go no farther.

"Doc" Roderick had violated all medical protocol by stuffing a kidney back into the large hole in my lower left side and doing everything possible to plug it up. He asked me what time it was. (Corpsmen were trained to ask their patients the time as a means of getting their minds off their wounds and avoiding combat shock, which was often as fatal as the wounds.) I told him it was 1700, and that I was not going into shock. He told me not to worry about it: he wouldn't let that happen, but he had to get me out of there before I bled to death—which he then did. I wasn't the only one he saved. He was the miracle man of the day, saving lives by the dozen as men dropped all around him. Hospital man Stanley Roderick should have received the Medal of Honor for his courage and his selfless devotion to duty that afternoon.

The next day, June 18, other elements of the 5th Marines approached Hill 907 from the left flank and occupied the regimental objective without firing a shot. The enemy had pulled out, having apparently held at all costs until the headquarters of the Tenth North Korean Division could move out. Ironically, our assault was the last action undertaken by United Nations forces in Korea during the summer of 1951. A three-month cease-fire followed almost immediately.

Two days later, on June 20, the Tenth Corps Commander recognized what B Company and the rest of the 5th Marines had accomplished since early June. But late on that afternoon of Father's Day, June 17, the occupation of Hill 907 by the 5th Marines, and General Almond's message, were yet to come. There was still work to be done on the forward slope of Hill 907.

The dead and wounded of what was left of the 3rd Platoon had to be evacuated. The battalion commander had dispatched a single rifle platoon from A Company to reinforce B Company. That force might have helped somewhere, but the meager reinforcement reached the Bandits only after Lieutenant Kerrigan had moved the company halfway back down the mountain.

It was time for me to go back down the hill. As they half carried, half dragged me to a safer place; the machine-gun section leader ran forward to the spot where I'd been hit. Risking sniper fire, he retrieved my helmet and returned it to me. He knew that it held a picture of my wife.

Earlier in the day, we'd cut saplings in an attempt to clear firing lanes for the company's 60mm mortars. The 60s were never able to make a real contribution, but the saplings now came in handy. Our men used them and ponchos to rig improvised stretchers that took the dead and wounded to the bottom of the mountain, where the Jeep ambulances waited. As carefully as possible, the sad procession started slowly downhill. It was a trip that we had seen so many others make. Now it was our turn.

For most of us, the war was over. For many of us, a different sort of a battle was about to begin.

## Many Years Later

*A Note from Ole Emmett: Several of the men who carried 2nd Lieutenant Charlie Cooper off the hill that day told me they thought he was going to die, or at least be incapacitated permanently.*

*The next thing many of us heard of Charlie Cooper was years later and that he was now Lieutenant General Charlie Cooper, USMC Retired.*

*I remember the first Baker Bandit Reunion he attended. Several guys could not believe their eyes, here was critically wounded (when they last saw him) Charlie Cooper, now known as General Charlie, walking, talking and everything just like the other Bandits. Boy, what a welcome he got!*

# On Hill 907

## Lieutenant Dave Gally

I received the 1st Platoon from "Stu" Wright, who was elated to be relieved of the assignment. Lieutenant Ray Fagan was assigned the 2nd Platoon. Since Lieutenant Charlie Cooper had been the 3rd Platoon leader for a month and a half, he was the "old hand" and was instructed to break us in.

There wasn't time for that, however. That afternoon the 1st Platoon probed the next objective, but because of my newness and caution, we were so slow that we didn't quite reach the objective. The next day, we did reach the objective after one small skirmish. Three North Korean Soldiers were killed and we had no casualties.

That night we were in a defensive perimeter with the 1st Platoon on the point. Forty-five minutes before dawn on June 12 the enemy attacked from below with grenades and burp-guns hitting one of our machine-gun positions. Three Marines were wounded, including Platoon Sergeant George Barr. We suffered several wounded almost daily, but we were eliminating a growing number of North Korean soldiers. Enemy mortars and artillery were doing us some damage.

On June 17, Lt Gally's 1st Platoon was called upon to assault the finger ridge to the left rear of Lt Cooper's 3rd Platoon to relieve the fire from that position. About 150 yards from the top of Hill 907, the 3rd Platoon ran into heavy fire from their front and both sides. The 1st Platoon was sent to the left across a draw and up another ridge leading to the top to attack from a second position and take the pressure away from Lt Cooper's platoon.

About the time we started up the ridge, the 3rd Platoon made an assault on the objective. When my platoon came upon the enemy that had been firing across the draw at the 3rd Platoon's left flank we attacked up the ridge. As we did, we ran into an outpost that opened up on us. They were joined by fire from our left and right fronts. John Stammel was Killed in Action almost immediately and Dick Chapa, in the point fire team was badly wounded in the leg. Our corpsman at that time was George W. Pfeiffer, who ran, under fire, to the point to care for Chapa. Pfeiffer would not allow us to move Chapa until the leg was splinted.

That action saved Chapa's leg. Two other men were seriously wounded and all were successfully evacuated.

When the fire got too hot, we hit the deck. I will always remember the three BAR men in the point squad standing up and mowing down the brush and grass to our front with two magazines of ammo each, so that we could see the enemy. The close in enemy fire ceased, but more fire came from the left front. We were told to take cover and hold our position until further notice.

We had no way of knowing at the time, but the rest of the company was having a harder time of it than we were. The 3rd Platoon was hard hit and Lieutenant Cooper was severely wounded. The 2nd Platoon was committed to the fight and others were hit, including Lieutenant Fagan who sustained a wound that cost him his lower leg. I was the only rifle platoon leader not wounded, but I brought back a bent slug that nicked my helmet; hit the shovel on my pack; and stopped in my rolled up field jacket. My ears rang for a couple of hours.

When the platoon was ordered to withdraw to the main ridge, one of my men put Stammel over his shoulder and we moved out quickly. We were met by an Able Company platoon that covered our withdrawal to our previous night's bivouac area.

When the assault was stalled by the hail of intense fire, the possibility of an enemy counterattack loomed as a very real thing.

*—Dave—*

# You'll Be Sorry

## Private John Buentello

When I arrived in Korea with the 9th draft on June 6, 1951, we were transported on cattle trucks to our regimental area. As we rode going up, there were other trucks with Marine troops going in the opposite direction, on their way back to the States. As they went by they yelled jokingly at us with a grin on their faces, "You'll Be Sorry!" It wasn't very long after that we found out what they meant.

After getting our assignments, our group was trucked to the 1st Battalion area. They were getting incoming when we arrived. Several guys that just got in were hit and we had to get them to safety. After the shelling stopped, we were mustered and got our guides to take us along with supply-bearers to Baker Company, up on some hill. I remember going through several days and nights climbing off one hill and up another every day.

One night in particular, after we had dug in for the night, we started to get some incoming. I heard cries for help and I knew someone had been hit. The night was dark and we could not see. Feeling my way through, I heard someone say "Give me a hand with this guy, he's been hit." I grabbed the wounded Marine right under his right shoulder blade and felt my hand slip in a hole in his side, as wide as a baseball. I was new to all of this and didn't know anyone by name. I just hope whoever it was made it out alright.

Things went on until the day we were told we had to take some high ground strategically critical to our ground forces. That high ground turned out to be Hill 907. As we started up the hill, I remember how thick the trees and foliage were. I recall we were high up our finger ridge when they opened up on us. I'm sure I wasn't the only one trying to take cover behind trees no bigger than 5″ diameter. We saw bark peeled off trees by bullets biting into them and dust spitting up at you as they whizzed by like an invisible force marking its territory. I remember Marine Corsairs flying overhead strafing and dropping napalm to soften up the enemy for us. Fat chance of that! There must have been a million of them to survive all of that pounding.

Word came down from the Lieutenant for Sergeant Sondergaard to move his squad forward to take the Point. At that time, I was Assistant BARman to Paul Ruth. We were assigned to protect the flanks of "Jake's" machine gunner and his crew. I rose up several times and fired my rifle, although I could not see anyone in front of me, due to the brush.

Suddenly, I felt like somebody had kicked me on the side of my neck and picked me up off the ground. Stunned as I was, I reached over with my right hand and felt the biggest hole on the left side of my neck. I didn't realize then that the left side of my face had also been split wide open. I thought that I had bought the farm. After a few seconds, in what seemed an eternity, my whole life reeled before my eyes. I came to my senses and figured I wasn't going to die right away. I then became angry as Hell and decided I was going to make the enemy pay. So, I got up and started to go up the ridge to get them. I didn't get anywhere though as I felt someone pulling me back, it was Paul Ruth.

I found out later that my rifle had been destroyed by enemy gunfire. There was nothing left of it. I know that Ruth, Jake, and a whole bunch of our guys were hit during the battle. I remember losing a lot of blood because the pockets of my shirt and trousers were filled with it. I also recall a corpsman, whose name I never found out, pulled several rifle wood splinters from my face and patched me up in the field. Woozy as I was, I helped carry a Marine who was worse off than me on a stretcher down off the hill to a riverbed where medical personnel and helicopters were waiting to evacuate out casualties.

After 40 days in the hospital and countless shots of penicillin to prevent infections and further extractions of shrapnel in my face and neck, I was sewed back up and ordered to rejoin my outfit. I returned back to Baker Company in August 1951. It wasn't very long before we jumped off again in battle. I was rotated back to the States in May 1952.

—*John*—

# Fire Team on Hill 907

## Art Reid

The action on June 17, 1951 was the one in which my very close friend, Daniel Joseph Ballem, was Killed in Action trying to pull our Platoon Leader, Lieutenant Cooper, out of the line of fire. Lt Cooper had been badly wounded. Dan lost his life from the same machine gun that wounded Lt Cooper.

My fire team was on the right side of a spur leading up to the ridgeline and the others in the mission were on the left side of this ridge. We advanced through low-lying clouds. The rifleman, in my fire team, a good Marine from Georgia named Hogan, was slightly to my left as we advanced. A North Korean soldier half-appeared out of a spider trap and looked very surprised as we were only about 10 feet in front of him. He threw a grenade over our heads before my rifleman, Hogan, shot him. Hogan stepped over to the fallen enemy and put two more rounds into him. I can still see that enemy's face and his surprised look to discover we were almost on top of him.

Hogan and I were side by side and I remember thinking this guy really has guts. I commented to Hogan how it took courage for him to advance up Hill 907 as he did. I told him he did very well and went up like a real veteran. He said "I just did what you were doing. You were the Old Guy, I was the New One. I went along with you because I thought you knew what you were doing."

An enemy machine gun in front of us opened up. A number of Marines were hit. My fire team was stopped by this machine gun. The enemy gunners had one of the usually well-constructed low-profile bunkers with a very small gun port facing outward. My fire team hit the deck about 20 to 30 feet in front of the bunker. We were on the reverse side of the slope from the enemy gunner. When we stuck our heads up to see the bunker, we got a burst of machine-gun fire for our efforts. It would have been suicide to advance over the slope on to the level ground commanded by the enemy gunner.

I remember the machine-gun bullets were whipping all around us. There was so much lead flying that I thought perhaps our own guns behind us were also involved. I rolled over and yelled back "Raise that gun; you're going to get us." One of our machine gunners replied "That's not our gun." I peered over the top and fired my M-1 into the gun port of the machine gun and got sprayed, in return. I backed down about a foot, after the gunner picked me for his next target, as he fired a burst at me. The burst threw dirt into my face so hard it numbed my face.

I remember wiping my face with my hands expecting to have a hand full of blood. I wasn't hit—needless to say I was surprised. My fire team was truly pinned down by this machine gun. My BAR man, Frank Fowlkes, emptied a number of magazines trying to get the machine gun out of action. On the left of the spur we were on, the remainder of our company was being cut to pieces by enfilade fire from a parallel spur. I did not know it at the time but we were also being attacked by a large number of North Koreans coming from our left along the ridgeline perpendicular to our spur. An F4U Corsair was on station above us and either we had an air controller somewhere in our units or the pilot could see the situation from his vantage point. I remember rolling over on my back and saw this Corsair with its wing guns blazing and his .50 cal. brass raining down on us. He released a napalm canister and it seemed to go somewhere between 10 and 20 feet above my head. It hit the North Koreans advancing along the ridgeline and ruined their day. Had it not been for the napalm and strafing of the Corsair we would have been overrun.

We had no platoon leader and no one in charge—the platoon sergeants were either out of action or just trying to get our wounded and dead together so we could pull back. We later found out that the enemy had used dum-dums on us. They were firing ammo where they had scratched across the copper jackets so that when they hit the copper came off in small bits—almost everyone hit in the arm became an amputee.

When the word came to pull back, I started dragging a wounded Marine out but stopped when he screamed that it hurt too badly. We cut small saplings and rolled the edges of ponchos around them to form stretchers. We carried a number out that way. I remember a dead Marine was wrapped in a poncho and slung over someone's shoulder. As we pulled out, this guy was right in front of me. The dead Marine slipped out of the poncho and fell at my feet. The Lieutenant from the other platoon looked at the body and said "Someone pick up this poor boy."

I remember Corpsman Stanley Roderick doing a great job on Lt Cooper and all the other wounded. I believe Lt Cooper later stated he should have written Roderick up for the Medal of Honor. I remember Clapp, a machine gunner, staying behind and keeping up a line of fire to hold the enemy off, while we pulled back.

I have thought many times how poorly prepared we really were to take out bunkers. A light-weight flame thrower, or the equivalent of an RPG or a small recoilless rifle, would have been just what we needed to take out a bunker. Even a grenade with a launcher to put it in front of a bunker to blind the gunners, would have been useful. I remember going by an army platoon and seeing what I suppose was a 37mm recoilless rifle. Having said that, we had the best air support possible from the navy and Marine air units. I don't think the army caught on to the merit of close air support until much later in the Korean War. I understand they later commandeered Marine air support for army units. This concept of using close air support for infantry was pioneered by Hitler in 1939 in World War II and used by the Marines in World War II. Obviously, the helicopter gun ship has been more than effective supporting infantry in wars after the "police action" we were in.

There was another incident prior to Hill 907 that stands out in my memory. The way I remember it is that our platoon leader—I don't remember which one—told us there were four T34 tanks coming down on us. He drew a line in the ground with a stick and said the tanks were coming in this direction and then he drew an X. He said this is where we are.

We were issued some kind of holder to go on our belts to hold a new classified antitank device that we could shoot from our rifles to stop the tanks. The "secret" rockets, or whatever they were, never arrived. Our platoon leader got on the radio and asked where these devices were. He was told that "They were classified and we could not have them." Even as a private, I could see there was some problem here.

There is a saying that "Military intelligence is a conflict of terms." I am sure there are other examples that could be cited but this situation seems to me to qualify. I am more likely to believe some rear echelon Pentagon type came up with this brilliant piece of ruling than a combat Marine.

—*Art*—

# Memories of Hill 907

## Lieutenant "Stu" Wright

After a rotation of command of the 1st Platoon from me to Dave Gally, I was assigned as S-2 (security manager). We were hunkered down in a dugout on the ridgeline when Lieutenant Ed Fisher came aboard. He was introduced as the replacement Mortar Officer. He seemed somewhat distressed in that the preceding Mortar Officers had all been casualties. In two or three days, his brown hair had turned white. He felt sure he was going to suffer the same terrible fate.

On June 16, we were walking the ridgeline when a single round burst at his feet. I was about 20 yards away. I can still feel the concussion and the damage was heavy. Lieutenant Edward D. Fisher was Killed in Action by that shell.

A strange twist—Captain Doug Vanderbilt, a long-time friend of mine from college days, was stationed in Japan and was in a position to follow B Company's action. Doug and I met stateside sometime after completing our tour of duty. He had married a nifty gal, a nurse, who he had met in Japan. Her husband, a Marine Lieutenant had been Killed in Action in Korea. This Lieutenant's name was Ed Fisher.

—*Stu*—

# Lieutenant Charlie Cooper Is Wounded

## Lieutenant Bill Kerrigan

About mid-morning, June 17, a radio message was received ordering the company to make a reconnaissance patrol to a prominent knob, Hill 578, on the ridgeline to Hill 907. A request was made to leave our packs and a small security force at our current position since it was believed that we would be returning there once relieved by Company A. The ominous response was to the negative!

We made it to Hill 578 without incident and reported it unoccupied by the enemy. We stayed where we were, awaiting word on when we were to be relieved?

It was not until well after noon that the battalion commander, Lieutenant Col. John Hopkins radioed to report that regiment had given him permission to take Hill 907. Company B was ordered to the attack. We still had 327 meters to climb and it was very late in the day to begin the attack on such a huge objective. It was the company's standard operating procedure to attack in a column of platoons. The point platoon was followed by a small company command group, in that group were the company commander; supporting arms forward observers; and radio operators. Following in trace were the remainder of the command post personnel and supplies. Taking up the rear was the reserve rifle platoon. Each of the rifle platoons had a section of light machine guns attached. The normal rotation of platoon was altered when the battalion commanding officer ordered Lieutenant Cooper's 3rd Platoon to attack 907!

As we approached the summit, a look to the rear told us we were easily seen by the enemy as we came up the ridge. They didn't have to guess our strength, location, or intention. Along the trail, there were bunkers and foxholes that had served as enemy observation posts and outposts.

Cooper's 3rd Platoon was on the Point and deployed for the assault at the edge of a wooded area covered with 2- to 4-inch saplings. They began to take in heavy small-arms fire from their front. I recall the leaves of the saplings were falling to the ground like it was autumn. Neither I, nor the forward observers, had a field of vision. Cooper called in his own supporting arms fire, 4.2-inch mortars, artillery, and airstrikes. The airstrikes were so close I felt the heat of the napalm bombs. The .50 caliber shells casings from the strafing runs were falling among us. During this most critical period, the battalion commander commandeered the radio net to hurl personal invectives at the enemy.

Lieutenant Charlie Cooper was faced with an extremely dangerous and tense situation. Just about the time the assault began, we had intense small-arms fire coming from the front. We began to be hit from the left front. It was coming from the adjacent ridge, and it seemed to be approaching more from our left flank. From Cooper's forward location, it was hitting him from his immediate flank and left rear. He requested relief from his tenuous situation.

Enfilade fire, along with a possible counterattack, would have placed the entire company in great jeopardy. It was necessary to protect the flank, so I dispatched Lieutenant Gally's 1st Platoon to contain and repulse the enemy on our left.

Fully expecting the enemy to counterattack, I ordered the reserve platoon, which was Lieutenant Fagan's 2nd Platoon forward to reinforce and relieve Cooper's 3rd Platoon. In the process, Lieutenant Fagan was hit with small-arms fire just below the knee. It resulted in the loss of his leg. Throughout this action, supporting arms played a major role in rescuing the company from a very precarious situation. After Company B was heavily engaged, the battalion commander saw fit to dispatch a meager force (a single rifle platoon) to reinforce us. It was not until they were halfway down the mountain that Company B met up with Lieutenant Bill Heer's A Company Platoon.

I ordered 60mm mortars into action with complaints from the men that the overhanging sapling limbs prevented this. After a bit of a shouting match, they began cutting down the saplings and the guns got into action. When the 60mm mortars were in action they were able to lob their shells to our immediate front. Later in the day, those saplings, along with ponchos were used to improvise stretchers to evacuate the dead and wounded.

At about the same time I realized we were in dire straits when I saw two Marines bringing Lieutenant Cooper to the rear. They had one of his arms over each of their shoulders and his feet were dragging along the ground. I felt certain that he had "bought the farm."

*—Bill—*

# Marine Miracles on Hill 907

## Lieutenant Charlie Cooper

A safe night in Korea was when you had about two hundred Marines with you and it didn't make a damn how many Chinese or North Koreans there were. You knew that with supporting arms, air, artillery and mortars and so forth, you could take on anything in the world.

I was this 23-year-old lieutenant, I hadn't been commissioned a full year when I joined B Company, but I realized I was seeing a miracle in the experiences I was having with this company of men. The bonding that I felt immediately was indescribable. People were wounded and moved out; new people came in almost daily, but the pulling together, the believing in each other, it was there.

We knew we'd never surrender, we knew that if we were wounded, or even if we were killed in action, we would not be left behind. We knew that we were part of a family. We didn't realize it fully, but we loved each other and we would die for each other. Several of my troops died saving my life after I was shot in that terrible day-long battle on Hill 907 on Father's Day of June 1951.

I got hit in the spine by a machine-gun round that was tumbling and knocked a hole about the size of a baseball in my left side and it stayed in me! I went through a considerable period of hospitalization on a ship. A month later, they told me I'd never walk again. My spinal cord was permanently damaged. I should quit talking about going back to B Company. I refused to accept it. I told the Good Lord, if you'll help me grow back I'd like to spend the rest of my life leading Marines and giving them the kind of leadership they deserve. You know, the Good Lord heard me. I defied all the prognoses. I got stronger and finished up a wonderful career, made it to Lieutenant General, and commanded an awful lot of good Marines which is what I love to do the most.

I remember on Hill 907 in early June 1951, our B-1-5 was down to about 65 percent strength and we were in the attack, every day. Then all of the sudden another Marine miracle happened, we began to get replacements out of hospitals and aid stations. When patients heard that we were short handed, we had almost two dozen Marines serving with B Company who had gone over-the-hill from hospitals and medical centers where they were recuperating, I'll bet you that ninety percent of us who were there still had holes in us from wounds that we had not reported. That is what the Brotherhood was all about.

*—Gen. Charlie—*

# B-1-5 Casualties and Medals—June 1951

## Killed in Action

*Confirmed through Korean War Project*

| | | |
|---|---|---|
| CPL Daniel J. Bellam, from New York City, NY | KIA | 17JUN51 |
| PFC Howard H. Harman, from Las Animas, Colo. | KIA | 17JUN51 |
| PFC Robert P. Mooney, from Kansas City, Kansas | KIA | 17JUN51 |
| PFC John E. Stammel, from Rensselaer, NY | KIA | 23SEP51* |

\* Marines who were there say PFC Stammel was KIA Jun 17, 1951 on Hill 907 but the Korean War Project reports him KIA September 23, 1951 at Punchbowl.

## Wounded in Action

*Confirmed through USMC Unit Diaries*

2LT Charles G. Cooper
2LT Raymond F. Fagan
PFC Thomas R. Betz
Cpl Billy G. Bonner
PFC John A. Boyer
PFC Donald H. Brown
PFC John H. Buentello
PFC Carl G. Cedarquist
PFC Jesus Flores

PFC John J. Horan, Jr.
SGT Harry C. Iben
CPL Gerald M. Jacobs
PFC Hunt S. Kerrigan
PFC Richard D. Kimpston
PFC Charles T. Payne
PFC Paul I. Ruth
CPL J.D. Sarver
PFC Virgil E. Walter

## Silver Star

Second Lieutenant Charles Cooper

Second Lieutenant Charles Grafton Cooper, United States Marine Corps, displayed conspicuous gallantry and intrepidity as a Platoon Leader of Company

B, 1st Battalion, 5th Marines, 1st Marine Division (Reinforced), in action against enemy aggressor forces in Korea on June 17, 1951. Participating in an assault against an enemy hill position when his platoon was pinned down by devastating small-arms and automatic-weapons fire from a strongly entrenched hostile position, Second Lieutenant Cooper, after calling for and receiving a friendly airstrike and artillery fire support, attempted to move his platoon forward but was again pinned down by fire from the same enemy position. With the advance of the entire company halted, he unhesitatingly charged through the hail of bullets and grenades with one other Marine and, upon reaching the enemy emplacement, hurled grenades through the embrasure, killing the occupants and silencing the fire. Severely wounded while engaged in this hazardous undertaking, Second Lieutenant Cooper, by his outstanding bravery and daring initiative, was directly instrumental in the seizure of the company's objective and served to inspire all who observed him. His heroic actions were in keeping with the highest traditions of the United States Naval Service.

## Silver Star

Harvey Nolan

The President of the United States of America, authorized by Act of Congress July 9, 1918, takes pleasure in presenting the Silver Star (Army Award) to First Lieutenant Harvey W. Nolan (MCSN: 0-50159), United States Marine Corps, for conspicuous gallantry and intrepidity as a member of Company B, 1st Battalion, 5th Marines, 1st Marine Division (Reinforced), in action against enemy aggressor force in the vicinity of Inje, Korea. On May 31, 1951, Lieutenant Nolan was serving as platoon leader with B Company. After successfully attacking along a ridgeline near Inje, his unit was held up at the base of Hill 780 by intense fire from enemy automatic weapons, small arms, and hand grenades. Due to impending darkness, further attack was postponed until the following day. On the morning of June 1, 1951, Lieutenant Nolan led his platoon through the intense fire and hand grenade barrage, in an assault on the enemy positions near the crest of the hill. He skillfully maneuvered his platoon to a position where the enemy's well entrenched and cleverly camouflaged positions could be observed. Lieutenant Nolan then expertly and effectively fired rifle grenades into the enemy positions. The gallantry and devotion to duty displayed by Lieutenant Nolan contributed materially to the success of his unit's mission and reflect great credit on himself and the military service.

# Western Front: March 1953

## Reno Hill
### Chuck Hall

They called the small hill Reno
Way out in no-man's land
'Twas here our country's finest,
Would make their final stand

The cold North wind was howling,
As they gazed into the night
The Chinese might take Reno
But not without a fight

The small platoon was ready,
For whatever came their way
The fateful die was ready cast,
The price they now must pay.

The Chinese overwhelmed them,
With numbers by the score
They fought both long and deadly,
With weapons, fists and more

Sealed up in their bomb-proof cave,
The survivors fought for air
They'd hold on to the very last,
No matter who would care

At last the fight was over,
And Reno Hill had fell
But a lot of mother's Chinamen,
Would walk the road toward Hell

The never mention Reno
Nor the brave Marines who died
They fought it to the very last
And no one harder tried

The hill would be abandoned
Not worthy for defense
'Twas out too far from the MLR
It didn't make much sense

In my mind I see the fighting,
Ghostly figures 'neath the sky
I think about their dying,
But mostly wonder why

Not many will remember,
The fight for Reno Hill
But I will not forget them,
Their courage lingers still.

# 5th Regiment—Reno–Vegas–Carson

USMC Historical Diary for the Period March 19–26, 1953 ~~SECRET~~ Declassified

## Summary (Excerpted)

**Mar. 19** On March 19, 1953, B Company conducted a raid on 31A. At 1905, A-1 Combat patrol left the Main Line of Resistance (MLR) for a probe on enemy positions. Friendlies approached the objective from the west in 1 squad strength, having placed a base of fire on their right flank. At 2040, the patrol was taken under fire by the enemy firing small arms and throwing grenades, from the trench line about 40 yards away. By 2045, Friendlies had received three wounded in action. They requested and received 60mm mortar fire north of the objective. At 2048, Friendlies were receiving enemy incoming on the objective. Friendly 81mm and 4.2 mortars and artillery fire began falling on the rear slope of the objective at 2050. At 2019, the patrol broke contact on order and returned to the MLR at 2120.

**Mar 26** On the evening of March 26, 1953, the company command post at Carson, Reno and Vegas were attacked by the enemy in battalion strength. Friendlies repulsed the attack at Carson, but Reno and Vegas fell into enemy hands. The command post at Vegas was subsequently retaken by elements of the 2nd Battalion, 5th Marines and 3rd Battalion, 5th Marines but the command post at Reno was still held by the enemy at the end of the period. At the end of this period, two squads of Corspmen were sent to recover casualties. The C Company aid station reported treating 56 casualties.

# The Ungok Raid

## Donald K. Dodd

The mission of the Ungok Raid, in March of 1953, was for the sole purpose of capturing a prisoner for interrogation. It was felt the Chinese Army was up to something. The strategy was to use the 2nd and 3rd Baker Company Rifle Platoons, augmented with a machine-gun section, and Marines from Weapons Company for mine clearing and manning four flame-throwers.

We were to raid Hill 31A, before dawn, after the lifting of the mortar and artillery fire further up the hill so as to keep the enemy down thus enabling our four flame-throwers to spray the enemy trench line. The 3rd Platoon, followed by the 2nd Platoon, was then to assault the trench line and capture whatever enemy was there.

Ungok–Reno–Carson–Vegas (USMC Map)

The platoons approached with only a slight delay caused by the clearing of a mine from the trail near the base of the hill. Once we got into assault position, the preparatory mortars and artillery were to commence on the trench areas which we were to attack.

It was about this time that all hell broke loose. I cannot for certain say that the first incoming were short rounds of our own, but it certainly sounded that way.

Some claimed that these were from the USS *Missouri*

or another naval vessel. That is absurd. First, we were at least 25 or more miles inland. Second, no one in their right mind would have attempted or conceived the use of naval gunfire from any distance to be so precise as to be within 50–100 yards' distance from friendly troops on the attack. Third, if the person making the assertion of navy short rounds realized the size of a battleship barrage, I doubt if any of us would have made it off Hill 31A.

Once incoming started, casualties occurred quickly. Whether the flame-throwers actually did their thing, I don't know, but the assault took place. I recall what appeared to be machine-gun fire and other small-arms fire coming from a hill knob of Ungok.

The duration of the attack along, with certainly what must have been incoming from the Chinese, was probably not more than an hour at the most. Casualties were all taken back to our lines by both the walking wounded and non-wounded. There was no time for second trips especially since the distance from the MLR gate to the base of Ungok was a long one, but also a clear open trail, field and a tank road.

I, along with Staff Sergeant Maxwell, Lieutenant Britt, and someone else, were the last ones off the hill. I know that Lt Britt was wounded and asked Sgt Maxwell if there was anyone else. Maxwell took a walk around in the open and reported back that we were it. The four of us carried someone Killed in Action or badly wounded across the field onto the tank road and back to the MLR. There were about 56 casualties both KIA/WIA/DOW from the 92 Marines that took part.

Jeremiah Jackson was in the same squad as I was. He and I were both BARmen. I recall him at Ungok in one piece, but at the end of the day, he was Killed in Action.

It is most unfortunate that we did not capture a prisoner. Baker Company was put back on the line, within a day. I was part of a four-man patrol that went back out on March 22, 1953 to Ungok with the plan of maybe getting a Chinese soldier out of a sniper hole. However, the patrol was unsuccessful due to a series of events. A tank light was turned on us by mistake. It was supposed to be turned on if we requested it, not while we were coming up to the sniper hole, thus giving us away.

I will admit I didn't want to voluntarily be on that patrol, but when two replacements including a Sgt (just in from Japan) volunteered and both were Gung Ho, I found out it's "catching". There are two things about this raid that trouble me, even to this day, and the one that's the biggest is—if we had been successful, would our G-2 have found out about the upcoming March 26, 1953 attack by the Chinese against Reno, Carson and Vegas which were to the immediate east of Ungok and were being held by Charlie and Dog Companies?

*—Donald—*

# Reno–Vegas–Carson, March 1953

## Maurice M. Deveraux

With the next reunion on its way to Nevada and the gathering to take place in a city called Reno, with a visit to Carson and another city called Vegas about 400 miles from here, I was thinking it would be a fitting time to honor our B-1-5, C-1-5 and A-1-5 brothers who had some very fierce and bloody battles in March of 1953 that were called Vegas, Reno and Carson.

These battles were to be the bloodiest Chinese attacks to date in Western Korea, and our Baker Bandits were in the thick of it. These three positions were held by 1st Battalion, 5th Marines when the communists sent battalions of 700 to 800 soldiers against the Marines on March 26, 1953 to open the battles.

The battle was fierce (USMC)

In the beginning, the bloody fighting resulted in the killing and wounding of nearly 1,000 Marines, with enemy losses at least double of the Marines. Most of the B Company Killed in Action were on March 19, 1953 in battles near Outpost Reno. It was the closest to the enemy and it depended on supporting fire from Carson and Vegas.

On the night of March 26, 1953, the Chinese sent a force of 3,500 soldiers against the 5th Marine sector. The Marines were hitting back at the Chinese with bayonets, knives, and bare fists. Our brothers in C Company who were at Reno at this time, only had seven out of 40 men still able to fight, after the initial assault. The enemy, by sheer force of numbers, had surrounded and overrun the C Company positions and all but five had been killed or taken prisoner along with 35 percent casualties to the reinforcing units. A navy corpsman attached to C Company lost his life saving many Marines and was awarded the Medal of Honor for this action. During the fight it was estimated that the Chinese shelled the Marine positions with 14,000 rounds of mortar, and artillery rounds.

**GOD BLESS OUR CORPSMEN**

—"Mo"—

# Navy Cross for Corpsmen's Heroism

## HMCS (FMF) Mark T. Hacala, USNR

Four platoons of Marines formed on the parade square at Marine Barracks, Washington, DC. The Commandant of the Marine Corps, General Charles C. Krulak, faced a line of five brothers standing at solemn attention. The men listened with pride and sadness as their late brother's citation was read. "For extraordinary heroism in action against the enemy while assigned as a hospital corpsman for Company F, 2nd Battalion, 5th Marines, 1st Marine Division serving in the Republic of Korea on the 26 and 27 March 1953."

On a terrible night in an unremembered battle of a forgotten war, one hospital corpsman epitomized the navy's ideals of honor, courage, and commitment. He did so at the cost of his life. On May 14, 1999, 46 years after his death, Hospital Corpsman Third Class Joseph F. Keenan was posthumously awarded the Navy Cross, the nation's second-highest decoration for combat valor, for his gallantry in battle.

## A Bad Night for Hospital Corpsmen

In the spring of 1953, long after the dynamic struggles at Inchon and the Chosin Reservoir, a vicious kind of combat had developed in Korea. Grand-scale campaigns of movement were replaced by small-unit raids from dug-in lines of trenches and bunkers. In this bitter style, the Korean conflict was now reminiscent of World War I.

Forward of the American line was a string of hilltop outposts, opposed by a similar line of Chinese strongholds, north of Seoul. The 5th Marines defended three outposts—known as Carson, Reno, and Vegas—with 40 Marines and a navy hospital corpsman each. A mere seven miles away, stalled truce talks tried in vain to end the bloodshed.

But a cease-fire would not come for another four months.

At 1900 on March 26, 1953, the Chinese launched a massive attack on the "Nevada Cities" outposts. The communists opened with immense artillery and mortar fire, which would riddle the Marines' sector with 14,000 rounds in the next eight hours. In the opening salvos, though, a staggering one to three rounds per second battered the scant garrisons.

As the bombardment began to tell, 3,500 Chinese soldiers attacked the 123 outpost defenders. Marine casualties were heavy and, in less than an hour, the Chinese dug out the handful of Reno's survivors from their bunker—which had been blown shut in the barrage—and took five Marines and a hospital corpsman prisoner.

Reno had been quickly overrun. Company C, 1st Battalion, 5th Marines rushed forward to help their beleaguered comrades, and Company F, 2nd Battalion, 5th Marines quickly followed. As they fought their way to the base of Reno Hill, the flurry of shrapnel began to find "Fox" Company's Marines.

Hospital Corpsman Third Class Joe Keenan now sought casualties in need of his care. Barely 20 years old, Keenan had arrived in Korea in February only weeks before, ominously on Friday the 13th. Now, minutes into his first, hellish battle, shrapnel from a nearby blast struck his hand. A fellow hospital corpsman moved to his aid, but Keenan waved him off, directing him to nearby wounded Marines. That sailor was killed by shell fragments an instant later.

HM3 Keenan continued his work until another piece of shrapnel found him, this time in the head. Fearing his wounds would be fatal, Keenan reluctantly fell back to his battalion aid station to receive cursory medical care. Although in no shape to go back into the fight because of his serious wounds, HM3 Keenan restocked his medical supplies and crossed the dangerous 1,600 yards to his company's position.

## Back into the Jaws of Death

The route back to combat Outpost Reno provided no good news for the hospital corpsman. Steep hills flanked his path, and rice paddies and mine fields covered the adjacent flat ground. That left only the trail to his outpost, which the Chinese had pinpointed for their guns and mortars. Once back with his Marines, HM3 Keenan continued to move in the open, all the while exposed to incessant shellfire. As he found and treated casualties, a nearby explosion blew dirt into his eyes, partially blinding him. Although slowed, he was undeterred.

HM3 Keenan found his way to Reno Block, a small hilltop 150 yards behind the Reno Outpost. There he found two hospital corpsmen from Charlie Company, 1/5 tending to the fallen. Hospitalman Francis Hammond pulled the wounded to safety and directed operations at this impromptu aid station. HN Paul Polley had been wounded by shrapnel and was blinded by the blast. Despite this, Polley had his hands guided to his Marines' wounds and treated them by touch alone. As

HM3 Keenan performed his medical work similarly impaired, a nearby Marine remarked, "This is a bad night for corpsmen—they're all blind!" Once these casualties there were stabilized, HM3 Keenan moved off the hilltop into a gully to aid those who were hit trying to retake Reno. The young petty officer soon had six to eight wounded under his care. There, two Marines from Keenan's platoon, Private Floyd Caton and Private Dan Holl, came across their friend while trying to find an alternate evacuation route back to the main line.

Both implored Keenan to fall back to a safer area. Caton and Holl argued feverishly, pointing out Keenan's wounds, his inexperience in combat, and the surrounding danger of shellfire and Chinese patrols. "I'm staying," Keenan barked resolutely! "I got a job to do, and I'm going to do it!"

Unable to convince their friend, Caton and Holl were at least able to flush HM3 Keenan's eyes with water from their canteens. The two then continued on their assignment, leaving Keenan to bandage his patients. When they passed the spot half an hour later as a rear guard for the American withdrawal, the Marines did not see their friend.

Unknown to Caton and Holl, some time between 0230 and 0530 on March 27, 1953, shrapnel struck HM3 Keenan in the head and killed him.

Dan Holl, Floyd Caton, and Joe Keenan had made a pact to write each other's families should anything happen to one of them. The Marines had seen Keenan's wounds from the early part of the evening battle and knew that he would survive them, so the two wrote to the Keenan family to reassure them that Joe would be all right.

These letters arrived at the Keenan's Massachusetts home shortly after the telegram that announced Joe's death. Holding out hope because of the conflicting information, the family contacted government officials to discover whether there had been a mistake—that Joe was still alive. Sadly, HM3 Joe Keenan's death was confirmed in correspondence from their senator, John F. Kennedy.

## A Brother's Quest

Michael P. Keenan was 13 years old when his brother Joe was killed in Korea. The event left an indelible mark on him. Three decades later, when he obtained Joe's 1953 letters home, Mike Keenan began to try to discover more about his brother's death. As he found Marines and sailors who knew Joe, Mike discovered that his brother had been nominated for a decoration for heroism on the night he died.

Over the next 15 years, Mike Keenan continued to seek survivors of the battle that killed his brother. From each contact he made, Mike found others who verified Joe's actions, including Dan Holl and Floyd Caton, the Marines who had written to his family in 1953.

Convinced of his brother's heroism, Mike assembled the supporting accounts and forwarded them to various military offices, hoping to spark some action to recognize Joe officially. Without the original award nomination, Mike was told, no action could be taken.

The original nomination, of course, had been lost in 1953. With the staggering casualties and normal transfers within Keenan's unit, the battalion became a completely new organization within a mere two months. If higher echelons of command had requested corroboration of the acts, no one left in the unit could verify them. It is easy to see the nomination could have remained unprocessed. Fortunately the issue did not end there. Through efforts undertaken at the Bureau of Medicine and Surgery, a successful award nomination negotiated navy channels.

The award of HM3 Joe Keenan's Navy Cross gave a sense of value to his heroism, to his determination, and to his devotion to his mission and his friends. Perhaps more importantly, it provided emotional closure to his family and to the Marines and sailors who survived that terrible night.

## Story Behind the Story

One copy of this package came to the historian's office at the Navy Bureau of Medicine and Surgery. Assistant Historian Dr David Klubes did some initial research in the Navy Medical Department's archives, but gave the package renewed interest when he discovered a group of Hospital Corps personnel data cards that had been removed from their files. All of these cards referenced hospital corpsmen who had received the Medal of Honor, except for one. That card was HM3 Joe Keenan's.

Dr Klubes mentioned his find to Senior Chief Hospital Corpsman Mark Hacala, a navy reservist who returned to active duty to research the history of the Hospital Corps for its 1998 centennial anniversary. Intrigued, the two approached the Navy Awards and Special Projects office and asked if procedures allowed for resubmission of an award recommended if their research verified Keenan's heroism? They were told it could be done.

Later that day, Senior Chief Hacala discovered a Korean War reunion group that was staying in the same hotel as he was. As fate would have it, this group was the veterans of Company F, 2d Battalion, 5th Marines. This was Joe Keenan's unit! The men with whom Hacala was visiting were the men whose letters formed Mike Keenan's package on his brother!

Senior Chief Hacala and Dr Klubes began a six-month investigation into the final day of Joe Keenan's life. They obtained unit rosters, battle reports, photographs, maps, and published material. They interviewed survivors of the terrible battle at Combat Outpost Reno and pieced together the clearest account of the events of March 26–27, 1953.

What resulted was a document of over 100 pages nominating HM3 Joseph F. Keenan for the Navy Cross. Upon recommendation of the Navy Awards Board, the Secretary of the Navy approved the posthumous award of the Navy Cross to Hospital Corpsman Third Class Joseph F. Keenan.

## Sailors' Valor in Battle

In the first night of the Nevada Cities battles, between six and 10 hospitalmen accompanied their Marines into the fight. The sailors who played a part in that battle distinguished themselves by heroic conduct under trying circumstances.

**HN Francis Hammond** was wounded as he moved about the battlefield for several hours, organizing the care and treatment of numerous casualties. Killed in action, he was posthumously awarded the Medal of Honor for his valor. Francis Hammond High School in his native Alexandria, VA was named in his honor.

**HN Paul Polley** cared for his wounded although temporarily blinded and struck by shrapnel in the chest. He was awarded the Navy Cross for his heroism. He retired from the navy as a master chief hospital corpsman.

**HN Thomas Waddill** was the hospital corpsman on Reno when the Chinese attack began. He was captured after being dug out of the collapsed bunker and remained a POW for several months. He was awarded the Navy Cross for his heroism in action.

**HM3 William G. Jones** moved to treat the other hospital corpsman in his platoon, Joe Keenan, when he was first wounded. When he moved to get to a nearby casualty, he was killed by enemy shellfire.

**HM3 Jay Guiver** accompanied a provisional platoon to evacuate wounded from Reno Block. Killed in action, he was posthumously awarded the Silver Star Medal for his bravery.

**HM3 Jack Linn** was severely wounded on the night of March 26–27, 1953.

In the ensuing days of battle to retake nearby Outpost Vegas, several hospitalmen demonstrated similar valor and were also decorated.

**HM3 William Charette:** Medal of Honor
**HN James McVeen:** Navy Cross
**HM3 Henry Minter:** Silver Star Medal
**HM3 Eldon Ralson:** Silver Star Medal
**HN Sidney Hughes:** Bronze Star Medal
**HM3 Donald Lee:** Bronze Star Medal
**HN Edward Schoonover:** Bronze Star Medal

# B-1-5 Casualties—March 1953

## Killed in Action

*Confirmed through Korean War Project*

| | | |
|---|---|---|
| PFC William Cortwright, from Brooklyn, NY | DOW | 5MAR53 |
| SGT Ural Dorsey, from Oak Ridge, LA | KIA | 19MAR53 |
| PFC Hershel B. Gooding, from Jamestown, Tenn. | KIA | 19MAR53 |
| PFC Richard B. Hanson, from Kenosha, Wisc. | DOW | MAR53 |
| PFC Jeremiah Jackson, from Natchitoches, LA | KIA | 19MAR53 |
| PFC Dennis D. Martinez, from Visalia, Calif. | KIA | 19MAR53 |
| PFC Charles H. McBrair, from Farrell, Penn. | KIA | 19MAR53 |
| 2LT Eugene Stewart McComb, Mississippi | DOW | 18MAY53 |
| PFC Lloyd A. Pinner, from Detroit, Mich. | KIA | 19MAR53 |

*Note: Casualties on March 26, 1952 were heavy among C Company and H Company. C-1-5 had its 2nd platoon over-run on Reno Hill. All were killed except four, who were wounded and captured by the enemy.*

*USMC Command Diary reports 5th Regiment May 1950—60 KIA and 148 WIA*

# End of the Korean War

President Eisenhower was keenly aware of the 1.8 million American men and women who had served in Korea and the 36,576 Americans who had died there. He played a key role in bringing about a cease-fire. In announcing the agreement to the American people on television shortly after the signing the Armistice, he said, in part:

"Soldiers, sailors, marines, and airmen, of 16 different countries, have stood as partners beside us throughout these long and bitter months. In this struggle we have seen the United Nations meet the challenge of aggression—not with pathetic words of protest, but with deeds of decisive purpose. And so, at long last, the carnage of war is to cease and the negotiation of the conference table is to begin…

We hope that all nations may come to see the wisdom of addressing differences in this fashion before, rather than after, there is resort to brutal and futile battle.

Now, as we strive to bring about that wisdom, there is, in this moment of sober satisfaction, one thought that must discipline our emotions and steady our resolution. It is this: We have won an armistice on a single battleground—not peace in the world. We may not now relax our guard nor cease our quest."

—*President Dwight D. Eisenhower 1953*—

# Fight Is Finally Over

## Corporal Emmett Shelton, Jr.

In the summer of 1953, President Eisenhower began to publicly hint that the United States might make use of its nuclear arsenal to break the military stalemate in Korea. He condoned Allied forces' harassing air raids on mainland China. The president also put pressure on his South Korean ally to drop some of its demands in order to speed the peace process.

Rumors of a Fleet of B-36 Peacemaker Super Carriers, loaded heavy with cargo, flew from Alaska in Russian and Chinese airspace and then to Guam. Whether or not Eisenhower's threats of nuclear attacks helped, by July 1953 all sides involved in the conflict were ready to sign an agreement ending the bloodshed. The armistice, signed on July 27, established a committee of representatives from neutral countries to decide the fate of the thousands of prisoners of war on both sides. It was eventually decided that the POWs could choose their own fate–stay where they were or return to their homelands. A new border between North and South Korea was drawn, which gave South Korea some additional territory and demilitarized the zone between the two nations. The war cost the lives of millions of Koreans and Chinese, as well as over 50,000 Americans.

After three years of a bloody war, the United States, the People's Republic of China, North Korea, and South Korea agree to an armistice, bringing the Korean War to an end. The armistice ended America's first experiment with the Cold War concept of "limited war."

The fighting ended on July 27, 1953, when the Korean Armistice Agreement was signed. The agreement created the Korean Demilitarized Zone to separate North and South Korea, and allowed the return of prisoners.

From the start of the War in 1950 to the end in 1953, USMC reports that 4,267 Marines were declared Killed in Action or Missing in Action; and 23,744 were wounded.

Crossing the 38th parallel (USMC)

# The Road Back Home

Throughout the years, I've often thought how natural it seemed in Korea to have everyone perform his duty under the most dangerous and stressful conditions. How presumptuous of me. We all know that many units, outside of the Marine Corps, were decimated or completely destroyed because the weakest link in the chain failed. The Marines and the corpsmen are indeed a special breed. Once a Marine—Always a Marine.

*—Kerrigan—*

# Ten Days in Korea—Life in a Wheelchair

## Corporal Emmett Shelton, Jr.

*"The real heroes never lived to come back home or are still suffering the wounds of war."*

The following story is about such a HERO. Private Jerry A. Schultz was assigned to B-1-5 back when it was Charlie-Sixth.

He was the company guide and proudly carried our company's guidon on parade.

Jerry went into Korea with B Company and the 1st Provisional Marine Brigade on August 2, 1950.

Ten days later, he was severely wounded and rendered paralyzed on August 12, 1950. He had been promoted to Corporal by this time. Our Unit Diary page 739 for August 17, 1950, reports it thus:

> SCHULTZ Jerry A
> WIA Korea GSW fracture spine Evac to
> 8054th Evac Hosp 13Aug50

Jerry was transformed from a tall strapping six footer to about four feet tall in his wheelchair. He could have given up and felt sorry for himself, but not Jerry, he had a wife, Judy, and a life to live.

He became a successful farmer back in Kansas and did a damn good job of getting on with his family and career. I asked Judy if Jerry had hired most of the farm work done and she replied with, "No, Jerry had rigged up a rope in a tree near the house where he could pull himself out of his wheelchair and onto the seat of his tractor. He did his own farm work." Jerry you were a hell of a man!

Jerry Schultz was excited to be a Marine (Schultz)

After our very first reunion, in 1987 Jerry handed me a spear point for our Guidon that he had used on our company Guidon back at Camp Pendleton prior to going to Korea. As the Company Guide, Jerry had kept it so as to keep it polished. When he went to Korea, it went into his sea bag and came back to him after the Korean War. That spear point still adorns its official place on the top of our B-1-5 Guidon.

God bless you, Jerry, you set a hard example to follow. You are my hero!

*—Emmett—*

## A Letter from Judy Schultz

The "Baker Bandits" were a very important part of Jerry's life the last few years, and I wanted you to know how much he enjoyed the friendship of his fellow comrades and receiving the *Guidon* so he could keep updated on your activities. Jerry died of a massive heart attack April 30, but he went the way he wanted to—in his bed, in the house he built and gazing out on the farm he had worked for the last 30 years. NOT in a VA hospital or a nursing home as I know he feared.

The Marine Corps came through with flying colors. When the Colonel of the Marine Corps League was contacted regarding a military funeral, he called to assure me Jerry would get the whole "Nine Yards"—his quote was "The Marines take care of their own, I'll handle everything." And he did, everything went like clock work. When I told the Colonel how pleased Jerry would have been, his remark was, "He's standing his first watch!"

*—Judy—*

# After Korea They Call Me "Lefty"

## "Lefty" Luster

I lost my right arm at the First Naktong Battle. I was with B-1-5 in Aug '50. I had seen an enemy soldier at a distance and borrowed an M-1 to check him out. After carrying a Browning Automatic Rifle (BAR) for two weeks, it seemed like a toy. Cease-fire had been ordered so my BAR remained silent. I could see the sniper had a hole dug into the hillside and covered with weeds. Cease-fire was not to be broken at that time, so I just kept an eye on that resting enemy soldier.

I was hit on August 17, 1950 at the First Naktong Bulge Battle. After my right arm was amputated, the surgeon left my wound open preventing me from the good liberty available. A pal picked up a Jap jacket for me, so I at least got something! The wound stayed open all the way to USN hospital at Oakland, CA.

I went home for Christmas and back to the USN hospital on January 5, 1951. So many amputees came from Chosin that it took a day for them to find a bunk for me on the amputee ward, 42-A. They put me next to our first quadruple amputee, USMCR, Sergeant W. Reininger of San Antonio, Texas. He bunked beside me. Without hands, he had difficulty when it came to smoking and the nurses would not help. I helped him and we became friends. Later on, he told me that he quit the smokes.

I received a "Dear John" letter from my stateside sweetheart right before Chosin. I spent my Christmas leave back home learning to shoot ducks with my left hand and left eye. The recreation officer at the USN hospital in Oakland had taken me quailing and I kept seeing the right side of the 12-gauge double gun instead of the sight line. It was tough to adjust, until I pulled my cap down over that dominant right eye. Then, I began to make more hits.

After duck season, I still had hospital leave time and had no girl to spend time with. The boys often called me the "ONE WOMAN MAN." I decided to hit the road and see some of the States. I left Little Rock, Ark. for Cleveland, OH and on to Montreal, Canada. When I hit NY City, I parked for three days, taking the sights in and answering all kinds of questions about my missing arm and the War. The old Tomb of the Unknown Soldier was a pleasure to see and watch the changing of the rear guard.

On my way back, the draw bridge over the Potomac River was up and traffic was snarled. Some crazy civilian rolled his window down and started yelling. It was unusual for a Yankee to be so very friendly so I tried to listen as I ignored him. I heard the name LUSTER ring out and my head jumped around to see my Marine buddy Cpl Dale Ellis, jumping up and down in those stupid-looking civies. When he was shot at Chosin, I thought he was gone forever. After being evacuated, he had been moved to Bethesda, MD to be closer to home base in Ohio. My driver could not believe we had served together in Korea. As the bridge leveled out I explained that Ellis had shot the enemy who shot me. That Chinese soldier was coming to finish me off when Ellis changed his mind with eight rounds from his trusty M-1.

It seemed like a dream, a miracle and maybe God does love the infantryman, after all. Dale is no writer, but he lost his leg trying to save me and my BAR. Today, he is retired in Las Vegas. Like me he has not adjusted too well to the civilian life, but one day long ago he was a great U.S. Marine and I am the only one left alive who knows it for certain. My salute to all those quiet men who kept the USMC alive.

*—Lefty—*

After 20 years, I found the bridge where B-5 left the dead after Sachon for later recovery (Luster)

*A Note from Ole Emmett: Lefty returned to South Korea after the War. He loved the people and the land. He spent about 15 years there teaching English as a second language. He shared the following:*

It was the First Naktong Bulge Battle when one of the officers said to the NCOs "We need an assembly point for our dead." Sergeant Waldo Wolfe looked over at me and said "you Bandits go find a spot where we can assemble our KIAs. And mark it so we can find them later." I said to Art "Bugs" Connally (my gunner) "He means us" and off we went.

We went down the bank to a bridge and looked around for something to mark it with. We had been gone all but three minutes when Sgt Wolfe shows up. We asked him what to use to mark the location. He said, use something sharp like your xxxx head. Being machine gunners, we didn't have bayonets, so Art used a bullet to mark "B-1-5."

After all these years, I found the bridge and assured myself that our fallen Brothers were recovered and that "B-1-5" mark is still, there!

*—Lefty—*

# Why Was I Spared?

## Corporal Emmett Shelton, Jr.

Before the Korean War, Second Lieutenant James L. Ables, Private Wilber B. Gray, Private Milton L. "Dell" Green and Private Emmett Shelton were members of A Company, Fifteenth Infantry Battalion, USMCR of Austin, Texas. In Korea, all were members of the Baker Bandits.

Korea was hard on these men. Lieutenant Ables was a platoon leader in our Reserve Unit and was well respected. He was killed accidentally when his rifle fell on a moving tank. Private Gray was accidentally killed when the 6×6 in which he was riding in early 1951 went off the roadway and turned over. Private "Dell" Green was badly wounded on Hill 313. They were all really good men.

I don't know how in the hell I was spared with just being frozen?

*—Emmett—*

# A Day in Ole San Francisco

## Private Milton L. "Dell" Green

I was sent to Korea in March of 1951 and assigned to Baker Company-1-5. I was doing pretty well until a place called Hill 313 on 23 April.

Here I was, hanging onto this tree for dear life with grenades rolling all over me. I kicked them away as best I could, but a couple went off and they pretty well messed up my legs in doing so.

We prevailed and I was taken down this hill along with Mr. McGahn, Harlan Pope and many other wounded Marines.

I spent the next five years in hospitals all over, but the tale I want to tell is about my liberty in San Francisco. My buddies, Frank Golemi and Joe Aikin had been with me in the Oakland Naval Hospital for months, without liberty. We decided to try for a liberty pass and to go into San Francisco and stay at the Marines Memorial Club.

We did get liberty passes and headed for Frisco. You've got to understand the situation; I was in a cast from the hips down. I could bend at the waist, but this heavy cast covered both my legs. Frank and Joe picked me up out of bed and deposited me in a wheelchair with both legs straight out in front like a set of dual water-cooled fifties. Both Frank and Joe were also wounded and gimpy as hell, so it was the wounded taking care of the wounded (sound familiar)?

So off we went, but we just couldn't pass up that first bar. We went in and lifted a few, but we were not accustomed to drinking, being out of training for months, that stuff went right to our heads. When we came out of that bar, it was a downhill grade to get where we were going and we were doing pretty well until my hands slipped off the wheels and my wheelchair started picking up speed. Here we came, a Marine in a wheelchair with both legs in a cast stuck out in front stiff as a board picking up speed at every turn of the wheels. My two gimpy buddies were trying to help, but they could hardly keep up, much less stop me. Of course, being pretty well oiled, we were shouting "GANG-WAY—GANG-WAY—GET OUT OF THE WAY!!" etc. etc.

Then our luck ran out. As I careened down that sidewalk, one of San Francisco's finest stepped out of a bar right in my path. He didn't look either way, but started walking the same way we were going and my cast caught him about butt high turning him ass over tea kettle and making a pretty good mess of his uniform and spoiling the heck out of his composure.

He didn't think it was a damn bit funny. Anyway, he got up and ate our asses out good and called a paddy wagon to come get us. They lifted me out of my wheelchair and deposited me in the wagon along side of my folded wheelchair and my two buddies and off we went to headquarters.

When we got to police headquarters they lifted me out of the paddy wagon and deposited me back in my wheelchair and took us indoors. The complaining officer had not cooled down at all; in fact, he wanted to throw the book at us. While they were trying to figure out what to do with us, they sent the complaining officer home to change clothes and get cleaned up. As soon as he was gone, they loaded us back into the paddy wagon and returned us to the Naval Hospital. And that is the story of my first liberty after Korea; a day in ole San Francisco.

*—Dell—*

# Sweetheart—I'm Coming Home

## Corporal Emmett Shelton, Jr.

I was evacuated from Chosin due to frostbite of the feet and hands. A few days later, I wrote my sweetheart:

Yokouka, Japan
Dec. 24, 1950

Dear Jeanette

I got your letter the day after the Chinese sprang the trap on us so I couldn't very well answer it until now. Right after I got your letter, they took us up on a mountain and we started fighting with the Chinese Army. We weren't fighting to take land or anything, we were fighting to stay alive.

I was in the B Company, 1st Battalion, 5th Marine Regiment. I never did so much walking, fighting, and praying in all my life. I fought through the enemy roadblocks to get out of there. They took us all to way down near Wosan which is 30 miles from Pusan. Then they said for all men with frostbite feet to go to sickbay, so I went. First they evacuated me to Masan then to Pusan, then to an army hospital in Japan, then 600 miles to a navy hospital still in Japan.

I got here night before last. Yesterday morning the doctors looked at us and you know what he said to me? He said "I'm sending you to the States!" And I didn't know what to think. My feet were bad enough to go to Japan. They don't look or feel very good but I can limp along.

They say they are going to try to send us to hospitals near our homes. I sure hope they can. They also say we will get a medal for this. I have lots to tell you if I ever see you.

You know how I always treated my parents? Well, I know now that was all crazy. I love and miss my home very much. At night in Korea when it was 35 below zero and the Chinese were attacking us, I could see what I had never seen before. I am a stern believer in God and I'm starting to go to church all the time. He saved me and I know it.

I don't really know why I'm telling you this but you need to understand me anyway. I used to be terrible to you—I know it. That was stupid of me. I was just a guy—I guess. And you know I was pretty wild. But I know my mistakes in life and I've repented. Boy, I've learned death comes too easy and quick.

One night I was sitting in my foxhole with a buddy of mine. I was out in the open and he had some dirt piled in front of him. A mortar shell hit about two feet from our hole. I noticed him still slumped over after it hit. I called to him and said "Roger, that was a close one." He didn't answer. As I shook him his head fell forward. Blood ran from his nose and mouth. I called for a corpsman. After some time they came and evacuated him. He had shrapnel in his head and he died. It should have been me by all odds but it was his time. That's not the only time similar things happened to me. Boy, I'm going God's way from now on. At least as much as I can.

What have you been doing lately? When you get this letter, please call my mother because I should be getting to the States pretty soon. When I get there, I'll phone home and give her my address. Tomorrow is Christmas and I hope you have a good one.

The Chinese got six truckloads of our mail and I think they got most of our Christmas presents. But know I'm going to the States is the best present I could get anyway.

This War has sure settled me down lots. The other day in the hospital, I caught myself looking as Better Homes and Gardens magazine and making plans!

You are probably going steady again by now but I hope not! When I get well, I'm going to try to get a 30 day leave. I hope I can. I better go for now and quit bothering you. Write real quick, just as soon as you can get my address in the States.

Love,
Emmett

P.S. I married Jeanette, my high school sweetheart, before I got out of the service. We raised four children and she helped proofread *The Guidon*. I was happily married to Jeanette for the rest of my life (over 60 years).

Emmett got married while still in the service (Shelton)

# The End of My Tour in Korea

## Corporal H. J. "Syd" Sydnam

On November 8, in our reserve tent camp near Inje, the men were given showers, haircuts, and "new" clothing for the upcoming winter. I had a picture taken of Andy Feller, Sam DiGiovanni, and myself celebrating our splendidly clean selves to commemorate the occasion.On November 10, we had an unusually good lunch and a cake-cutting in celebration of the Marine Corps' Birthday. We then pulled up the tents and moved out at midnight to relieve the 1st Battalion, 1st Marines on the line. On the 13th, we were in the new position improving bunkers and trenches, constructing warm-up bunkers and generally getting ready for the fast approaching winter. At the same time we were conducting patrols and night ambushes, taking occasional mortar and artillery rounds and repelling night probes. It was getting colder and colder and still the peace talks ground on.

To the front of our position was a large, heavily mined, valley. On the far side of the valley arose a great, bald, mountain which was rapidly becoming heavily fortified by the enemy. Both sides made nightly patrols into the valley but few encounters were reported. All of us "short-timers" lived in dread that the orders would come to "take that hill" before our group left for the States.

November 22 gave us a new treat: Our Thanksgiving Dinner was helicoptered in on a pad we had constructed on our reverse slope. A USMC photographer took a photo of "Top," Master Sergeant Ishmael Powers, and Sergeant Sydnam eating a hot turkey dinner in a shell hole. That photo was published in the Top's hometown paper. I had similar photos taken with my camera. I also received a "care package" from Jane Nolan that Lieutenant Nolan had signed off to me. Miniatures of Scotch and some fine cigars completed a memorable Thanksgiving.

## Departing Korea

Before leaving on rotation from the area of hostilities, we either had to sign up for re-enlistment or sign a waiver of rights to seniority for re-enlistment in the corps. We were made to burn our bridges or go for a career. I gave it a good deal of thought and then signed the waiver.

On November 27, the largest rotation draft of the war, to date, left for the sea. The day before, I had given my small hoard of morphine syrettes to the corpsmen and those of us headed home assembled at battalion headquarters in preparation for the move. This was the 11th Rotation Draft and there were five officers and 135 enlisted men.

Upon finally leaving, I had very mixed emotions. I was very glad to leave, especially with the prospect of having to advance over the terrain to our front; also I felt that I was overdue to leave and that my terrific luck couldn't hold out forever. The Bandits were a great bunch of men, however, and it was not without regret that I was, for the first time in 11 months, going away from them and their dangers.

We formed a great truck convoy heading for the Sea of Japan. It was very cold, about zero Fahrenheit, with a strong wind and the ground was snow covered. At regular intervals the convoy would stop to allow all of us to get off and warm up. It was necessary to keep stamping your feet on the truck bed and flailing your arms to keep from freezing. Despite my best efforts I froze the bottoms of both of my feet.

When we reached the beach, and I recall it being only a "beach" and not a "port," there were primitive warm-up facilities and a long, long wait to be lightered out to the ship. Thompson, Woods and I had traveled with a good supply of beer, which of course froze. We tried heating it on the oil stove and eating it with our "spoons." We located a group of local villagers' shacks where we bought some hot radish soup that was very warming. There was a Japanese landing craft beached at our embarkation point that was being used as a generator plant. Since the three of us were familiar with that kind of vessel we went on board, found the paint locker and went to sleep on warm shelves.

Unfortunately, we nearly missed our ride to the ship. When we were finally found and lightered out all of the troop bunks had been taken and the three of us had to sleep in the crew's "head" until we reached Japan. My frosted feet gave me hell as they thawed but fortunately I lost no flesh.

The ship took us to Kobe and we then went on to Otsu, where we regained our old sea bags left from our trip to Korea. Here we spent about a week getting de-wormed, more shots, drunk and disorderly. At the NCO Club it was $2.50 for a fifth for any "Western" booze. We did a lot of "catching up." We actually did some more Christmas shopping! Semper Fidelis,

*—"Syd"—*

# From Hill 907 to Stateside and "Safety"

## Art Reid

I have reflected many times on some of the events in my life after leaving Hill 907 to return home. Some were quite humorous in retrospect. I am sure all who returned could find things that may interest their grandchildren. I will share a few of my memories—mostly post Korea.

When I left Korea after Hill 907, we traveled to Japan; I was standing in line for my sea bag. I told a Marine in "supply" my name and waited for my sea bag to appear. I was told I was KIA and my sea bag had been returned to my family. I assured him I felt alive, however, in looking in the U.S. Marine Corps Bound Diaries of B Company, 1st Battalion, 5th Marines, January–December 1951, I find Reid, Arthur L. Jr., listed as Killed in Action March 20, 1951. On that date I was knocked out by concussion from a mortar round and when I came to, I found I had a hole in my leg from shrapnel. I was evacuated to a Med Station and stayed there until some time in April when I returned to B-1-5. I also found out later there was an A.L. Reid, Jr. who was Killed in Action in the Chosin in December '50. His folks got my sea bag and returned it to the corps and eventually it found its way back to me.

On the ship home from Japan, we got into a rather large storm and I noticed when we were in the trough between waves, the wave tops were above the porthole I was looking through. The ship's screws would come out of the water and the ship would vibrate. I remember thinking we shall probably go down and I won't make it home after all. I met Dan Ballem's uncle in Frisco. Dan was Killed in Action on Hill 907. His uncle and his sweet wife asked if I would like to walk down the main drag and just see what civilization looks like again? That sounded good, so as we walked along in this beautiful crowd of people that seemed peaceful enough some idiot comes running out of a jewelry shop with a pistol in his hand. He had decided to circumvent working for a living and rob jewelry stores instead. He came out shouting "Stand back" and pointed his pistol at me. I remember not being frightened, but just thinking "I knew it—this fool is going to shoot me and I will never get home, after all."

I finally made it home to Houston, Texas. My dad had been planning for me to resume former days together when we would go hunting. Sure enough, we went hunting in East Texas and some yo-yo in the woods begins firing at something. I remember a few rounds snapping in the trees around me and I told my dad "I don't care to go hunting anymore." So we go fishing together on some creek near Liberty, Texas. While casting for bass, I heard some rustling behind and above me from something or someone on a bluff bank. The hair on my neck began to stand up. I turned around and saw nothing, but felt a bit uneasy. My dad was between me and my mother who remained in their car. She preferred reading the newspaper to fishing. I then heard the car horn honking so I headed and found that a large cougar, coming from our direction, had crossed the road a few feet in front of the car. My dad and I decided hunting cougars with a rod and reel was not too swift, so we left.

I reported to Naval Air Station, Corpus Christi as my new duty station. I was hitch hiking home to Houston one day when a fellow gave me a ride. After riding a number of miles, he reaches over and opens the glove box and there is a .45 automatic inside. He informs me he is contemplating killing someone. I relaxed a bit when I realized it was someone else, not the passenger he intended to kill. I suddenly had a desire to be let out of the car so I could get a bite to eat. What became of this Dillinger or his intended victim, I do not know.

I had the opportunity to be transferred to the Naval Retraining Command (actually it was a naval prison) at Portsmouth, New Hampshire. I applied and got the transfer. I wanted to visit Dan Ballem's parents who lived in Lynn, Mass. and this was an opportunity to do so. While at the NRC I began having recurring bouts with my tonsils swelling up. When I would go to sick bay, the doctors would say, "You need to have those tonsils out, but we can't do that while they are swollen. Come back when they are not swollen and we will take them out." When I would return to have them removed, they would say, "They are not swollen and there is no need to take them out." With only a few months left before my "Truman's year" expired I went to the hospital and reminded the doctor that he had promised to take my tonsils out. I suppose I reminded him in such a gentle way that he got ticked off and said, "Do you want your tonsils out now?" I said yes, so he obliged me by taking them out in his office while I sat in my chair. It occurred to me that I probably should have been a bit more tactful. A tonsillectomy without anesthetic is not the way to go, even for a Baker Bandit! At least they gave me a hospital bed for awhile to let me recover at no extra cost.

The GI Bill was authorized for us Korean Vets, so I decided to get out of the corps and go to school. I had not graduated from high school so while in the corps, I took and passed the high school and first-year college GED. A good friend I was stationed with and I were talking about this GI Bill and I told him I wanted to get an education, but did not know what to take in college. He had attended the University of Maine before going to Korea and he majored in Electrical Engineering. He told me a bit about what an engineer would do, so I decided to give that a try.

I showed up at the University of Houston, and was informed that the Dean of the School of Engineering had to approve all engineering candidates before they were admitted. He asked about my educational background and I told him about my wonderful GED qualifications. He said they were useless and I would have to go back to high school to graduate before he could accept me. He then asked me what I had been doing since I cleverly left high school before graduating? I explained I had been in the Marines and served with Baker Company, 5th Marines. His eyes lit up and he said he had been in the 5th Marines on Guadalcanal. We talked about the 5th Marines for about a half hour, he then said, "One Marine is going to help another. I will let you be admitted as a probationary student. You will have to maintain a C average for your Freshman year and take remedial math to remain in engineering school." I did so and graduated in '56 and then attended graduate school at the University of Houston for another year.

One other "little incident" occurred while I was TDY for Department of Defense in Turkey. I was traveling with another government engineer with a cab driver through Kurd territory. For some reason I cannot remember, the military transport we were supposed to have was not available. As we traveled we asked the driver to stop so we could get a photo from the mountain road where we were with a view overlooking the Black Sea. We had been warned that the Kurds routinely attacked targets of opportunity, like us, and killed and robbed them. As I was standing on the seaward side of the cab and looking through my camera viewfinder a shot rings out just behind me. My first thought was that this is not good. I turned around to see where the shot came from—it sounded like it was just next to my ear. That is exactly where it occurred, because there was a smoking pistol about a foot from my head. The pistol was in the hands of our cab driver. He had a big smile. He just wanted us to appreciate the echo effect of a pistol shot in this beautiful, mountainous, desolate, area in the middle of Kurd territory.

I had a cousin, Melvin Reid, who served with the 5th Marines and was frozen at the Chosin and later died in August of '51. I had a cousin who served with H-3-5 in Korea. My brother served with C-1-1 in Korea and won the Bronze Star in the Hwachon action. Another cousin served on Iwo with the Marines and another cousin served in the corps in Vietnam with "The Walking Dead." Between us we gathered eight Purple Hearts and a love for the United States Marine Corps. Looking back I can say I feel honored to have ever been a member of B-1-5 and a privilege to have served with the best! I thank the Lord for sparing my life in Korea and for letting me have such a great 54-plus years. Semper Fi,

—*Art*—

# Reconnecting With Brothers
# 40 Years Later

## The Brotherhood
### Chuck Hall, 1990

We have a special Brotherhood,
Known only to a few
Others cannot share it,
It's meant for me and you

To many, we are survivors,
To some, we're still unknown
We're thought by some as outcasts,
With no place to call home.

We've had our many problems,
And troubles by the score
But still we love each other,
And never ask for more

We hung tough in Korea,
Until our job was done
We faced a sullen public,
Who didn't believe we won

We only had each other,
To understand our mind
To ease the many heartaches,
Our peace was hard to find

Our numbers aren't too many,
Too early some are lost
We band together stronger,
We know we paid the cost

We'll love and keep our Brotherhood,
No matter what our fate
Faithful to each other,
'Till we meet at Heaven's Gate.

# The Guidon Brought Us Back Together

## Corporal Emmett Shelton, Jr.

I returned from Chosin with frostbite. I spent months in a series of hospitals. I couldn't wait to get my regular life back. I got married to my high-school sweetheart while at Quantico. When I got discharged, I came back to Austin, Texas, started a family and took on a sales job. I volunteered as a fireman and as the Marshall of my small community. Twenty years later, I was a successful land developer and the Commander of the Legion Post in Austin. I started an Americanism program in Austin high schools and invited local heroes as speakers.

In 1985, I attended the CHOSIN FEW reunion in San Diego, CA with over 1,300 members present. The handful of Marines from Baker Company, 1st Battalion, 5th Regiment USMC were in the crowd but we had a hard time relocating our follow "Baker Bandits."

Our "Old Top" Lieutenant Phil Dierickx, appointed me a committee of one to get the Bandits a Company guidon so Bandits could find their Company at the next reunion. I contacted the current Marines of B-1-5 (Bravo-1-5). The officers and men had a special Guidon made and sent it to us. I was so elated that I wanted to tell all of the 16 men that I was in contact with at that time. I made up a little newsletter telling about our new guidon, added a few stories and I named it *The Guidon*. I wrote that if Bandits would send in stories, pictures, and money for postage, I'd put out *The Guidon* monthly. They did, and I did.

In 2006, *The Guidon* mailing list had grown to 340 copies a month. We had stories from our leaders and our privates, we had the official USMC Historical Diaries, medals and lists of our casualties. Stories covered famous battles like Inchon and Chosin Reservoir, and many lesser-known battles. Stories came from privates, captains, even generals, we were all equal after the war. Emmett tracked each Bandit and each was "Posted to Heaven" when they died.

# The Photos We Share

## Corporal Emmett Shelton, Jr.

My Dad was a history buff. The day I boarded the train to Pendleton Summer 1950, gave me a diary, the Bullet camera he had carried in WWII and three rolls of film. He said write often. They rolled around in my pack till I got to Korea. Once there, I carried the camera in my jacket every day, I lost the diary. But, I did write home often.

A Marine does not pull out the camera in battle. But a son snaps a photo of a memory to share. Maybe it's a snap of a buddy in camp, or his platoon on a march or men trucking out. He knows *that* photo may survive him in the upcoming battle. It is for the future—to explain.

Most of the photos in this book are snapshots from men of the B-1-5 in the battlefield in 1950-53 with primitive cameras, in tough conditions: no tripods, no long lenses, no "do-overs." The film sat in pack for months in freezing or sweltering temperatures. It survived the mail before developing. After the war,

Men peering from a bunker (Conley)

the photos sat in wallets or in drawers for years before their owner searched them to share, here.

They may be dim, and the focus not sharp, but these are our memories.

Most notably, although our Marines share memories of the unthinkable, atrocities of war, their photos highlight how they lived, where they fought, the Brotherhood. We rely on the USMC photographers and other professionals for a few details, but most of the images are the memories of Baker Bandits.

Art said it best:

Dear Emmett,

You will have to forgive the quality of most of the photos I am sending you as they were taken with my dad's old Mercury 35mm, that split the frame. Even the originals were not too great. Since I have long misplaced the negatives, I had to re-photograph the old prints. The first roll I tried in a photo transfer machine and they came out one to one and are so small you cannot make them out. My next attempt, I used a close-up set of lenses which helped.

I didn't keep a diary and cannot remember the different locations or hill numbers associated with each picture. I was in B Company between April–November 1951.

*—Art Conley and Emmett—*

# How the Baker Bandits Got Their Name

## Master Sergeant "Ole Top," Phil Dierickx

Shoemaker guarded the beer ration carefully

We were reminiscing at the first reunion and a question was posed as to where our name "Baker Bandits" came from. Contrary to what everyone thinks, it was not that we Marines were thieves or that we were short on supplies because our supply sergeant wouldn't give us anything. Sgt Willie Shoemaker was the best scrounger of all. This guy was always out at night when you couldn't see him, looking for cast-offs or extras. It may take him a few days but he could find anything you needed—except ammunition.

Frank McDonald came to B-1-5 about when we adopted the name "Baker Bandits." Frank was friends with Shoemaker during the war so we asked him to give his opinion of why we were called "Baker Bandits."

Frank McDonald stood up and said:

> I have to say that, at the time that the "Baker Bandits" really took up the name, I had just been assigned to Baker's Weapons Company. The name "Baker Bandits" began while we were under Lt. John Hancock. Of course, we were Baker Company – but what about the Bandit part?
>
> You're right about "Shoe," he was the best and most crafty supply man in the world. The Marines always felt this way about supplies, if we've got it over in "our supply," the Tootsie Rolls or whatever, that's good. But if it's over in the Army's supply, it's a matter of choice. And with the "Baker Bandits," the choice was always to get it over to "our supply." That way, Shoemaker had Tootsie Rolls so we Bandits would have Tootsie Rolls and the Army had none. You could say the "Bandits" really opted for the cumshaw-midnight requisition method (acquisition through irregular methods). "Shoe" was pretty good at it. He always managed to keep enough so that the Bandits supply was adequate, even during a war. He gave the impression we were a bunch of a squirrels gathering and saving the nuts in the cave for a winter day. We always managed to supply ourselves, **our way.**
>
> —*Ole Top and Frank*—

# Healing Through Reconnecting

## Private Jim "Poodles" Redding, B-1-5

The mind can work in wondrous ways. The bad and the sad are closed out while the humorous and happy thoughts are often recalled; at least most of the time.

The personal contact I received along with some wonderful news has replaced one of those sad memories with thoughts of gladness. At the risk of seeming corny to some, I would like to share this transformation of sadness to happiness.

Sometime during April or May 1951, the 3rd Platoon received a new Platoon Leader, as a replacement for Lt Ables who had been Killed in Action. The new Platoon Leader, Charles Cooper, was a recent graduate from Annapolis. He wanted his troops to salute him, even in combat!

This new Platoon Leader wanted to have a field pack inspection. Gosh! We thought he was crazy since most of the gear in our pack were broken or cast-offs. The next week, we got all new equipment for the packs.

This new Platoon Leader was either courageous or stupid as he spent most of his time with the Point on patrol. He rotated his fire teams on the Point.

This new Patrol Leader was, in fact, a leader. He led his men in taking an objective, he didn't direct them. He set an example for his men.

This new Platoon Leader was shot by the enemy while on the Point taking an objective. I saw him carried down the hill.

While I was being evacuated aboard the USS *Haven*, I heard that our new Platoon Leader had been shot bad, but he was not killed. He was paralyzed from the waist down.

For many years, I have often thought of this battle with much sadness for this "Gung-Ho" and courageous Lieutenant.

When I saw General Charlie Cooper at the 1989 Reunion, this sadness was replaced with joy. He did not lose the use of his legs. In fact, he recovered and received the opportunity to return to duty. He received the recognition this brave leader deserved.

Lieutenant (excuse me, General) Charlie, we salute you, gladly. You can inspect my field pack any time you want to. I am now a much happier and, hopefully wiser Marine from Baker Company for knowing you.

*—Poodles—*

# Found My Bandit Brother

## Private Bill G. Irwin

How did we live through that morning in Chosin? Let me tell you what I believe with all my heart. I believe God must have had plans for two young Marines who were sure they were going to die that day. We were still a long way from getting out of that mess. A lot of our friends didn't make it, but we were Marines and we weren't about to give up.

Over the years, I have thought of that morning often. I would see a little grove of trees or a hill that resembled that one and I would remember. "Who was that man with me that morning?" I had no idea. "Did he make it? What was he doing? Does he ever think about that day? Does he ever think about me?"

Through the years I have had the opportunity to attend some of the reunions of our outfit, "The Baker Bandits" as we came to be known. We have a little newsletter called *The Guidon*. It's sent to those of Baker Company, 5th Marines and helps us keep up on one another. I had read some letters seeking information about someone from time to time.

I sent in a little blurb to Emmett for *The Guidon* that said, "If anyone out there remembers 'Custer's Last Stand' give me a call." I don't think I ever really expected to hear from anyone, but a week or so later, my wife and I had just gotten home from church and there was a phone call. I couldn't believe what I was hearing! "Bill, I'm your foxhole buddy!" "Who is this?" I wanted to know. He said, "This is Archie Lyle and I'm the one who was with you at 'Custer's Last Stand'."

I can't believe it still. It had to be a miracle! After 51 years I was talking to the man who had fought along side me that day. I had goose bumps as big as goose eggs.

In the midst of our rejoicing I asked, "Archie, what did you do when you got back from Korea?" He said, "Well I got married and when I got out of the Marines I sold insurance for a while and then God had the audacity to call me to preach." I said, "You're kidding!" He went on to tell me he had attended Baylor University and Southwestern Theological Seminary at Fort Worth, Texas.

He had pastored churches in Texas and then had gone to Missouri to pastor a church and retired there.

I said, "Archie, would you believe I'm a preacher too?" And I shared that God had called me to the ministry while I was in Korea and when I got out of the Marines I married, had a family, went to college and seminary (the same one he had attended), pastored several churches, and became a Director of Missions for our denomination in Colorado. I was retired too.

We have had several opportunities to get to know one another since then and it has been apparent to both of us that God did indeed have some very special plans in mind for two young 19-year-old Marines who met one morning in December 1950.

What a wonderful privilege it was to be able to serve with men of such great character. And what an honor to get to know some of these men since that time of trial in Korea on a more personal basis. It's been said, "Once a Marine, Always a Marine!" There has to be some truth to that statement because there is still a great deal of pride when I remember those Dress Blues and the fact that I had the privilege to be called a United States Marine.

So... the next time you attend a parade, as our flag passes by, watch the crowd. If you do you will be sure to see men snap to attention. You may even see tears in their eyes and a look of pride on their faces. No, they are probably not all former Marines. They may even look old and tired now, but I'm sure there was a time when they were full of vim, vigor, and vitality, fighting, not just for their own lives, but for YOUR life and for the life of this wonderful country we call THE UNITED STATES OF AMERICA. Semper Fidelis and God Bless,

—Bill—

*A Note from Ole Emmett: We just love to locate our old buddies and we just can't help but believe some of you Bandits out there know where some men are. If you do know, or even just think you know where one of our buddies lives, please send the information to me and I will do the detective work to locate them positively.*

# B-1-5 Adopted a Brother

## Corporal Emmett Shelton, Jr.

Over the years, I have spent many days looking for B-1-5 Bandits. One day, I called a Carmelo Tellez in Arizona as I was looking for a Bandit with that name. No answer—so I left a message.

Carmelo had a hard time calling me back. When he did, he told me of his nightmares and flashbacks to his time as an army ranger in Korea. I told him to go to a reunion of his old unit. But, he was army and his unit had no reunions, so I invited him to join the Baker Bandits. He has fit right in and he told you what it did for him. His experiences are the same as ours. Many Bandits have related similar experiences about the healing power of reconnecting.

Dear Emmett—

I finally have a chance to write a short note. What a good year this has been for me, and my family. The high point was when I got to meet all of you "Baker Bandits" at the reunion in San Diego. What a wonderful experience that was for Alice and me. I have never in my life met a finer bunch of people. I do not have the words to express my gratitude at the way you Marines accepted my family and me as part of the outfit.

The respect and love that was shown to us was the high point of my life. I can really say that the anger, hate, and bitterness are all things of the past. By golly, there is life after Korea.

I see by the letters in *The Guidon* that other people have had their battles with this devil. I hope that they find healing as I found healing through the "Baker Bandits."

Emmett, I sure am glad I made that phone call three years ago. I'm also glad you were home to take my call; I do not think I would have had the nerve to call a second time. I had butterflies in my stomach then, but they are all gone now.

*—Carmelo A. Tellez—*

# Letter Lifts Morale of Vet

## Art Markey

Reading by the wood stove will be my sole position this winter since an old Korean War injury has branched out to cause problems with my leg. My family doctor says that the only way to recover from the pain of my spine-leg injuries was to lie down, never sit, and apply a heating pad. Naturally, the place to lie down during the day is a couple of feet from my wood stove.

I started reading about otters, it was a good article, but having already been trapped on the couch for six hours made my interest wane. I only got three paragraphs into perfecting the pie crust before I was snoozing again, having first crawled to the stove to re-load it.

"How," I asked myself, "am I to survive two weeks flat on my back." I was either falling asleep or bored.

All that changed with the delivery of the day's mail. The envelope indicated it was sent from somebody in Texas that I did not know but there was a Marine insignia stamped on the envelope. Inside, were several old snapshots of men that I did not recognize plus an article from a Texas newspaper. It told how local veterans of a bitter battle early in the Korean War were preparing to attend their first reunion in the 35 years since that war changed their lives, forever.

The battle began November 27, 1950, with 15,000 Allied ground troops from the 1st Marine Division and our Army's 7th Infantry Division, and smaller combat teams, navy medical personnel, and British Royal Marine Commandos became encircled by 120,000 Chinese Communist soldiers who had been ordered to wipe out the Allied troops.

Thus began the battle of the Chosin Reservoir, where our forces spent two weeks fighting over 60 miles of North Korean mountains where night temperatures dropped to 20 below zero. I remembered that the rations were too frozen to eat. Many men lived on tootsie rolls and biscuits. Weapons were obsolete from previous wars, froze in the cold and ammunition failed. The Chinese were tough but the weather was worse.

The fellow who mailed me the info about the upcoming reunion was Emmett Shelton Jr., who once, like me, was a Marine infantryman doing his job while trying to stay alive. Emmett continues to suffer from his frostbite from Chosin. Recently, he had surgery to amputate part of his toe to relieve the pain. He tells me it is the best he felt in years.

Emmett said in his letter that he always wondered why he was spared and those he considered better men than him were killed or frozen to death in battle. So, he told me, ever since he has tried to do good things for his community and patriotic things for his country. And, I must add, such kind things as writing to me—a stranger who—unknown to him—needed a morale lift this day.

Allied casualties totaled almost 12,000 killed in those two weeks. Over the three-year war 54,000 American soldiers were killed, 8,000 were left missing in action.

What Emmett did was go down the list of Marines in Chosin and attempt to contact all who were in his infantry company. And he reached out to me.

I wasn't complaining anymore after I finished reading Emmett's letter and the old newspaper articles. I recognized an old buddy in one of the photos. I was warm and safe at home. I even had my own wood stove—far from the old days in Korea.

I had misty eyes as I read and re-read Emmett's letter, especially the last part where he signed it simply—Your Chosin buddy, *Emmett.*

Art Markey, published in his column in the *Knickerbocker News* Albany NY Feb 1, 1986
Follow-up letter:

Dear Emmett

It has only been in the past year that I have re-established contact with the Marines—thanks mainly to the Chosin Few and *The Guidon* newsletters. So, now I know that all those years I was not "nuts" or strange, but simply a survivor of a very unusual experience—one that civilians cannot fathom.

I hope we can stay in touch, Emmett. I do not recall what you look like but that is not unusual for me. A lot of things about Korea I fail to remember—and I thought it was just as well.

Again, thank you for your thoughtfulness and your first Christmas Card. It really means a lot knowing we are not alone and are truly a Band of Brothers. God Bless

*—Art—*

# Baker Bandit Reunions

## Corporal Emmett Shelton, Jr.

The Baker Bandits held annual reunions over the U.S. for over 15 years. We visited places like my home town Austin in 1987 and 1990, San Diego in 1988, Quantico in 1989, San Francisco in 1991, Colorado Springs in 1992, Albuquerque in 1993, Atlantic City in 1995, and so on. In 2004, we expanded to add regional reunions. Each reunion lasted a few days at a nice hotel with a hospitality room. We would take tours of local sights and visit each day and in the evening we would have a banquet and guest speakers.

A highlight in my work on *The Guidon* came in 1988 and again in 1991. General Charlie Cooper was one of our Cornerstones. When I started talking about having a Reunion in 1988, Gen Charlie Cooper told me the following:

When I was the commanding officer of the Bandits back in 1951, I had a Lieutenant Pat McGahn in the Company. After a tough day at battle on Hill

Donald Trump hosted Baker Bandits heroes in Atlantic City

313, I was having a de-briefing with my men. When we were wrapping up, Lt McGahn stood up and said, "Sir, if we make it out alive, I'm going to invite everyone to one Hell of a party in Atlantic City." The B Company men were dog tired but both most chuckled at the idea of a party. The next day, Pat was seriously wounded in an intense battle and evacuated. His heroism that day earned him a Navy Cross.

By 1989, McGahn had recovered from his war wounds and was working for Donald Trump in Atlantic City. Emmett contacted Pat about *The Guidon*. Gen Charlie called Pat about his promise. Pat McGahn invited a group of Bandits to be the war heroes for a military scholarship event at Trump's Taj Mahal. They had banquets, fishing trips, sight-seeing, and a hospitality room just for sharing stories. Many military dignitaries attended and even Rush Limbaugh was there. The Baker Bandits received accolades from President Reagan and Marine Corps commanders.

Our "Gone to Heaven" weekend in August 1989 in Atlantic City was just so overwhelming most of us didn't know anything like that existed. I tried to put this into words, but trying to explain the feelings that are unexplainable, is impossible.

It was "a hell of a party," just as Pat had promised his Bandit Brothers. It was such a success; Pat invited us back in 1991.

Rush Limbaugh honored the Baker Bandits (Shelton)

# *The Guidon* Kept the Skipper's Memory Alive

## Julia Hancock

Dear Mr. Shelton and Lt. Palatas

Both of you knew my grandfather as "The Skipper," 1st Lieutenant John Hancock. He was killed in action on February 7, 1951 while leading B-1-5 on a Guerrilla Hunt.

To my father, John Jr., the Skipper was not just a Marine, but also his Hero. My father used to talk about him often—although I knew he never actually met him. He would remember a few stories mother told him and he showed me a letter she got from Korea. The Skipper was killed right after my dad was born, stateside. Grandma died years later.

I learned the most about Grandpa from *The Guidon*. When I read this last issue about him, I was greatly touched by the last line:

"They say that you are not really dead so long as someone remembers you. Lots of us remember "The Skipper" fondly so he still lives on with us."

I have read *The Guidon* for two years, but I feel this issue was the best you have ever done because of the fact that, in this issue—his memory lives on.

On behalf of the whole Hancock family, I want to express my deepest gratitude to you because of what you have done. God bless you all for keeping His memory alive!

—*Julia Hancock*—

# Greater Love Hath No Man!

## Corporal Emmett Shelton, Jr.

As the Annual Baker Bandit Reunion was approaching in 1995, Bandit Ervin C. "Cork" Diels was diagnosed with leukemia. (In the war, he went by "Corky") Cork wanted so much to see his wartime buddies one more time that he went in and got a transfusion of three pints of fresh blood to give him strength to make the trip.

Cork and his wife Ruth then drove their van across the continent, from California to Atlantic City, New Jersey to be with his beloved Baker Bandits. He had car trouble along the way, but persevered right through it.

Every time we saw Cork at the reunion he had a big smile on his face and a twinkle in his eye. He was very busy getting in all the visiting he could. He was really active to be in the physical shape he must have been in.

Upon returning to California from the reunion, Cork got another three pints of blood transfused, but something went terribly wrong. Cork became ill and died September 11, 1995.

Greater love hath no man than what Cork had to go through to be with the Baker Bandits one last time! We again were quite fortunate to have had this quality time with our old friend and buddy at our reunion. God bless you Cork, we'll see you shortly.

*—Emmett—*

# Korean Remembrance

## Chuck Hall, 1997

I can't forget the paddies,
The hills and bunkers too
I can't forget the winters,
As white skin turned to blue.

The people I remember,
Their courage knew no bounds
I still think of my buddies,
And the battles' horrid sounds.

My nights are filled with memories,
Of deeds done long ago
When every night held terror,
As we tried to hold the foe.

The thing that kept us going,
Was pride and Esprit de Corps
To be Marines until we died,
Just that and nothing more.

I won't forget my memories,
Of men who are no more
Marines who gave their very all,
The life blood of our Corps.

# Frost Call Network

## The "Ole Top" Phil Dierickx

We are all aware that none of us is getting any younger, and that we are vulnerable to all of the problems that crop up as we age. Some remember platoon leaders waking men in line telling the men to do the "Chosin Stomp" to prevent frostbite. We need that kind of Frost Call, now. We need to keep in touch about important changes in our Bandits' health.

To facilitate notifying our Bandits of changes in health conditions, I suggest forming a network to spread this information quickly and easily without too much pressure on just a few.

I suggest that one "squad leader" be appointed for each region. He, or she, then designates five people whom he will call—these five will each name five that they will call. This way, one person is obligated to make just five calls, and no one is overburdened.

We can call for volunteers in *The Guidon*. I know—we were taught early on in the Marine Corps, "Don't volunteer for anything," but some of us have ignored this and gone forth to get things done. We were also taught Leave No Marine Behind.

Please give this serious consideration!

—*The "Ole Top" Phil Dierickx*—

*A Note from Ole Emmett: from* The Guidon *1998: I got this letter from the "Ole Top" a month or so after Ike Fenton died. It took about six seeks before the next edition of* The Guidon—*so many of you did not get word for some time. Well guys, we do have this problem. In the past, I notify those on my e-mail list and then put it in* The Guidon. *If something comes to my attention right after* The Guidon *comes out, it will be one to two months before most of you will find out about the death or illness of our buddies. What do you think? Will you support such a network?*

**A word from Cyndie in 2020**: *And the Bandits so wished for an answer! Years later, we have social media. Reach out to your Marine buddies and keep in touch. Use all the tools—email and social media make it easier to stay in touch. They can open up worlds and connect across miles. You never know when that foxhole buddy needs a Brother and you are called to step up to—Leave No Marine Behind.*

Ole Emmett remembers that Christmas in Korea (Markey)

# B-1-5's Honored Dead in the Korean War

## What Happened to Our Heroes?
### Chuck Hall, 1994

*Dedicated to those who never returned from the Korean War*

What happened to our heroes,
From back in days of yore?
Why do we not recall them,
And speak of them no more?

Their shining deeds in battle,
Stand like a beacon light
A perfect, pure example,
For those who would do right

They're with us now no longer,
And lost from history's page
The many have forgotten,
These warriors brave and sage

Our nation now is poorer,
From the vision we have lost
Of men who did their duty,
And paid the final cost

Let's speak to these our children,
That they may not forget
These stalwart battle veterans,
Whose sun has slowly set

# A Tribute Delivered at Chosin

## Lieutenant John M. Baker

In October 1951 in Korea, the 1st Battalion, 5th Marines, which was in division reserve at the time, held a memorial service remembering battalion members who had died during the battalion's previous operations. During this service, 1st Lt J.M. Baker gave the following address:

Taps at Chosin (USMC)

> The tribute which we mortals pay to our comrades should be voiced not as our last respects, but rather as our lasting respect.
>
> In memory of them it is fitting that we who carry on, should call to mind those things for which they gave their lives. Death is no stranger to men who call themselves Marines. Men who, as these, our honored dead, our fallen comrades, left their homes and loved ones during periods of peace and tranquility at home, to defend their nation against its enemies, where ever they threaten.
>
> To speak of them as heroes alone would be an empty tribute. To recount their deeds, or recall their valor in itself, would be a shame. It is more proper that we re-dedicate ourselves to the defense of freedom. That we pledge ourselves to preserve, to cherish, and to defend the way of life, in defense of which they died. They would have it so!
>
> By their great sacrifice, they bought for us a priceless legacy. With that legacy, we also received from them the eternal spirit which has animated free men since the very dawn of history. So long as that spirit continues to flourish, we shall not fail, in the future, the men we honor today!

*—Lieutenant J. M. Baker—*

# B-1-5's Honored Dead from the Korean War

*Confirmed by Korean War Project*

DOW is Died of Wounds.
KIA is Killed in Action.
MIA is Missing In Action.

| | | |
|---|---|---|
| 2LT James L. Ables, from Corpus Christi, Texas | KIA | 29APR51 |
| CPL James Aragon Jr, from Paguate, New Mexico | KIA | 5SEP50 |
| SGT David M. Archer, from Dallas, Texas | DOW | 13AUG50 |
| CPL Ralph E. Auten, from Sheridan, Missouri | KIA | 22SEP50 |
| CPL Daniel J. Ballem, from New York, New York | KIA | 17JUN51 |
| PFC William V. Barfield, from Baraboo, Wisconsin | KIA | 17APR52 |
| PFC Patrick J. Berkley, from Twin Falls, Idaho | MIA-KIA | 13AUG50 |
| PFC Edward F. Blasko, from Maryd, Pennsylvania | KIA | 12JUL52 |
| PFC Herman C. Bohnke Jr., from Carnegie, PA | MIA-KIA | 13AUG50 |
| PFC William A. Bouquin, from Utica, New York | KIA | 28NOV50 |
| PFC Eugene W. Bowden, from Jacksonville, Florida | KIA | 13NOV50 |
| CPL Allen M. Bowman, from Covington, Indiana | KIA | 28NOV50 |
| PFC Richard Q. Braman, from Danbury, Conn. | KIA | 22SEP50 |
| PFC Charles R. Briggs, from Warwick, Rhode Island | DOW | 5MAR52 |
| PFC Donald R. Brown, from Circleville, Ohio | KIA | 11SEP51 |
| CPL Jewell C. Bruce, Mounds, Illinois | KIA | 18AUG50 |
| SGT Anthony M. Cappucci, from Bristol, RI | KIA | 23APR51 |
| PFC Ernesto P. Castilla, from Seguin, Texas | KIA | 13JUN51 |
| PFC James C. Carney, from Covington, Kentucky | DOW | 12APR52 |
| PFC Alfredo Carrizales, from San Benito, Texas | MIA | 13AUG50 |
| PFC Bobby J. Chandler, from Stockton, California | KIA | 7DEC50 |

SGT Howard F. Clark, from Los Angeles, California    KIA         23APR51
CPL Alvis Clowers, from Pittsburg, Oklahoma          KIA         15SEP50
PFC Donald Coleman, from Richmond, Virginia          DOW         8DEC50
PFC William Cortwright, from Brooklyn, New York      DOW         5MAR53
2LT Carey S. Cowart, Jr., from Tulsa, Oklahoma       DOW         22Mar51
PFC George A. Crocker, from Eastboga, Alabama        KIA         5SEP50
PFC John C. Cross, from Detroit, Michigan            KIA         11MAY52
PFC Jack D. Crouch, from Estalline, Texas            KIA         18AUG50
CPL Richard C. Cruze, from Long Beach, California    KIA         28DEC50
CPL Paul F. Cullen, from Jamacia Plain, MA           DOW         15JUN52
PFC Edward D. Darchuck, from Scobey, Montana         KIA         18AUG50
PFC Frank D. D'ermilio, from Philadelphia, PA        KIA         25NOV52
CPL Robert L. Dobbs, from Kansas City, Kansas        KIA         28NOV59
PFC Donald W. Donnell, from Oakland, California      MIA-KIA     31JAN51
SGT Ural Dorsey, from Oak Ridge, Louisiana           KIA         19MAR53
CPL Donald J. Durst, from Bethlehem, Pennsylvania    KIA         13NOV50
PFC Lee E. Dutcher, from Hastings, Nebraska          MIA-KIA     31JAN51
PFC Donald E. Edwards, from Richfield, Idaho         KIA         18AUG50
CPL Henry Eggenberger, E.White Plains, NY            KIA         24FEB51
CPL Kenneth W. Fare, from West Amana, Iowa           KIA
CPL Douglas S. Finley Jr, from West Monroe, LA       MIA-KIA     31JAN51
1LT Edward D. Fisher, from Chicago, Illinois         KIA         16JUN51
PFC Robert J. Fisher, from Worchester, MA            KIA         28NOV50
PFC Donald W. Forbes, from Nevada, Iowa              KIA         29NOV50
PFC Roger D. Fortenberry, from Houston, Texas        MIA-KIA     13AUG50
PFC William E. Fortin, from Brusnwick, Maine         DOW         16SEP50
PFC Freddie Garcia, from Santa Paulo, California     MIA-KIA     13AUG50
CPL Richard D. Garcia, from San Antonio, Texas       MIA-KIA     13AUG50
SSGT Gordon Gardner, from Portsmouth, Virginia       KIA         13NOV50
PFC Gilbert R. Gaudet, from New Orleans, LA          MIA-KIA     13AUG50
PFC Louie O. Gerue, from Klamath Falls, Oregon       KIA         23APR51
PFC George Giedosh, from Harleigh, Maryland          KIA         28NOV50
PFC Hershel B. Gooding, from Jamestown, TN           KIA         19MAR53
PFC Wilbur B. Gray, from Austin Texas                KIA         21FEB51
PFC Clark W. Gribble, from Boulder, Colorado         DOW         22SEP51
CPL Michael Grubisich, from Peoria, Illinois         MIA-KIA     31JAN51
PFC Harry J. Haden, from New London, Missouri        KIA         6NOV52
1LT John R. Hancock, from Craig Nebraska             KIA         7FEB51
PFC Richard B. Hanson, from Kenosha, Wisconsin       DOW         22MAR53
PFC Howard H. Harman, Las Animas, Colorado           KIA         17JUN51

| | | |
|---|---|---|
| PFC Roy E. Harrison, from Sissonville, WV | KIA | 11JUN51 |
| PFC Donald G. Hasty, from Portland, Oregon | KIA | 3DEC52 |
| CPL Richard E. Hawley, from Seattle, Washington | KIA | 12AUG50 |
| CPL Leonard E. Hayworth, from Crown Point, IN | KIA | 24SEP50 |
| CPL Maynard L. Highley, from Houston, Texas | KIA | 13NOV50 |
| CPL Raymond F. Hill, from St. Louis, Missouri | KIA | 23APR51 |
| CPL Weston W. Hoey, Baltimore, Maryland | KIA | 5SEP50 |
| PFC Gerald D. Hooper, from Athol, Kansas | KIA | 13AUG50 |
| PFC George M. Hudson, from Ft. Valley, Georgia | KIA | 13NOV50 |
| PFC Herbert F. Hunter, from Blue Earth, Minnesota | KIA | 17AUG50 |
| PFC Jeremiah Jackson, from Natchitoches, Louisiana | KIA | 19MAR53 |
| 2LT Austin "Swede" Jenson, from Abernathy, Texas | KIA | 29NOV50 |
| PFC Alfred E. Lawrence, Jr., from Norfolk, Virginia | MIA-KIA | 31JAN51 |
| SSGT Eugene L. Lawson, from Enid, Oklahoma | MIA-KIA | 13AUG50 |
| CPL Duane E. Longbrake, from Hebron, Nebraska | KIA | 8JAN52 |
| PFC Franklin Malkemes, Jr., from Wilkes-Barr, Penn. | KIA | 11SEP51 |
| PFC Arnulfo Martinez, from Brownsville, Texas | DOW | 9SEP50 |
| PFC Dennis D. Martinez, from Visalia, California | KIA | 19MAR53 |
| PFC Charles A. McAndrews, from Chicago, Illinois | KIA | 7DEC50 |
| PFC Charles H. McBrair, from Farrell, Pennsylvania | KIA | 19MAR53 |
| SGT Wayne H. McCluskey, Holyoke, MN | KIA | 29NOV50 |
| SGT Charles A. McCoy, from Hockerville, Oklahoma | MIA-KIA | 13AUG50 |
| CPL Howard McDonough Jr, Berkley, MI | KIA | 18AUG50 |
| CPL John F. McDowell, from Farwell, Minnesota | KIA | 13NOV50 |
| PFC Hugh P. McKenna, College Point, New York | KIA | 29MAR51 |
| PFC Spencer C. Meldrum, from Provo, Utah | MIA-KIA | 13AUG50 |
| PFC Charles W. Melvold, from Henning, Minnesota | MIA-KIA | 31JAN50 |
| PFC Kenneth J. Milligan, from Galveston, Texas | KIA | 18AUG50 |
| PFC Robert P. Mooney, from Kansas City, Missouri | KIA | 17JUN51 |
| PFC Herbert F. Morgan, from Akron, Ohio | KIA | 29NOV50 |
| PFC Joseph D. Moss, from Pevely, Missouri | KIA | 18AUG50 |
| PFC Edward A. Muntz from Houston, Texas | MIA-KIA | 12AUG50 |
| PFC Secundino Olivares, from San Antonio, Texas | KIA | 13NOV50 |
| PFC Loyde R. Orr, from Oberlin, Kansas | KIA | 12SEP51 |
| PFC Joseph Ostergaard, from Richmond, California | MIA-KIA | 13AUG50 |
| PFC Frankie "Arkie" Parrish, from Norfolk, Virginia | MIA-KIA | 13AUG50 |
| PFC Leon Patchen, from Anoka, Minnesota | DOW | 12DEC50 |
| PFC Lloyd A. Pinner, from Detroit, Michigan | KIA | 19MAR53 |
| PFC Bobby R. Poare, from Salinas, California | MIA-KIA | 13AUG50 |
| PFC Norman I. Podos, from Los Angeles, California | KIA | 23APR51 |

| | | |
|---|---|---|
| PFC George W. Rae, from Roundup, Montana | MIA-KIA | 31JAN5 |
| CPL Joseph W. Remine, from Leadville, Colorado | KIA | 13AUG50 |
| PFC Carlos L. Robles, from El Paso, Texas | MIA-KIA | 13AUG50 |
| SGT Anthony N. Rodriguez, from Chicago, Illinois | KIA | 11SEP51 |
| PFC Jose R. Rodriguez, from Visalia, California | MIA-KIA | 13AUG50 |
| PFC Donald E. Rowe, from Rock Island, Illinois | KIA | 13JUN51 |
| CPL Alejandro E. Salinas, from Tucson, Arizona | MIA-KIA | 13AUG50 |
| PFC Gerald A. Schick, from San Diego, California | MIA-KIA | 13AUG50 |
| PFC Charles E. Schoonover, from Amlin, Ohio | DOW | 27JUN53 |
| PFC Gilman Shelton, from Tucson, Arizona | DOW | 19SEP50 |
| SGT James R. Shepard, from, Huntington, WV | MIA-KIA | 13AUG50 |
| PFC Theodore M. Skeals, Jr., from Baltimore, Maryland | KIA | 23APR51 |
| PFC Robert B. Smith, from Vallejo, California | KIA | 18AUG50 |
| CPL Kenneth H. Spencer, from Wichita, Kansas | DOW | 11JUN51 |
| PFC Myron Springsteen, Jr., from Montclair, NJ | KIA | 3SEP50 |
| PFC John A. Stammel, from Rensselaer, New York | KIA | 23SEP51* |
| PFC Bernard U. Stavely, from Hyattsville, Maryland | MIA-KIA | 13AUG50 |
| 2LT Eugene Stewart McComb, Mississippi | DOW | 18MAY53 |
| PFC Roger V. Sturdevant, from Groton, MA | DOW | 7DEC50 |
| PFC Richard L. Swenson, from Kansas City, Kansas | KIA | 22MAR52 |
| PFC Eugene D. Tangeman, from Omaha, Nebraska | KIA | 28NOV50 |
| 1LT David S. Taylor, from Walla Walla, Washington | KIA | 18AUG50 |
| PFC Billy Thompson, from Corpus Christi, Texas | KIA | 29MAY51 |
| PFC Kenneth Thornton, Corpus Christi, TX | KIA | 8JAN52 |
| PFC Huey E. Upshaw, from Lillie, Louisiana | MIA-KIA | 13AUG50 |
| PFC Lester H. Vannort, from Frankfort, New York | KIA | 18AUG50 |
| CPL William A. Ward Jr., from Portland, Oregon | KIA | 7DEC50 |
| PFC Paul E. Warren, from Oakland, California | MIA-KIA | 31JAN51 |
| CPL Roy L. West, from Dansville, Michigan | MIA-KIA | 31JAN51 |
| PFC Lawrence A. Wilcox, from Steinauer, Nebraska | MIA-KIA | 13AUG50 |
| PFC Ronald Worley, from Indianapolis, Indiana | KIA | 3SEP50 |
| SGT Thomas Yesenko, South Fork, PA | MIA-KIA | 31JAN51 |

* Marines who were there say PFC Stammel was KIA Jun 17, 1951 on Hill 907 but the Korean War Project reports him KIA September 23, 1951 at Punchbowl

*Every time we think of one of these heroes, they are momentarily still with us, so read this list and honor these Marines!*

*—Emmett—*

The long march out (USMC)

# Index